T0253607

Lecture Notes in Computer Science

Lecture Notes in Computer Science

Edited by G. Goos and J. Hartmanis

264

Eiiti Wada (Ed.)

Logic Programming '86

Proceedings of the 5th Conference
Tokyo, Japan, June 23–26, 1986

Springer-Verlag
Berlin Heidelberg New York London Paris Tokyo

Editor

Eiiti Wada
Department of Mathematical Engineering and Information Physics
Faculty of Engineering, University of Tokyo
3–1, Hongo 7-chome, Bunkyo-ku
Tokyo 113, Japan

CR Subject Classification (1987): D.1.3, D.3.4, I.2.4-5, I.2.7

ISBN 3-540-18024-9 Springer-Verlag Berlin Heidelberg New York
ISBN 0-387-18024-9 Springer-Verlag New York Berlin Heidelberg

Printing and binding: Druckhaus Beltz, Hemsbach/Bergstr.
2145/3140-543210

Foreword

The present volume of the Springer Lecture Notes in Computer Science includes papers presented at the fifth Logic Programming Conference (June 23 - 26, Tokyo) and subsequently submitted for publication. The conference itself was, as usual, sponsored by ICOT (the Institute for New Generation Computer Technology).

The format of this last conference differed from that of the preceding ones in that:

On Monday, two tutorial talks were given, i.e.

1. Introduction to ESP: system description language for sequential prolog machine by T. Chikayama

2. Introduction to GHC: parallel logic programming language by K. Ueda

and two invited speeches were presented on Tuesday and Wednesday, i.e.

1. Japanese phrase structure grammar by T. Gunji

2. Logic program transformation by H. Tamaki and T. Sato.

Twentysix normal papers were presented from Tuesday to Thursday.

Some sad news:

Professor Tohru Moto-oka who played an insightful role as the leader for the Japanese fifth generation computer project passed away on November 11, 1985. His warm criticism and timely advice given to us at the former conferences and elsewhere will be missed but his voice and smile will remain in our mind with the pleasant memory of one of the founders of the Japanese computer technology.

As the chairman of the program committee, I thank its members, referees and authors for their cooperation and patience. I also thank ICOT for the conference administration.

Eiiti Wada
The University of Tokyo

Foreword

The present volume of the Springer Lecture Notes in Computer Science includes papers presented at the fifth Logic Programming Conference (June 23 - 26, Tokyo) and subsequently submitted for publication. The conference itself was, as usual, sponsored by ICOT (the Institute for New Generation Computer Technology).

The format of this last conference differed from that of the preceding ones in that:

On Monday, two tutorial talks were given, i.e.

1. Introduction to ESP: system description language for sequential prolog machine by T. Chikayama

2. Introduction to GHC: parallel logic programming language by K. Ueda

and two invited speeches were presented on Tuesday and Wednesday, i.e.

1. Japanese phrase structure grammar by T. Gunji

2. Logic program transformation by H. Tamaki and T. Sato.

Twentysix normal papers were presented from Tuesday to Thursday.

Some sad news:

Professor Tohru Moto-oka who played an insightful role as the leader for the Japanese fifth generation computer project passed away on November 11, 1985. His warm criticism and timely advice given to us at the former conferences and elsewhere will be missed but his voice and smile will remain in our mind with the pleasant memory of one of the founders of the Japanese computer technology.

As the chairman of the program committee, I thank its members, referees and authors for their cooperation and patience. I also thank ICOT for the conference administration.

Eiiti Wada
The University of Tokyo

Program Committee / Editorial Board

Table of Contents

Plan-Based Text Generation in an On-Line Help System

Takashi Kakiuchi, Kuniaki Uehara, and Jun'ichi Toyoda

The Institute of Scientific and Industrial Research,
Osaka University, 8-1 Mihogaoka, Ibaraki, Osaka 567, Japan

ABSTRACT

This paper describes an on-line help system, ASSIST, which is designed
to produce multiparagragh explanations in English in response to
questions about computer terminology. ASSIST's text generation
mechanism is based on the speech act planning theory proposed by Cohen.
Namely, generation process can be viewed as the process of planning
utterances to achieve a discourse goal. In order for the system to
have the ability to provide different responses in accordance with
user's level of expertise, a user model is constructed throughout a
session, and then utilized to determine how much detail is necessary.
Critic can examine how much information is sufficient for the user and
vary response by cutting off an unimportant, redundant goal during the
course of planning. Furthermore, a focusing mechanism is introduced to
ensure that the generated explanation is coherent. Focusing
information is also used to decide on how to express each sentence,
i.e., whether pronominalization can be applicable, which sentence form
is more appropriate, an active voice or passive one, etc.

1. INTRODUCTION

Command assistance is available on most interactive operating systems.
Typically, a user asks for command assistance to avoid looking up
commands in user's manuals. On-line help systems are often found on
systems primarily used by people unfamiliar with computer technology.

The simplest and most common way to generate explanations in such an
on-line help system is to type explanations as text strings and store
them in advance. The system can thus search an appropriate text string
and simply display it which has already been stored. Since almost all
error messages of an operating system, for example, are produced in
this way, messages can be as complex and natural as possible. This
approach is a rather easy way for the system to have the ability to
produce explanations.

The second approach is to utilize the template completion mechanism.
This approach can be seen in most expert systems. Templates are
English phrases with slots which can be instantiated with different
words and phrases depending upon the context. Templates may be
combined with each other and instantiated in various ways to produce
different sentences.

Unfortunately, these approaches have their own critical deficiencies.
The problem associated with the first approach is that all questions
and answers can not be anticipated in advance if the system becomes

larger and more complex. Although it is possible to write out answers to all questions, the same answer would be always responded to the same question. The problem with the latter approach is that simply combining templates to organize the answer does not ensure its connectivity. Furthermore, the explanation made up of complete sentences are often awkward and tiresome.

A text generation system, ASSIST, is designed to produce multiparagragh texts in English in response to questions about computer terminology. The approach taken here is to generate texts by translating knowledge structures directly into English. One of the main advantages of this approach is the ability to paraphrase variety of sentences from a single knowledge structure.

2. BASIC ASSUMPTION

ASSIST's text generation process is based on the speech act planning theory, proposed by Cohen (1979). The basic idea is that speakers do not simply produce sentences that are true or false, but rather perform speech actions to affect their listeners' state. Such language use can be modeled by viewing speech acts as operators in a planning system.

The theory of planning is a methodology of how to decide what actions to take for the purpose of achieving some goal. A goal is accomplished by a course of actions, called a plan, and the process of deciding on what plan to take is called a planning. As each goal can be replaced by more detailed subgoals, a generated plan may have a hierarchical structure. We name this structure a hierarchical planning structure.

3. SYSTEM OVERVIEW

Figure 1 shows the principle data flows in ASSIST.

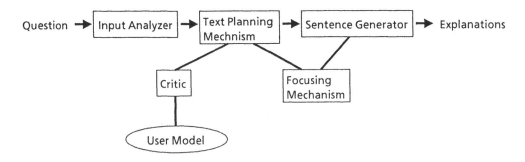

Fig. 1   System overview

To answer an incoming question, ASSIST should, first, decide on what to say and how to say. ASSIST's Text Planning Mechanism makes these decisions, based on the speech act planning theory. Text Planning Mechanism generates a hierarchical planning structure where the highest node is the most abstracted plan which corresponds to a high-level description of the discourse goal extracted from the incoming question. The lowest node is a primitive plan to produce a single sentence. The hierarchical planning structure can be viewed as the story tree

(Simmons 1979) where nodes closest to the root are the most important events, i.e., episodes in a narrative and nodes closest to the leaves are concerned with details of the episodes.

In order to communicate effectively with users of differing levels of expertise, the system should have the ability to provide different responses to the same question which vary by level of detail. ASSIST also has <u>User Model</u> that represents his knowledge. User Model is gradually constructed throughout a session, and is used to determine how much detail is needed for each user at different time.

During the course of planning, <u>Critic</u> determines the appropriate level of this detailedness and amends the planning structure to suit the user's level. By considering the user's model, Critic eliminates the goal that is concluded to be of no significance for achieving the original goal, so as to avoid an explanation aside from the subject and cut off unimportant information.

In a discourse, speakers center their attention on a particular discourse element, called the focus of a discourse by Sidner (1983). <u>Focusing Mechanism</u> can be used to ensure that the generated text is coherent, tracking focus of attention as the text is created. Focusing Mechanism provides <u>Sentence Generator</u> with information necessary to decide on how to express the text. For example, focus information is used in situations to test whether pronominalization can be applied, to discriminate between the use of passive and active sentence, and so on. Text Planning Mechanism and Focusing Mechanism operate in a cooperative fashion to produce coherent explanations.

4. KNOWLEDGE STRUCTURE

Knowledge representation is the important aspect of a text generation system. In ASSIST, we adopt a frame-like representation, a cluster of the properties of an object or event into a single concept. The idea is that grouping relevant sets of relationships into a single data structure enables the system to retrieve all the relevant information required for an explanation about a particular entity effectively.

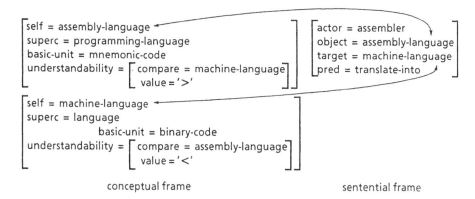

conceptual frame   sentential frame

Fig. 2   Knowledge structures

ASSIST has two types of knowledge structures. One is called a conceptual frame, which provides definitional information of an entity including a generalization hierarchy and characteristic features of each entity in the hierarchy. As shown in Fig. 2, the representation for "assembly-language" has the slots 'self' and 'superc' which are filled by "assembly-language" and "programming-language", respectively. This means that the super class of "assembly-language" is a "programming-language". The second type of the knowledge structure is called a sentential frame, which provides descriptive information about entities in the conceptual frame. The sentential frame is allowed to represent actions or situations. Roughly speaking, the idea of a sentential frame is similar to that of a case frame proposed by Fillmore (1968). The example in Fig. 2 represents relations between "assembly-language" and "machine-language" in the conceptual frame. This means that "assembly-language" is translated into "machine-language".

5. INPUT ANALYSIS

User's input to ASSIST is first analyzed by an Integrated Parser (IP) (Uehara 1986). The formalism of an IP grammar is based on a Lexical Functional Grammar (Bresnan 1982). IP parses an input sentence and produces the internal representation of the sentence, called a functional structure (f-structure), which motivates the system's response.

6. TEXT PLANNING

The classes of questions accepted by ASSIST include:

    WHAT_IS: What is the assembly language?
    HOW: How to delete a file?
    DIFFERENCE: What is the difference between assembly language
                and machine language?

In this paper, the following question will be used to illustrate how Text Planning Mechanism operates.

    What is the assembly language?

In text planning, the first step to generate a text is to detect discourse goals to be achieved by explanation. Each question-type depicted above is associated with its own discourse goal. For the question above, the goal 'DEFINE(assembly-language)' is extracted from the question by IP, since the question represents a request for definition. A summary of the assignment of discourse goals to these question-types is shown below:

    DEFINE Goal: To answer WHAT_IS-type question
    TO-DO Goal: To answer HOW-type question
    DISTINGUISH Goal: To answer DIFFERENCE-type question

Text planning in ASSIST is accomplished by developing a hierarchical planning structure from the discourse goal. The original discourse goal in the planning structure is expanded into more detailed subgoals in a manner where the planning module forms a rough goal first, later refining it into more concrete low-level subgoals. To do this, we introduce the concept of a goal-expanding operator, as shown in Fig. 3. The goal-expanding operator encodes the fact about which goal is expanded into which subgoals. The operator consists of a goal and the sequence of its subgoals for accomplishing the goal. For example,

OPERATOR1 expands a goal of the form 'DEFINE(X)' into four subgoals. Applying OPERATOR1 to the original discourse goal 'DEFINE(assembly-language)' generates four subgoals:

```
EXPLAIN(assembly-language)
        {superc = 'programming-language'},
EXPLAIN(assembly-language)
        {basic-unit = 'mnemonic-code'},
EXPLAIN(assembly-language)
        {understandability = [compare = 'machine-language',
                              value= '>']},
EXPLAIN(assembly-language)
        {[actor = assembler,
          object = assembly-language,
          target = machine-language,
          pred = translate-into]}.
```

Each goal above is expanded into its subgoals recursively until each leaf of the planning structure is reduced to a primitive goal 'OUTPUT(X){REL=Y}'. The primitive goal represents the fact that the attribute REL of the entity X has its own value Y. Thus, the final planning structure which has been completely expanded is shown in Fig. 4. A course of explanations which instantiates the original discourse goal is extracted by gathering primitive goals in a top-down, left-to-right search of the planning structure.

```
OPERATOR1
   GOAL: DEFINE(X)
   SUBGOALS: EXPLAIN(X){superc=A},
             EXPLAIN(X){consist_of=B},
             Explain X with its attributives,
             Explain X with its descriptive information.

OPERATOR2
   GOAL: EXPLAIN(X){REL=Y}
   SUBGOALS: OUTPUT(X){REL=Y},
             DEFINE(Y).
```

Fig. 3   Goal-expanding operators

7. USER MODEL

In order to make decisions about how much information is sufficient for answering a particular user, an explicit model of the user's knowledge, knowledge of what the user knows and believes, is required. In ASSIST, User Model is constructed throughout a session, and is utilized to determine an appropriate level of explanation.

In ASSIST, the fact which has been concluded to be known to the user is recorded as a fact representation. For example, the fact representation 'knows(john, machine-language)' means that John knows "machine-language". In addition to these fact representations, inference rules are added to our User Model. The inference rule 'X -> Y' represents that if one knows the concept X, then he may also knows the concept Y. These rules are used to infer which concept is known to the user. A portion of the inference programs is described as follows:

```
knows(X,F) :-
        commonsense-knowledge(F).
```

```
knows(X,F) :-
      inference-rule(Fl->F),
      knows(X,Fl).
knows(X,F) :-
      knows(X,superc(F)),
      knows(X,consist-of(F)).
```

where commonsense-knowledge(F) means that F is known to be familiar with users who can somewhat operate computer systems.

When ASSIST is to explain some concept, the inference mechanism uses User Model to determine whether he knows the concept or not. Unfortunately, if he has only incomplete knowledge about the concept, ASSIST should provide him with enough explanation.

This detection method of incomplete knowledge is based on PDS (Program Diagnosis System), developed by Shapiro (1982). PDS is an interactive system that can identify a bug in a logic program, such as incorrectness, incompleteness, nontermination. If we compare programs to be diagnosed with User Model, we can easy draw a conclusion that these bugs in a program correspond to user's incorrect knowledge, lack of knowledge and incorrect use of knowledge, respectively. In order for our User Model to detect a lack of user's knowledge, the diagnosing mechanism is incorporated into the inference mechanism. Further discussion on user modelling will be treated in a forthcoming paper. In the next chapter, we shall explain how these information is actually used during the course of planning.

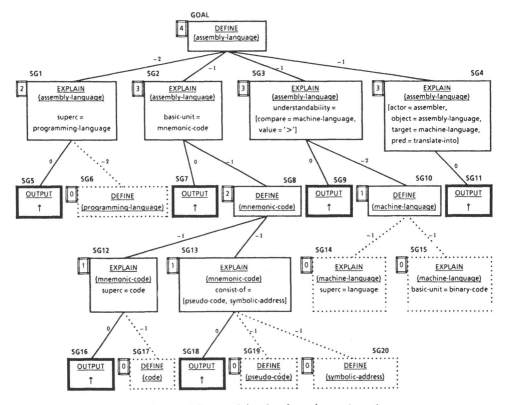

Fig. 4   A hierarchical planning structure

8. CRITIC

In order to communicate effectively with users of differing levels of expertise, ASSIST should have the ability to provide users with different responses to the same question which vary by level of detail. If the user is clearly unfamiliar with terms involved, more detailed explanation is necessary. If it is clear that the user understands the concept which is just introduced in an explanation, further explanation is of no significance and tiresome.

The varying responses by level of detail is accomplished by the program called Critic. Critic can examine how much information is sufficient for answering a particular user and eliminate goals in a planning structure to avoid providing overwhelming information.

ASSIST can discriminate among various levels of detail, assigning each goal in the planning structure a 'criticality value', which reflects the relative importance of the goal to the original goal to be achieved. The original goal is assigned the criticality value which has been predefined as a default value, and a lower level goal is assigned the value less than the one at the higher level. The criticality value assigned to the goal is calculated as a sum of the criticality value assigned to its parent goal and the weight being associated with the branch between the goal and its parent goal. That is, if the goal G has a criticality value of C and the branch reaching to its subgoal SG1 is weighted with W, then the criticality value of the subgoal SG1 is the sum of C and W (Fig. 5). Normally, the weight being associated with a branch has a negative value so that lower level goals may be given less criticality values than higher level ones. If the branch expands from the parent goal to its subgoal which is concluded to be known to a user by considering User Model, then the criticality value of the subgoal is less than ones of goals at the same level of the hierarchical planning structure.

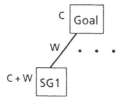

Fig. 5   Calculation of criticality values

Critic would be employed whenever the goal is expanded. It checks whether each expanded goal satisfies the following condition:

the criticality value assigned to a goal is more than the threshold value.

If the condition is not satisfied, no further expansion would be performed and the goal would be eliminated from consideration. Eliminating unsatisfactory goals enables the system to avoid deviation from the subject of an explanation and cut off unnecessary, redundant, explanation.

In the planning structure shown in Fig. 3, the original discourse goal is assigned the criticality value of 4 which has been predefined as a default value. Almost all branches have -1 as their own weights. But the branch between the goal SG3 and its subgoal SG10 has a weight of -2, since we assume that the term "machine-language" is concluded to be familiar to a user by considering the state of User Model. Consequently, the goals SG14 and SG15 are eliminated from consideration because their criticality values are equal to the threshold value (in this case, 0 is taken). The goals SG17, SG19 and SG20 are eliminated because they are judged by Critic to be straying from the subject for explanation of "assembly-language".

9. SENTENCE GENERATOR

The generation of a sentence takes place in two steps. First, the attribute and its own value of an entity in a conceptual (sentential) frame representation is mapped into the functional representation of a desired sentence, called a functional structure (f-structure) (Bresnan 1982). The f-structure is composed of a set of ordered pairs each of which consists of an attribute and a specification of the attribute's value for the sentence. The f-structure is then, converted into a surface-structure form, that is, an appropriate string of words. This linearization process is implemented as a production system, where the syntax is expressed as a set of production (TEST-ACTION) rules. The tests check on the semantic condition; when they fire, actions instantiate fixed templates with sub-f-structures, and the sub-f-structures, in turn, are then expanded, piece by piece, until they finally become a normal natural language sentence.

10. FOCUSING

10.1. Focusing in Discourse

As was described in a previous chapter, ASSIST constructs the hierarchical planning structure, and then extracts the sequence of primitive goals to achieve the original discourse goal from the structure. Subsequently, the sequence of primitive goals would be carried out by a Sentence Generator and a textual explanation is produced. To ensure that the generated explanation is to be coherent, we shall now introduce the focusing mechanism, proposed by Sidner (1983).

When speaking or writing, one may, being consciously or unconsciously, center his attention on various concepts or objects. Centering his attention on particular concepts is called focusing. The focusing mechanism keeps track of focused elements over the sequence of sentences.

Sidner used the focusing mechanism for disambiguation of definite anaphora and thus for aiding in the interpretation of discourse. Briefly, she claims that the speaker has four rules for maintaining and sifting focus from one sentence to the next:

    1. continue talking the same thing
    2. switch to talk about an item just introduced
    3. return to a topic of previous discussion
    4. talk about an item implicitly related to the current focus

We make use of the focusing mechanism to generate explanations so that generated sentences may be connected with each other. Focusing can ensure its connectivity because it specifies that each sentence of the discourse is related to the previous discourse. Using the rules depicted above, ASSIST keeps track of focused elements and decides on how focus can move from one sentence to the next.

10.2. Surface Selection

Not only to determine what to say next, focusing information is also used to decide on how to express each sentence. For instance, changing focus may involve the use of an another syntactic form, allowing the user to recognize its movement. Pronominalization may be required when continuing to talk about the same topic. Passivizing the sentence can be used to move a focused element to the subject position.

To see how focusing information is actually used, it is instructive to follow the processing of a question "What is an assembly language?" in some detail. The sequence of primitive goals derived from the planning structure of Fig. 3 is shown below.

SG5, SG7, SG16, SG18, SG9, SG11

First, the questioned object "assembly-language" is being focused on, since the goal SG5 is to provide information about "assembly-language". The next goal SG7 is also involved with "assembly-language", and then the focused element is unchanged, applying the rule1 presented in a previous section. In consequence, the following sentences are produced:

Assembly-language is a kind of programming-language. Basic-unit of assembly-language is a mnemonic-code.

Subsequently, both SG16 and SG18 are about "mnemonic-code" and the focus shifts from "assembly-language" to "mnemonic-code", applying the rule2. Then the sentence is generated as follows:

Mnemonic-code is a kind of code and consists of pseudo-code and symbolic-address.

In the sentence above, the subject of the sentence derived from the goal SG18 is same as the one of SG16, and then the subject of SG18 is omitted. The goal SG9 is about "assembly-language" again and the focus returns to the previous topic (the rule3 is applied). As the result, a paragraph break is made so as to indicate that the conversation moves to the previous subject. Furthermore, the goal SG11 is carried out retrieving descriptive information about "assembly-language" from the set of sentential frames. Finally, the following explanation is generated:

Assembly-language is a kind of programming-language. Basic-unit of assembly-language is a mnemonic-code. Mnemonic-code is a kind of code and consists of pseudo-code and symbolic-address.
Assembly-language is more understandable than machine-language and translated into machine-language by assembler.

Focusing information is used to discriminate between the use of passive and active construction. The passive can be used to place the focused constituent in surface subject position when the logical subject of the sentence is not focused on. Thus, the last sentence above is passivized since "assembly-language" is being focused on. The focus movement over the sequence of sentences in this example are illustrated in Fig. 6.

rule1   rule2   rule1   rule3   rule1

SG5 $\longrightarrow$ SG7 $\longrightarrow$ SG16 $\longrightarrow$ SG18 $\longrightarrow$ SG9 $\longrightarrow$ SG11

Fig. 6   The focus movement in the example

Focusing information is also used to decide whether pronominalization is acceptable. Pronominalization is applicable only to items that convey given information. Focus of attention is similar to given information in that the focused element has already been mentioned in the previous discourse. Thus, if a concept has been focused on over the sequence of sentences, a pronominal form can be used to refer to it. The following two sentences illustrate this:

> Minicomputer were much smaller than mainframes. They fit on a desk, in the corner of a room, or on a rack.

11. CONCLUDING REMARKS

In this paper, we have presented an on-line help system, ASSIST, which is designed to produce multiparagragh explanations in English in response to questions about computer terminology. In ASSIST, Text Planning Mechanism, User Model and Critic are incorporated into the text generation mechanism so as to produce different explanations in accordance with the user's level of expertise. Furthermore, Focusing Mechanism is used to ensure that the generated explanation is to be coherent.

There are much effort to have a computer system to produce explanations. UC (Wilensky 1984) is such an on-line help system which advises users in using the UNIX operating system. Wilensky emphasized on the derivation of a user's goal in order to interpret an user's input correctly. UC's generator simply translates conceptual representations for the ideas to be expressed, piece by piece, into a natural language text, and therefore, textual coherency is not considered at all. In ASSIST, Focusing Mechanism is occupied in ensuring its connectivity.

TEXT (McKeown 1985) is a text generation system which produces multisentence responses to queries about a database schema. The basic approach taken in her system is to define a number of standard patterns of discourse structure called schema and to use each schema to incorporate relevant information into a coherent text. However, since a schema is a template containing a stereotyped discourse structure and could not be modified, asking the same question results in the same answer at all times. In ASSIST, adopting the plan-based text planning and criticizing the plan by considering the state of a user, enables the system to produce explanations according to the user's level of expertise.

REFERENCES

Bresnan J (ed) (1982) The Mental Representation of Grammatical Relations. MIT Press, Cambridge, Mass.
Cohen PR, Perrault CR (1979) Elements of a Plan-Based Theory of Speech Acts. Cognitive Science 3: 177-212
Fillmore CJ (1968) The case for case. In: Bach E, Harms R (eds) Universals in Linguistic Theory. Holt Rinehart Winston, New York, 1-88

McKeown KR (1985) Text Generation. Cambridge University Press, Cambridge

Shapiro EY (1982) Algorithmic Program Debugging. MIT Press, Cambridge, Mass.

Sidner CL (1983) Focusing in the Comprehension of Definite Anaphora. In: Brady M, Berwick RC (eds) Computational Models of Discourse. MIT Press, Cambridge, Mass., 267-330

Simmons RF, Correira A (1979) Rule Forms for Verse, Sentences, and Story Trees. In: Findler NV (ed) Associative Networks: Representation and Use of Knowledge by Computers. Academic Press, New York, 363-392

Uehara K, Kakiuchi T, Mikami O, Toyoda J (1986) Extended Prolog and Its Application to an Integrated Parser. In: Wada E (ed) Logic Programming '85. Springer, Berlin Heidelberg New York, 214-225

Wilensky R, Arens Y, Chin D. (1984) Talking to UNIX in English: An Overview of UC. Comm. of the ACM 27: 574-593

Inheritance Hierarchy Mechanism in Prolog

Kiyoshi AKAMA

Department of Behavioral Science, Faculty of Letters,
Hokkaido University, Sapporo-shi, 060, Japan

ABSTRACT

PAL is an extended prolog to deal with inheritance hierarchy (IH).
It adopts new patterns called class bound variables (CBVs). CBVs are
different from variables with constraints in existing prolog systems,
such as variables with "frozen" goals in prolog-II and term
descriptions, in that class constraints of CBVs change in the inference
when they are unified with other CBVs. The unification is efficiently
executed by using the restriction on the IH structure, such as the
exclusiveness among brother classes in IH. CBVs and the fast
unification method improve the inferential efficiency greatly by
suppressing combinatorial explosions, which might be caused by
exhaustive searches in the inference in other systems.

1. INTRODUCTION

In order to handle, in prolog systems, inheritance hierarchy(IH),
especially concept hierarchy, we can find several methods, such as
multiple world in Prolog/KR and Uranus (Nakashima 1986), term
description (Nakashima 1985; Tomura 1985), extension of unification
(Shibayama 1984), and knowledge representation of DCKR (Koyama 1985).
Among these research, only DCKR is the representation in the ordinary
prolog system, while the others extend prolog from the more general
point of view and apply the result to the representation of IH. In the
contrast of these, this paper extends prolog by introducing a special
mechanism for IH.
Special devices for IH become necessary when we try to construct a
large system to deal with everyday knowledge. The major problem is the
combinatorial explosion of searches in the inference. Because of the
insufficient utilization of useful properties of IH, existing methods
can not avoid exhaustive searches, which could be avoided by better
treatments.
The extended prolog system that we have newly implemented is
called PAL. PAL adopts new patterns called class bound variables
(CBVs). CBVs are variables with class constraints. We define a new
unification for terms including CBVs. The unification is efficiently
executed by using the restriction on the IH structure, such as the
exclusiveness among brother classes in IH. CBVs and the fast
unification method improve the inferential efficiency greatly by
suppressing combinatorial explosions, which might be caused by
exhaustive searches in the inference in other (prolog) systems.
CBVs are different from variables with constraints in existing
prolog systems, such as variables with "frozen" goals in prolog-II
(Giannesini 1985) and term descriptions, in that class constraints of
CBVs change in the inference when they are unified with other CBVs.

Like Prolog/KR, PAL adopts an S-expression syntax, which is simpler than Dec-10 prolog syntax and easier to deal with it theoretically. Thus we use mainly the S-expression syntax in the paper. It is easy to apply the result of the paper to other prolog syntax.

2. DESCRIPTION OF INHERITANCE HIERARCHY AND ITS MEANING

We use a general term "inheritance hierarchy (IH)", because we do not restrict ourselves to the concept hierarchy. This paper gives brief explanations to an example of part-whole hierarchy in 6.
In order to define IH, we introduce two concepts: a class and an instance. We assume that they are both finite symbol atoms. Any symbol atom in PAL is either a class or not, and at the same time, it is either an instance or not. Hence symbol atoms in PAL are divided into four kinds. Among them, symbol atoms that are both classes and instances are used for special purposes, and will be explained partly in 6. The discussion except 6 is given as if there did not exist such symbol atoms.
The relation between two classes are represented using a built-in predicate "asc", in the expression of the form:
    (asc parent_class_name child_class_name).
For example, we can write
    (asc human man)
    (asc human woman)
in order to declare that "human" consists of "man" and "woman". The relation between classes and instances are represented using a built-in predicate "asi", in the expression of the form:
    (asi class_name instance_name).
For example, we can write
    (asi man Tom)
    (asi man John)
    (asi man Bill)
in order to declare that Tom, John and Bill are men.
IH knowledge is defined by a finite set E of asc and asi expressions, where the set E is assumed to satisfy the two conditions:
    a   The associated graph of the expression E has no loops.
    b   No class is the first argument of both asc and asi expressions.
By the associated graph of E we refer to the graph whose node set is all the classes and the instances in E and whose arc set is all the set of arrows each of which goes from the first argument to the second argument of an asc or an asi expression in E. Following the usual convention we often use words for family relations to represent the relations between nodes in the associated graph. For example we say brother classes, etc.
In order to deal with the most typical IH structure in this paper, here we add following two conditions, *c* and *d*. The more general case where E does not satisfy *c* and *d* will be discussed in subsequent papers.
    c   Associated graph of E is an arborescence.
    d   Brother classes in IH are mutually disjoint.
Arborescence is a technical term in graph theory and means to be a rooted tree. We refer to it simply as a tree hereafter, following the ordinary usage of computer scientists.
For convenience, we introduce other built-in predicates, "defc" and "defi", which are equivalent to some sets of asc or asi expressions that share the first argument. Their general forms are:
    (defc parent_class_name list_of_child_class_names), and
    (defi parent_class_name list_of_child_instance_names).
Thus we can write
    (defc human (man woman))

```
(defi man    (Tom John Bill))
(defi woman (Marry Sue))
```
For simplicity we will refer only to defc and defi in the explanation
bellow.
      Let E be an expression representing an IH, and assume C is any
class in E. Then the set of all instances which are descendants of C in
IH is uniquely determined. Thus IH defines a representation framework
that can specify a corresponding set for each class name.

3. CLASS BOUND VARIABLES AND THEIR UNIFICATION

      In order to utilize IH in the inference in prolog, we extend the
concept of variables by introducing new variables with class
constraints. In the program variables are written in the form:
      variable_name^class_name
This means that the variable referred by the "variable_name" matches
only the instances in the set corresponding to the class referred by
the "class_name". Such descriptions or variables in them are called
class bound variables (CBVs). For example,
      *xyz^woman
is a CBV which can become only a woman. Here it should be noted that
variables in PAL are symbol atoms that begin with "*". The example
reminds us of term descriptions (Nakashima 1985) which is an extension
of prolog patterns and implemented in TDProlog (Tomura 1985). It
enables us to regard
      *xyz:woman
as a term that unifies only with women. In the declarative meaning,
these two descriptions (*xyz^woman in PAL and *xyz:woman in TDProlog)
are the same. But, note that PAL defines woman as a class in IH, while
TDProlog defines woman as a predicate with one argument. The more
important difference between the CBV and the term description is the
procedural meaning, that is, the method and the speed of inference,
which comes from differences of the definition of unification.
      The unification using IH is defined as follows. Terms in PAL are
of four kinds: conses, atoms, ordinary variables, and CBVs. The newly
introduced terms are only the last ones: CBVs, and the unification
among old three kinds of terms are the same as the unification in
ordinary prolog. Thus all we need to define is the unification of CBVs
with four kinds of terms (conses, atoms, ordinary variables and CBVs).
   1. unification with a cons (car . cdr)
         fails, since instances of any class are only symbol atoms.
         unify(*x^classx, (car . cdr))   --> failure
   2. unification with atom "a"
         succeeds if the classx involves "a", and *x becomes "a", and
         fails if the classx doesn't involve "a".
         unify(*x^classx, a) --> *x=a   if classx involves a.
         unify(*x^classx, a) --> failure if classx doesn't involves a.
   3. unification with an ordinary variable *y
         succeeds, and *y is bound by classx.
         unify(*x^classx, *y) -->   *x=*y, *x^classx, *y^classx
   4. unification with a CBV *y^classy
         succeeds if two classes are in the inclusion relation, and
         fails   otherwise.
         unify(*x^classx, *y^classy)
            --> *x=*y, *x^classx, *y^classx if classy includes classx
            --> *x=*y, *x^classy, *y^classy if classx includes classy
            --> failure if classx and classy are disjoint
Assuming a familiar IH, we give some examples of unification.
   unify(*p^human, (1 2))   --> failure
   unify(*p^human, adam)   --> success: *p = adam

```
unify(*p^woman, adam)       --> failure
unify(*p^human, *q)         --> success: *p = *q, *p^human, *q^human
unify(*p^woman, *q^human)   --> success: *p = *q, *p^woman, *q^woman
unify(*p^human, *q^woman)   --> success: *p = *q, *p^woman, *q^woman
unify(*p^woman, *q^man)     --> failure
```

4. KNOWLEDGE REPRESENTATION USING INHERITANCE HIERARCHY

First we compare the knowledge representation using IH with the one of DCKR. Consider the following program in DCKR.

```
(a) sem(clyde#1, P)  :- sem(elephant, P).
(b) sem(clyde#2, P)  :- sem(elephant, P).
(c) sem(clyde#3, P)  :- sem(elephant, P).
(d) sem(elephant, P) :- sem(mammal, P).
(e) sem(dog, P)      :- sem(mammal, P).
(f) sem(cat, P)      :- sem(mammal, P).
(g) sem(mammal, P)   :- sem(living_thing, P).
(h) sem(plant, P)    :- sem(living_thing, P).
(i) sem(X, is_a:X).
(j) sem(clyde#2, birth_year:1962).
(k) sem(elephant, color:gray).
(l) sem(mammal, blood_temp:warm).
(m) sem(time#current, year:1986).
```

Using IH, the same knowledge is represented as follows.

```
(1) (defc living_thing (mammal plant))
(2) (defc mammal (elephant dog cat))
(3) (defi elephant (clyde1 clyde2 clyde3))
(4) (defp birth_year ((clyde2 1962)))
(5) (defp color ((*^elephant gray))
(6) (defp blood_temp ((*^mammal warm)))
(7) (defp year ((time_current 1986)))
```

(a),(b) and (c) in DCKR assert that clyde#1, clyde#2 and clyde#3 are instances of elephants, and correspond to (3). In DCKR instances are discriminated from classes by the occurrence of functor #, while in PAL they are recognized by the occurrence in the second argument of defi. (d) (e) and (f) defines three subclasses of the superclass mammal, and correspond to (2). (g) and (h) defines two subclasses of a superclass living_thing, and correspond to (1). We can write (1) (2) and (3) in any order. Here we write them from upper classes down to lower, which seems more natural for the syntax of defc and defi. In DCKR the exclusiveness of brother classes (for example, mammal and plant are brothers and mutually exclusive) can not be represented, while exclusiveness of brother classes is assumed in PAL.

The "predicate" is_a in (i) has a usual meaning: subclass is_a super_class. In PAL this is represented by two predicates: "subclass_of" and "instance_of". For example,

```
(subclass_of dog living_thins)
(instance_of clyde3 mammal)
```

hold assuming the IH defined above. Furthermore we can give queries, such as

```
(subclass_of *c mammal)
(subclass_of cat *c)
(instance_of clyde2 *c)
(instance_of *i living_thing)
```

and can get successively all the classes or all the instances that satisfy given queries using backtracking. The "subclass_of" predicate deals with class inclusion relation based on the IH knowledge, and the "instance_of" predicate class-instance relation. They can not update the IH knowledge.

Facts from (j) to (m) correspond to expressions from (4) to (7). The predicate "defp" is similar to "define", a built-in predicate of Prolog/KR. PAL has both "define" and "defp". CBVs can be used in "defp" expressions, while they can not appear in "define" expressions. The predicate "define" can be efficiently used when we define predicates without using IH knowledge. (5) says that elephants are gray, and (6) says the blood temperature of mammals is warm. (7) says that the current year is 1986.

The next example states naturally that the age of each living_thing is the difference between current year and its birth year.

```
(defp age ((*^living_thing *age)
           (year time_current *year)
           (birth_year *^living_thing *birth_year)
           (- *year *birth_year *age))
```

PAL can also handle the knowledge with exception. For example most birds fly while penguins do not. We can write in PAL:

```
(defc animal (bird fish mammal))
(defc bird (penguin hawk eagle))
(defp can_fly ((*^bird) (not (can_not_fly *))))
(defp can_not_fly ((*^penguin)))
(defp has_a ((*^bird wing)))
(defp move ((*^animal)))
```

5. INFERENTIAL EFFICIENCY

5.1 Comparison with DCKR

There are some cases where we can improve inferential efficiency greatly using IH mechanism and CBVs of PAL. For example, consider the following problem given by Frisch (1985).

Bicycles and cars are both vehicles. Bic-1, bic-2, ... ,bic-n are bicycles. Car-1, car-2,..., car-n, and "mycar" are cars. Vehicles have tires. Cars have doors. I own "mycar". Find all that has tires and has doors and I own.

This problem requires us to seek for what satisfies some given conditions. In this sense, this is a typical prolog problem. We now represent this problem by two methods, DCKR and PAL, and compare the execution time to get solutions. In order for the experiment to be independent of machines, the test run is executed in PAL, which is now the only system to be able to execute both methods. When we give examples of representation, we assume that the problem parameter is 3.

[1] Representation in DCKR
The problem may be represented in DCKR as follows.

```
(as (sem bicycle *) (sem vehicle *))
(as (sem (bic1) *)  (sem bicycle *))
(as (sem (bic2) *)  (sem bicycle *))
(as (sem (bic3) *)  (sem bicycle *))
(as (sem car *)     (sem vehicle *))
(as (sem (car1) *)  (sem car *))
(as (sem (car2) *)  (sem car *))
(as (sem (car3) *)  (sem car *))
(as (sem (mycar) *) (sem car *))
(as (sem vehicle (has tires)))
(as (sem car (has doors)))
(as (sem (mycar) (own I)))
(as (test *) (sem * (has tires)) (sem * (has doors)) (sem * (own I)))
```

In the program above, instances are represented by lists of length 1, since PAL has no functors. Similarly the second arguments of sem predicate are represented by lists of length 2.

[2] Representation in PAL
   We can represent the problem in PAL as follows.
   (defc vehicle (bicycle car))
   (defi bicycle (bic1 bic2 bic3))
   (defi car (car1 car2 car3 mycar))
   (defp has ((*1^vehicle tires)) ((*2^car doors)))
   (defp own ((I mycar)))
   (defp test ((*) (has * tires) (has * doors) (own I *)))
This representation is natural, and easy to read and write.

Table 1 Execution time to obtain the first solution in each method

	n	3	6	9	18	27	
(1)	DCKR	2.40	6.10	11.00	63.00	210.00	(in sec.)
(2)	PAL	0.04	0.04	0.04	0.04	0.04	

      The table 1 shows a result of the experiment, where the parameter
n varies form 3 to 27. While the execution time in DCKR increases
rapidly as n goes up, the PAL's execution time is constant. In prolog
systems with clause indexing, the execution time in DCKR may be
smaller, but the conclusion leaves unchanged, because our argument is
based only on the fact that the order of the execution time of DCKR is
more than n. Note that n means the quantity of knowledge. DCKR has the
shortcoming that it takes more time to infer as it has more knowledge.
      In the representation of DCKR, classes or instances which are
candidate solutions are as follows:
      vehicle,
      bicycle, bic1, bic2,bic3,
      car, car1, car2, car3, mycar.
The search of DCKR is an exhaustive search that checks such classes or
instances one by one. It is for this blind search that DCKR requires
much time in solving such problems.

5.2   Inference Method in PAL

      PAL can avoid the difficulty by using CBVs. The method of
inference could be understood more clearly when we see the successive
execution process for a query (test *) in PAL.

P|(test *)
---> call (test *)
        matched rule = ((test *) (has * tires) (has * doors) (own I *))
---> call (has * tires)
        matched rule = ((has *1^vehicle tires))
<--- succ (has *1^vehicle tires)
---> call (has *1^vehicle doors)
        matched rule = ((has *2^car doors))
<--- succ (has *2^car doors)
---> call (own I *2^car)
        matched rule ((own I mycar))
<--- succ (own I mycar)
(test mycar)

This is the whole search process, where we can see the transition of a
solution set:
      * --> *1^vehicle --> *2^car --> mycar
 This is a successive limitation of the solution set, and the minimal
calculation is done at each time when a new condition is given. Adding
the knowledge of classes and instances by increasing the problem
parameter n doesn't change the solution search process. Thus PAL is

free from the contradiction that the acquisition of knowledge increases the execution time of inference on the knowledge.

The key point of PAL is in the use of the set relation:

vehicle $\cap$ car = car,

car $\cap$ {mycar}   = {mycar}

and PAL can make use of the set relation very effectively, which is understood by two facts:

(1) Since brother classes in IH is assumed to be exclusive, the relations of any two classes in IH is inclusive (one is a subset of the other), or exclusive (two are disjoint). The relation between classes and instances are similar, since we can identify instances with singleton classes.

(2) We can check whether two given classes are inclusive or exclusive by only judging whether there is a path or not from one class to the other class in the tree of IH. And this can be done by traversing IH tree upwards.

5.3 Comparison with Other Methods

Much of the works to extend prolog are based on the extension of unification definition. Such extended unification, however, can not avoid similar kinds of exhaustive searches as DCKR, because they deal with IH knowledge as the set of unary predicate and don't take advantage of useful properties of IH, such as exclusiveness of brother classes, which typical subtrees of IHs share. Therefore, these extended prologs need as much execution time as DCKR needs.

Using "freeze" in prolog-II we can solve the problem as efficiently as PAL can, because prolog-II can freeze the checks of having tires and doors until the third constraint tells it that the only possible solution is mycar. The freeze mechanism is not useful, however, when we are given a slightly changed problem: What has tires and doors? The answer is cars, which PAL can answer by showing a pattern *^car, while ordinary or extended prologs including prolog-II can not. Freeze mechanism in prolog-II is useful only when the answer is not a class but an instance, and does not have the ability to deal with IH knowledge generally.

6. FROM PROPERTIES (UNARY RELATION) TO N-ARY RELATIONS

Mammals have bodies and eyes. Following the method of Koyama (1985) we can represent such knowledge in DCKR as follows.

```
sem(human,  P) :- sem(mammal,  P).
sem(monkey, P) :- sem(mammal,  P).
sem(mammal, has_a:X) :- sem(body, part:X).
sem(X, part:X).
sem(body, part:X) :- sem(hands, part:X).
sem(body, part:X) :- sem(eyes,  part:X).
```

As Koyama said, this representation has some (serious, I think) problems. In order to see it, let us imagine the amount of search necessary for answering the query:

```
?-sem(monkey, has_a:eyes).
```

There are two paths along which we can go from the monkey vertex.

```
monkey --> mammal ==> body ==> hands
monkey --> mammal ==> body ==> eyes
```

The two paths share the way from monkey to body, and separate after body. As the tree of has_a becomes larger, the search for answering the query becomes more and more difficult. This leads to a similar kind of explosion to the one in DCKR's search for mycar.

PAL can also deal with has_a relation very clearly. The main part of the representation in PAL of such knowledge might be:

```
(defc mammal (human monkey))
(defc body    (hands eyes))
(defp has_a  ((*1^mammal *2^body)))
```

The third defp expression describes that each instance of mammals has
any "instance" of "body". Note the meaning of the latter "instance".
The relation between body and eyes, or body and hands is a part-whole
relation, not a set inclusion relation. Hence we can not use here the
word "instance" in the usual meaning. The usage here has an extended
meaning. To see it more clearly, we write a program that represents our
intention without using CBVs:

```
(defp has_a ((mammal body)) ((mammal hands)) ((mammal eyes))
            ((human   body)) ((human   hands)) ((human   eyes))
            ((monkey body)) ((monkey hands)) ((monkey eyes)))
```

Here the roles of the first arguments (mammal, human and monkey) and
the second arguments (body, hands and eyes) of the predicate has_a are
symmetric. So we can deal with both inclusion relation and part-whole
relation in a similar manner. The semantics and concepts of classes and
instances of IH in PAL are based on such interpretation. In order to
complete the program to represent our whole intention preserving the
symmetricity of the first and the second arguments, only things to add
are instances that share their names with classes:

```
(defi mammal (mammal))
(defi human   (human))
(defi monkey (monkey))
(defi body    (body))
(defi hands   (hands))
(defi eyes    (eyes))
```

These declarations make five atoms to be both classes and instances.
Note the following points. Assume that there are three persons: Bill,
John and Sue and their hands are hand-B, hand-J and hand-S,
respectively.

```
(defi human (Bill John Sue))
(defi hands (hand-B hand-J hand-S))
```

We can derive from the knowledge above not only

```
(has_a Bill hand-B)
(has_a John hand-J)
(has_a Sue  hand-S)
```

but also

```
(has_a Bill hand-S)
(has_a Jack hand-B)
(has_a Sue  hand-B)
```

and so on. This contradiction is a result of misunderstanding that the
word "has" in "man has hands" and the word "has" in "Bill has hands"
have the same meaning and can be represented by one predicate. They are
not equal. The former "has" is a general part-whole relation that is
common to human beings, while the latter "has" deals with personal
data. It is necessary to discriminate them and to define two predicates
for the two kinds of "has" and to use them to proper purposes.

The instances which share names with classes should be used
carefully. For example, human is not a instance of human in the usual
meaning. Current edition of PAL assumes that all the class has the
instance with the same name, and we need not declare the defi relation
for atoms that are both classes and instances. Such instances are not
treated by the built-in predicate "instance_of".

DCKR succeeded partly in avoiding the exhaustive search in is_a
hierarchy, but failed in has_a hierarchy. PAL succeeded in avoiding the
explosion by using a binary relation has_a and two trees. Important is
the ability to deal well with binary and n-ary relations. If DCKR
represents the knowledge by the properties (unary relations) such as
has_body, has_eyes, and has_hands, not by the binary relation has_a,
the problem described above never comes out.

The problem is not specific to DCKR, but most of the systems ever developed share it, where the inheritance means only inheritance of properties and no sufficient attentions have not been paid for n-ary relations. In order to get out of the limitation and to treat n-ary relations efficiently, IH of PAL is very important.

7. IMPLEMENTATION

The implementation of IH mechanism is not difficult, both in structure copying method or structure sharing method. We provided PAL with the IH mechanism, keeping the structure sharing mechanism of base prolog unchanged. We will explain it here. Note that there is a variable binding method that do not need any variables with both ordinary S-expression binding and class binding in the same time. So when a variable has class constraint, we connect the variable (and its environment) with its binding class, which is an extension of the case where each bound variable (and its environment) is connected with a pair of an S-expression and its environment in ordinary structure sharing method. For example, when we have
   *x = *y, *x^human, *y^human,
we can represent them by
   (*x env_x) ==> (*y env_y),
   (*y env_y) ==> human,
where env_x is the environment of *x, and env_y is the environment of *y. The two bindings are discriminated by the distinction whether bound variables are connected with pairs (conses) or atoms.
   Assuming ordinary common-sense IH knowledge and using some easy examples, we illustrate the changes of class bindings through unifications. *x^human and *^woman are unifiable and the internal representation of class bindings changes from
   (*x env_x) ==> human,
   (*y env_y) ==> woman
to
   (*x env_x) ==> (*y env_y),
   (*y env_y) ==> woman.
*x^human and *y are also unifiable, and the binding changes from
   (*x env_x) ==> human,
   (*y env_y)
to
   (*x env_x) ==> human,
   (*y env_y) ==> (*x env_x).
*x^human and adam are unifiable, and the change is from
   (*x env_x) ==> human,
   (adam env_a)
to
   (*x env_x) ==> (adam env_a),
   (adam env_a).
*x^animal and *y^vehicle are not unifiable.

8. CONCLUDING REMARKS

We proposed an extended prolog with a special mechanism of handling IH knowledge. It enables us to write facts and rules naturally using IH knowledge. It also improves the inferential efficiency greatly by avoiding exhaustive searches. Our method is very natural and suited to prolog systems. The implementation of the extension which provides ordinary prolog with IH facility is easy and does not decrease the inference speed of base prolog.

When we handle various knowledge in machines, very large part of them depends on the IH structure. In order to handle large scale knowledge bases in practical speed, we need to explore techniques to utilize IH structure fully. The method described in this paper is one of them.

In subsequent papers we will give extensions of the work, such as multiple IH, IH compiling techniques, clause indexing techniques using IH, and application methods for natural language processing.

REFERENCES

Frisch AM (1985) An Investigation into Inference with Restricted Quantification and a Taxonomic Representation, SIGART Newsletter, 91: 28-31
Giannesini F, Kanoui H, Pasero R, van Caneghem M (1985) Prolog (in French). InterEditions, Paris
Koyama H, Tanaka H (1985) Definite Clause Knowledge Representation (in Japanese), proc. of the Logic Programming Conference '85, 95-106
Nakashima H (1986) Uranus Reference Manual, Research Memorandum, ETL-RM-86-7. Electrotechnical Laboratory, Ibaraki JAPAN
Nakashima H (1985) Term Description : A Simple Powerful Extension to Prolog Data Structures, Proc. of IJCAI-IX, 708-710
Shibayama E (1984) Extension of Unification in Logic Programming and its Applications (in Japanese), WG. of Software foundation,10-4, 31-40
Tomura S (1985) TDProlog: An Extended Prolog with Term Description (in Japanese), Proc. of the Logic Programming Conference '85, 237-245

KORE : A HYBRID KNOWLEDGE PROGRAMMING ENVIRONMENT FOR DECISION SUPPORT BASED ON A LOGIC PROGRAMMING LANGUAGE

Toramatsu Shintani, Yoshinori Katayama, Kunihiko Hiraishi, and Mitsuhiko Toda

International Institute for Advanced Study of Social Information Science (IIAS-SIS) FUJITSU LIMITED, 140 Miyamoto, Numazu-shi, Shizuoka 410-03, Japan

ABSTRACT

We discuss problems to construct intelligent decision support systems, and propose KORE (Knowledge Oriented Reasoning Environment) as an environment for developing such systems. KORE is a hybrid tool for assisting unified knowledge-based program construction, and is composed of four subsystems. Each of the subsystems provides a unique knowledge programming paradigm which is object-oriented (e.g., SMALLTALK), data-oriented (e.g., demons), rule-oriented (e.g., OPS5), network-oriented (e.g., semantic networks), or logic-oriented (e.g., Prolog) programming paradigm. These subsystems can be integrated by using a relational table based on a logic programming language, which is used as a common internal representation for information. The integration by the relational table enables to provide a unifying principle for the different programming paradigms. KORE can offer a hybrid environment to solve problems on intelligent decision support systems.

1. INTRODUCTION

Simon proposes a model for the process of decision making which identifies three distinct phases(Simon 1960): (1)intelligence activity (searching the environment for conditions calling for decision), (2)design activity (inventing, developing and analyzing possible courses of action), and (3)choice activity (selecting a course of action from those available). The model describes decision making in its broad sense, and the division into the three phases is useful when we consider to support decision making as a human intelligent activity.

There have been considerable efforts of research on systems and methodology for supporting decision making in the areas of (a)DSS(Decision Support Systems), (b)decision analysis, and (c)expert systems. Existing systems and methodology in these areas do not effectively support all of the three phases of decision making discussed above, although they support a part of the process. This is in part due to the limitation of present state of art for DSS and in part due to the narrow scope of the areas covered by (b) and (c). In order to support decision making effectively, we should interpret it in its broad sense and design systems which can support decision makers throughout the three phases. Such systems are required to be flexible and function intelligently so that they can support the highly intelligent activities of human decision makers, hence they must be equipped with knowledge information processing capabilities based on knowledge bases and inference engines etc. We call these systems *Intelligent Decision Support Systems* (*IDSS*).

The broad scope of support intended by IDSS requires us to invent new methods and integrate them with existing ones, and to develop it on a knowledge information processing environment. We propose *Knowledge Oriented Reasoning Environment (KORE)* to facilitate designing and developing IDSS. KORE is a hybrid problem solving environment consisting of four subsystems, each of which provides data-oriented, rule-oriented, object-oriented or network-oriented knowledge programming paradigm. We outline the method for implementing KORE and show how it provides an environment for developing IDSS which integrate functions of existing systems and methodology in a uniform manner.

This paper consists of six sections. In section 2 we analyze functions of existing systems and methodology, and discuss needs for IDSS. Then we propose KORE and describe principles of its design and implementation in Section 3. In Section 4 we sketch feature functions provided by subsystems of KORE. In Section 5 we describe the relations between KORE and the needs for IDSS. Section 6 concludes the paper with some remarks.

2. NEEDS FOR IDSS

In this section we discuss needs for IDSS which are obtained by surveying the current state of art and research for systems and methodology for supporting decision making; DSS, decision analysis, and expert systems. Effective IDSS should be designed by considering these needs, which are analyzed in terms of the Simon's three phases of decision making.

2.1. DSS : Decision Support Systems

There exist many systems which are called DSS. However, serious study for developing full scale DSS is an emerging interdisciplinary field (Schneider 1985), and there are many problems to realize effective supports for decision making (Keen 1978). Based on the lessons learned from MIS(Management Information Systems), the term DSS was first proposed by Gorry and Morton(1971), and has been used in various interpretations since then. They can be classified into the following two types(Alter 1980); (1)data oriented systems(e.g., searching or managing data), and (2)model oriented systems (e.g., applying accounting models or optimization models). Data oriented systems, the majority of existing systems, mainly support intelligence activity, and model oriented systems mainly support design and choice activities. The support, however, is limited due to lack of flexibility of the systems. Their user is required to have detailed knowledge of the systems, databases and model bases, etc. He needs to take time for combining individual models and integrating them with data, either by himself or with the aid of a specialist for DSS.

We need to construct mechanisms which can combine the functions of the two types of DSS and support us effectively in combining models for decision making and integrating them with data. In order to realize the mechanisms with modeling knowledge we introduce those of knowledge based systems in KORE by integrating an inference engine with database management. The inference engine enables to merge models in model bases, and database management enables to retrieve data required to evaluate the models.

2.2. Decision Analysis

Decision analysis mainly provides methodology for design and choice activities. During design phase the main concern of a decision maker is to specify decision alternatives based on knowledge accumulated through his experience, hence IDSS needs to support searching and structuring his knowledge rather than providing information in IDSS. This support, called structuring support of user knowledge, can be attained by implementing such methodology as problem reduction and means-ends analysis. ABSTRIPS(Sacerdoti 1974), which is based on hierarchical planning methodology, is an example of problem solving systems. During the structuring support of user knowledge a system can help clarify the structure of a decision problem by providing prespecified operators (or actions) which are used to attain the main goal of problem solving.

Multi-criteria decision making methodology (e.g., Keeney 1976) is useful for choice activity. It is intended to support a decision maker who is faced with real world complex decision problems, which require him to consider various aspects and to select an optimal alternative based on his subjective assessments on criteria for the multiple aspects. This type of activity during choice phase is intermixed with the above design activity.

In order to realize the structuring support of user knowledge we need to construct mechanisms for structuring knowledge and maintaining consistency in knowledge bases. To meet this need we implement an object-oriented knowledge representation in KORE, which can structure knowledge hierarchically. As a mechanism for maintaining consistency in knowledge bases, we implement a network (of relational information) management component in KORE, which supplies important information for managing knowledge to solve complex problems in connection with a network inference, a truth maintenance mechanism(Doyle 1978), etc.

2.3. Expert Systems

It seems that expert systems can be used for supporting a part of choice activity. They can provide functions for unstructured (or ill-structured) decision problems. They support solving the problems by offering knowledge bases which keep domain dependent knowledge of experts(Hayes-Roth 1984). A consultation system, an example of expert systems, provides decision support mechanisms for making a diagnosis by choosing and examining appropriate knowledge in knowledge bases.

In order to integrate functions of expert systems effectively into IDSS, we need to realize effective knowledge representation. It often happens that a single knowledge representation is not sufficient for varieties of domain areas required for decision support. Therefore, we implement multiple forms of representations in KORE, which provides a terse hybrid representation capability.

3. KORE : KNOWLEDGE ORIENTED REASONING ENVIRONMENT

In order to develop IDSS discussed in Section 2 we design and construct KORE which can provide various knowledge programming paradigms (Bobrow 1984). KORE consists of four subsystems for knowledge programming and problem solving, which are (1)KORE/DB(Data Base subsystem), (2)KORE/IE(Inference Engine subsystem), (3)KORE/KR(Knowledge Representation subsystem), and (4)KORE/EDEN(Extended Dependency Network subsystem). These subsystems are programmed by Prolog and integrated by relational tables as shown in Fig. 1.

These subsystems enable KORE to offer a hybrid environment for constructing problem solving applications of IDSS. Each of the subsystems provides a unique paradigm for

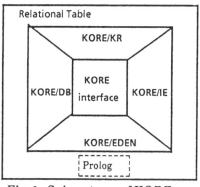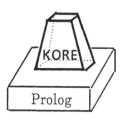

Fig. 1. Subsystems of KORE.

knowledge programming: data-oriented (in KORE/DB), rule-oriented (in KORE/IE), object-oriented (in KORE/KR), and network-oriented (in KORE/EDEN) knowledge programming (or control) paradigms. These subsystems can be used independently to solve problems on an IDSS, and can also be integrated by using relational tables based on logic programming. The integration by relational tables enables to provide a unifying principle for different knowledge programming paradigms, which are easily combined together for developing an IDSS.

3.1. Organizing Knowledge in KORE

Relational tables in KORE provide a means for organizing knowledge in a uniform manner and for interconnecting information throughout the three phases of decision making. Namely, a subsystem in KORE can support and use results of problem solving in the other subsystems by using the tables as a means of communication. The relational table in KORE corresponds to a blackboard which is proposed in a "blackboard model" by Hayes-Roth(1978). It has the following two unique features : (1)it is used by subsystems, which have unique control strategies, as a means of communication, (2)it is a kind of relational database managed by KORE/DB.

We implement the tables by using assertions in Prolog. In logic programming, the 3-column and 3-row table in Fig. 2 can be represented by the 3 assertions of 3-place predicate in the same figure (Kowalski 1977).

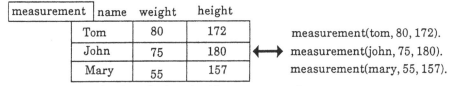

Fig. 2. Example of a relational table representation.

In this representation, the predicate name "measurement" represents the name of the table, and each row of the table can be uniquely identified by the first argument of these assertions. The other arguments represent the column positions of the table.

The internal representation of subsystems is unified by using relational tables as shown in Fig.3.

Subsystem	internal representation	unified relation
KORE/KR	Relations between objects ← Slots ← Methods ←	Relational information
KORE/IE	Relations between rules ← Working memory elements ← Rules ←	Declarative information
KORE/DB	Table schemata Tuples ← Triggers (or Demons) ←	Procedural information
KORE/EDEN	Relations between knowledge ←	

Fig. 3. The unified relations of internal representations.

In Fig. 3 'unified relations' unify internal representations which have the same table structure (or schema), and connect them by lines. There are three types of unified relations, which are (1)relational (connected by solid lines), (2)declarative (broken lines), and (3) procedural information (dotted lines) as in Fig. 3.

3.1.1 The relational information

The relational information which is managed by KORE/EDEN is used to control relations between knowledge such as isa (or class-inclusion) relationships, hasa (or part-whole) relationships, data dependencies (McDermott 1983), etc. These relationships are useful for managing and manipulating knowledge to solve complex problems in connection with belief revision, default reasoning, network inference and so on.

The relational information is kept in knowledge tables (Shintani 1986). A knowledge table keeps relations between knowledge by using a table-like representation on a logic programming language (i.e., Prolog). The table represents information of adjacency and reachability matrices of a directed graph which express relations. An example is presented in Fig.4 to illustrate the notion and implementation of knowledge table. The directed graph in Fig. 4 can be kept by the table in the same figure which integrates an adjacency matrix and corresponding reachability matrix. Each element of the table has number "01","10", or "00" which indicates (1)adjacency, (2)reachability, or (3)no relation between nodes, respectively as in Fig. 4. The "00" elements in the table in Fig.4 are omitted in the economical list representation in the relational table in Fig. 5. It is a compact representation for the table in Fig. 4 and the tuples without 'element' are suppressed.

A list in the relational table in Fig. 5 is a bitwise representation of a row of the table in Fig. 4. For example, the list "[346]" identified by "6" for "position" attribute represents the 6th row of the table. We can consider the sequence "000101011010" of the column elements of the row as a binary digit string, and then consider it to be binary number "101011010", which is 346 as a decimal number (or integer).

Operations (searching, deleting, appending relations, etc) on knowledge tables are carried out efficiently by manipulating the numbers, since we can represent rows of the tables with

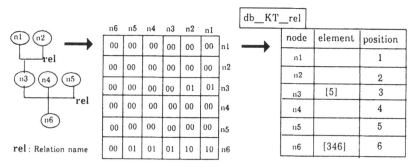

Fig. 4. A table representation for relations.   Fig. 5. A compact list representation.

integers, and can apply logical bitwise computations (integer bitwise disjunction, conjunction, negation, etc) to identify and modify the integer for updating the table.

3.1.2. The declarative information

The declarative information in KORE is represented by a relational table, which is composed of slot-values and a class name. Each tuple (or row) in the table corresponds to a working memory element in KORE/IE or a slot of an instance in KORE/KR. A table schema is represented as shown in Fig.6.

db__<NAME>__slot					
<Slot$_1$> $\cdots$ <Slot$_n$>	time	usage	author	table

Fig. 6. The table schema of declarative information.

In Fig. 6 <NAME> and <Slot$_1$> $\cdots$ <Slot$_n$> indicate a class name and slot names, respectively, which are identified when a table is used. Other additional attributes of the table play important roles. The attribute "time" indicates the time when a tuple is added to the table. It is used as a time tag of a working memory in KORE/IE. The time tag is important information for conflict resolutions. The attribute "usage" is used to describe information for making use of a tuple. The attribute "table" is used to refer to other tables.

3.1.3. The procedural information

The procedural information (procedures) in KORE is called by different terms; demons (or attached procedures), rules, and methods in KORE/DB, KORE/IE, and KORE/KR, respectively. The procedural information is represented schematically by the relational table shown in Fig. 7.

db__<NAME>__method									
name	cond	result	activity	priority	date	author	usage	userform	table

Fig. 7. The table schema of procedural information.

In Fig. 7 <NAME> indicates the name of a database, a class or a rule base, which is identified when the table is used. The attribute "name" indicates the name of a procedure composed of some trigger conditions and actions, which are specified by the attributes "cond" and "result", respectively. The attributes "activity" and "priority" are used as control information for activating procedures, and the other attributes are used to maintain the procedures.

3.2. Controlling Knowledge in KORE

In order to construct applications of IDSS, subsystems of KORE are used as parts which offer functions for controlling knowledge. Controlling knowledge corresponds to interpreting and managing information in relational tables. KORE is equipped with four strategies for controlling knowledge ; rule-oriented (in KORE/IE), object-oriented (in KORE/KR), data-oriented (in KORE/DB), and network-oriented (in KORE/EDEN) strategies. These parts for controlling knowledge jointly offer flexible environments for IDSS.

Fig. 8 illustrates an example of clear distinction between organizing knowledge and controlling it in KORE.

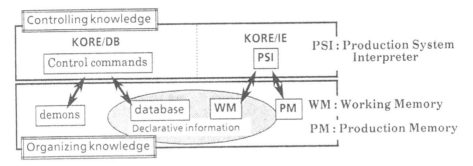

Fig. 8. Controlling and organizing knowledge in KORE.

KORE/IE can be considered as a production system, and its component for controlling knowledge corresponds to PSI(Production System Interpreter), which interprets productions (or rule), as shown in Fig.8. Other components of KORE/IE are organized and stored systematically in relational tables : i.e., WM(Working Memory) is stored as declarative information and PM(Production Memory) is stored as procedural information. By integrating KORE/DB with KORE/IE as parts for controlling knowledge, we can easily construct an environment for IDSS, which combine a relational database with an inference engine. Adding tuples to a database in KORE/DB corresponds to adding a working memory element to WM in KORE/IE. Therefore, rules are invoked when tuples are added to the database, and changes in WM caused by invoking rules in PM activate demons (triggers or attached procedures) in KORE/DB, which then modify the database. Thus KORE/DB and KORE/IE can be cooperatively utilized for solving problems.

3.3. Comparison of KORE with Other Environments

There exist systems which provide hybrid programming environments such as LOOPS(Bobrow 1983) and KEE(Fikes 1985). The main difference between these systems and KORE lies in the mechanisms to enable hybridity. KORE aims at realizing hybrid control of knowledge, whereas other systems realize hybrid knowledge representation. In these systems various knowledge programming paradigms are confined in one language representation, hence its syntax is complex and makes it difficult for us to program and construct application systems on their environments. In KORE knowledge programming paradigms are distributed to subsystems, each of which provides a unique knowledge programming paradigm for controlling knowledge as in Fig. 9. Consequently we can easily

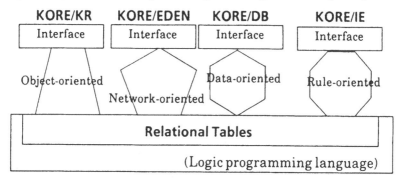

Fig. 9. Knowledge programming paradigms in KORE.

use various knowledge programming paradigms by integrating them as parts. The integration is achieved by unifying internal representations of the subsystems with relational tables and by communicating through the tables.

4. FEATURE FUNCTIONS OF SUBSYSTEMS OF KORE

4.1. KORE/DB

KORE/DB provides functions for managing relational tables as a subsystem of KORE. Independently it can be used as a database management system for supporting a process of intelligence activity for decision making. The syntax of its language is similar to that of SQL(Astrahan 1975).

Logic programming is advantageous for representing and managing relational tables, since (1)all the functions for manipulating relational tables can be written efficiently in one language, and (2)integrity constraints in databases can be easily realized(Kowalski 1978).

KORE/DB has basic functions for managing relational databases. It is insufficient for a complete relational database management system in the following respects : (1)the size of a database is smaller than general databases, (2)it does not provide functions for multiple users, and (3)it is not equipped with recovery functions for hardware errors. It is possible to improve these insufficiencies by using techniques in logic programming(Dahl 1982). However, KORE/DB is not intended to include these features, since it is intended to be a personal system and to offer basic functions for manipulating relational tables in KORE.

4.2. KORE/IE

KORE/IE provides functions for rule-oriented problem solving and knowledge representations in KORE. Independently it functions as a production system like OPS5(Forgy 1981), and in IDSS it can be used as an inference engine and integrated with other subsystems. Its basic functions and the syntax of its language are similar to those of OPS5. In order to speed up pattern matching during a recognize-act cycle, we use an algorithm like Rete match algorithm(Forgy 1982), which is easily implemented by using advantages of a refutation mechanism in Prolog.

An example of rules below illustrates the syntax of KORE/IE :

> on_floor : **if** goal(status = active, type = on, object_name = X) **&**
>   monkey(on \= = floor)
> **then**
>   modify(2, on = floor) **&**
>   modify(1, status = satisfied).

where bold characters are reserved words, "on_floor" shows a rule name defined by a user, and "&" is a delimiter. The LHS(Left Hand Side) is composed of patterns which correspond to terms of Prolog. The patterns are represented by tuples of declarative information in relational tables in KORE. In the RHS(Right Hand Side) of a rule, we can use OPS5-like RHS actions (make, modify, remove, etc) and Prolog predicates which can be prespecified by a user. Manipulation of WM by RHS actions can be realized easily by using functions of KORE/DB, since manipulating WM corresponds to manipulating relational tables. Other functions of KORE/IE can also be realized by using functions of KORE/DB. Table 1 shows corresponding functions between KORE/IE and KORE/DB.

Table. 1. Correspondence of functions between KORE/IE and KORE/DB.

KORE/DB	Functions	operations on tuples	KORE/IE	Functions	operations on WM
	table definition	create		class definition	literalize
	insertion	ins		addition	make
	updating	update		updating	modify
	deletion	del		deletion	remove

4.3. KORE/KR

KORE/KR provides functions for object-oriented knowledge representations(Goldberg 1983) which can be used to represent and manage knowledge hierarchically. A definition of a class (which is a description of one or more similar objects) in KORE/KR can be shown as follows:

> **defclass** scroll_window **::**
>   **supers** window **;**
>   **partof** frame1 = frame_object **;**
>   **value__set** wp = [2,6,5],
>   partition = hbm,
>   attribute = an,
>   scroll = jump_scroll**;**
>   **method** move**:**[Top,Bottom]**:** 'move window'**:**
>   Line is Bottom-Top + 1,
>   putvalue(self,wp,[Top,Bottom,Line]),
>   (^ refresh)**;** · · · · **.**

where bold characters are reserved words. As shown in the example, the definition consists of three parts, which are description for (1)relationships between objects(the supers and partof part), (2)slots(the value__set part), and (3)methods(the method part). The part for relationships can be managed and enhanced by KORE/EDEN, hence KORE/KR can provide powerful functions for message passing: it can broadcast a message to unspecified objects, which can be determined by specifying classes to direct the message, as well as normal message passing to specified objects adopted by existing object-oriented systems. The part for slots is represented in relational tables as declarative information. The unified internal representation for the subsystems provides KORE/KR with basic functions for cooperating in problem solving with the others. For example, making instances which are objects described by particular classes, and modifying slots can be used as conditions for activating rules in KORE/IE, and conversely, the results of the actions of the rules can be represented and managed hierarchically by using KORE/KR as in Fig. 10. The cooperation corresponds to using KORE/IE as an inference engine and KORE/KR as a knowledge base.

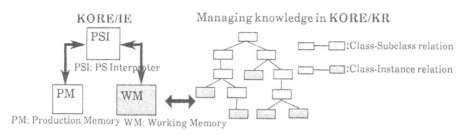

Fig. 10. Cooperation between KORE/IE and KORE/KR. Dark parts, WM in KORE/IE and instance objects in KORE/KR, indicate shared declarative information.

4.4. KORE/EDEN

KORE/EDEN provides functions for representing and managing relations between knowledge in KORE. The relations are efficiently stored in the knowledge tables discussed in Section 3.1.1. Independently the subsystem can be used as a management system for networks(Brachman 1983).

KORE/EDEN enables us to get useful information to implement a truth maintenance system(Doyle 1978) for belief revision and dependency-directed backtracking(Stallman 1972) for complex problem solving, since the networks managed by KORE/EDEN correspond to data dependencies(McDermott 1983) for the mechanisms.

5. THE RELATIONS BETWEEN KORE AND NEEDS FOR IDSS

The needs for constructing IDSS described in Section 2 can be met by integrating the subsystems of KORE. Namely, KORE provides a hybrid environment for constructing IDSS. Fig. 11 illustrates the flexibility of integration of the subsystems for developing IDSS.

Fig. 11 shows an example for integrating KORE/KR and KORE/DB. In the integrated system, we can write programs for data processing of a database by using KORE/KR, and information constructed by KORE/KR can be retrieved easily by using KORE/DB which has simple declarative search commands. Other examples of integration are described in Sections 3.2 and 4.3.

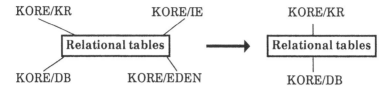

Fig. 11. Integrating subsystems of KORE.

The environment provided by KORE corresponds to a basic and unified environment for constructing applications which support problem solving throughout the three phases of decision making. The needs discussed in Section 2.1 for intelligence as well as design and choice activities, which is to integrate an inference engine with database management, can be realized by combining KORE/IE with KORE/DB. The needs discussed in Section 2.2 for design activity, which is to represent and manage knowledge hierarchically and maintain truth in knowledge bases, can be realized by integrating KORE/KR and KORE/EDEN. The needs discussed in Section 2.3 for choice activity, which is to provide a terse hybrid knowledge representation, can be realized by using the subsystems as parts for controlling knowledge.

The information in KORE is unified into relational tables, the uniform internal representation of its subsystems. The information can be used for problem solving throughout the three phases at any time. If we construct applications of IDSS by using existing tools and techniques implemented on KORE, the applications can be integrated effectively and can support decision making throughout the three phases.

6. CONCLUSIONS

In this paper, we have discussed an approach to construct intelligent decision support systems (IDSS) based on Simon's model for decision making. The model, which identifies three distinct phases of decision making, is a useful concept to analyze the needs for supporting decision making. We have proposed KORE which provides an environment for supporting decision making throughout the three phases. By using KORE we can effectively adopt, integrate, and modify functions of existing systems for supporting decision making.

Subsystems of KORE can be integrated by using relational tables on Prolog, which are used as a common internal representation of the subsystems. This method of integration is useful to provide a hybrid environment for controlling knowledge, and contributes to simplifying syntax of languages for the subsystems. In KORE knowledge programming paradigms are distributed to its subsystems, each of which provides a unique paradigm. Therefore we can easily use various knowledge programming paradigms by integrating them when we develop IDSS.

ACKNOWLEDGMENT

The authors would like to acknowledge the continuing guidance and encouragements of Dr. Tosio Kitagawa, the president of their institute, and Dr. Hajime Enomoto, the director of their institute.

This research has been carried out as a part of Fifth Generation Computer Project.

REFERENCES

Alter SL (1980) Decision Support System: Current Practice and Continuing Challenges. Addison-Wesley, Mass., p316

Astrahan MM (1975) Implementation of a Structured English Query Language. Communications of ACM, 18:580-589

Bobrow DG, Stefik MJ (1983) The LOOPS Manual. KB-VLISI-81-13

Bobrow DG (1984) IF PROLOG IS ANSWER WHAT IS THE QUESTION. Proc. The International Conference on Fifth Generation Computer System, 138-145

Brachman RJ (1983) What IS-A is and isn't : An Analysis of Taxonomic Links in Semantic Networks. Computer 16 (October): 30-36

Dahl V (1978) On Database Systems Development Through Logic . ACM Transactions on Database Systems 7:102-123

Doyle J (1978) Truth Maintenance System for Problem Solving. MIT, AI-TR-419

Fikes R, Kehler T (1985) The Role of Frame-Based Representation in Reasoning. Communication of the ACM 28: 904-920

Forgy CL (1981) OPS5 User's Manual. CMU-CS-81-135, July

Forgy CL (1982) Rete: A Fast Algorithm for the Many Pattern/ Many Object Pattern Match Problem. Artificial Intelligence 19: 17-37

Goldberg I, Robson D (1983) Smalltalk-80: The Language and it's Implementation. Addison-Wesley, Mass., p714

Gorry GA, Morton MSS (1971) A Framework for Management Information Systems. Sloan Management Review 13: 55-70

Hayes-Roth F (1984) The Knowledge-Based Expert System: A tutorial. Computer 17 (September): 11-28

Keen PGW, Morton MSS (1978) Decision Support Systems: An Organizational Perspective. Addison Wesley, Mass, p264

Keeney RL, Raiffa H (1976) Decisions with Multiple Objectives : Preferences and Value Tradeoffs. Wiley, p569

Kowalski R (1977) Logic for Problem Solving. Elservier North Holland, 31-44

Kowalski R (1978) LOGIC FOR DATA DESCRIPTION. In: Gallaire H(ed) LOGIC AND DATA BASES, Plenum Press, New York

McDermott D (1983) Contexts and Data Dependencies : A Synthesis. IEEE, PAMI-5: 237-246

Sacerdoti ED (1974) Planning in a hierarchy of abstraction spaces. Artificial Intelligence 13: 81-132

Schneider HJ, Whinston A (1985) Editorial. Decision Support Systems 1: 1-4

Simon HA (1960) The New Science of Management Decision. New York: Harper & Row

Shintani T (1986) Knowledge Table: An Approach to Knowledge Utilization Mechanism for Knowledge Base. FUJITSU IIAS-SIS Research Report No. 70, p32

Stallman RM, Sussman GJ (1977) Forward Reasoning and Dependency-Directed Backtracking in a System for Computer-Aided Circuit Analysis. Artificial Intelligence 9: 135-196

LEGAL EXPERT SYSTEM · LES-2

H. Yoshino, S. Kagayama, S. Ohta, M. Kitahara,
H.Kondoh, M. Nakakawaji, K. Ishimaru, and S. Takao

Legal Expert System Association
Meiji Gakuin University,
1-2-37 Shirokane-Dai, Minato-Ku, Tokyo, (108) Japan

1. INTRODUCTION

This paper presents the second version of the Legal Expert System (hereafter LES-2), which the Legal Expert System Association (LESA president Prof. H. Yoshino, Meiji Gakuin University, Tokyo) developed in cooperation with NEC Corporation in 1986.

In December 1985 LES-1 was developed.It was the 1st version of this system and it was developed as a reasoning system for substantial law(Japanese civil law). LES-2 was developed in June 1986, the structure of which is meant to augment LES-1 simple natural language transmission, Q&A system and a new reasoning system for civil procedural law. LES-2 employs PROLOG-KABA and WING on NEC PC9801 computer.

A legal expert system is a computer system containing specified legal knowledge, with which one can perform legal problem-solving. Progress in the expert system in the field of law has, comparatively speaking, made less headway than in other fields. A developing programming with PROLOG has, however, recently served to promote several systems. For instance, we can see new impact for research on description dealing with the time in law.

To build up a general legal expert system, one needs to have cooperation between informaticians and professionals(experts). In this very sense, it can be argued that this system has resulted from such cooperation.

In building up a legal expert system, it is necessary to analyze the structure of legal knowledge, and subsequently create a system suitable for that structure. The features of legal knowledge are: (i)it is expressed in natural language, and (ii)it is an OPEN-ENDED universe of discourse. This study examines LES-2 from those two perspectives.

2. THE FUNDAMENTAL STRUCTURE OF LAW AND LEGAL REASONING AND ITS FORMALIZATION

The process of judgement made by a jurist to solve legal problems, that is, the process of the legal judgement, is referred to as "legal reasoning." A legal expert system must be first and foremost a legal reasoning system.

The most typical form of legal reasoning is the reasoning of law application. That is, it means to reason the conclusion to be gotten by applying of law to a certain case. This legal reasoning is composed of the reasoning for justification of legal conclusions from the given premises and heuristic reasoning for the premises themselves. As the reasoning for justification of legal conclusion is looked upon as the fundamental source of legal reasoning, the system of the reasoning of legal justification should be created first.

The reasoning of legal justification is based on logical proof, but not legal syllogisms in a simple form which are composed only of legal rules and facts. While legal rules(the "articles") are abstractly prescribed, each fact is concrete. It is necessary, therefore, for legal rules to be interpreted as the "concretization" of the meaning of the rules so that a bridge might be built between an abstract legal rule and concrete facts. These articles are not independent of each other, but are related logically to each other to form the legal system. There are legal principles which logically relate each legal article. The structure of the reasoning for the justification, as well as those principles formulated by PROLOG, can be expressed in the following modified legal syllogism:

Fig. 1.
Rule 1 (legal norm sentence):
1a. legal_principle: legal_effect_0(X):-
                legal_effect_1(X), legal_effect_2(X).
1. legal rule: legal_effect_1(X):-
                legal_requirement_1(X), legal_requirement_2(X).
1b. interpretation: legal_requirement_1(X):-
                legal_requirement_11(X), legal_requirement_12(X).
1c. judgement·supplementary interpretation:
                legal_requirement_11(X):-
                legal_requirement_111(X).
Rule 2 (subsumption judgement dictionary)
2. subsumption: legal_requirement_111(X):-
                fact_1(X).
Fact:
3. Fact: fact_1(a).

Logical deduction:
4. Legal decision: legal_effect_0(a).

(The legal rule 2, legal requirement 2, legal requirement 12 needs an appropriate legal rule, interpretation, and facts, but they are abbreviated here.)
        As shown in Fig. 1 above, the fundamental unit of legal knowledge, a legal norm sentence, has a logical structure based on the conditional sentence of legal requirement and legal effect. Moreover the legal system has a hierarchical logical connective structure reaching from the abstract to the concrete level. It should be noted that in the above PROLOG formulas the connection of each legal requirement on the right side, that is, of each literal in the body means not only the connection AND in logic, but also it prescribes the procedural order to decide the truth or falsity of each sentence, and thus the legal world resembles the PROLOG world in that both assume a closed world where each sentence must be false if it fails to be proved to be true. It could be said it corresponds to the reality of legal reasoning.
        Supposing the rightness of the rules system, (the rightness of) the legal decision of a case can be proved as the logical deduction from this rules and the given facts. To construct a reasoning system of legal justification, the system has to be provided with a rule base of rule 1 and a dictionary base of rule 2. Then inputting the FACTS of the case the legal decision can be deduced by the back-tracking reasoning process of PROLOG.
        In legal reasoning, there are valid meta rules which control priority in applying rules. For example, "A special law is prior to a general law," "An upper law is prior to a lower law," "A new law is prior to an old law" and so on. When it is possible to apply mul-tiple legal rules to a case, it is necessary to control the reason-ing by means of the meta rules. And it is necessary to build up an inference engine to control the priority. The precise way is to be stated in section 4 below.

The object being sought in legal reasoning is usually the af-
firmation of the existence of a legal relation, that is, the affir-
mation of the existence of a "right-obligation" relationship. In
formalizing legal knowledge, therefore, regarding the relationship
as a top-goal, the expression form is to be considered in which one
can call into the variable domain the concrete data of the aspects
of the legal relation according to the particularity of the case. In
the world of legal knowledge as shown in Figure 1, each legal
requirement and legal effect shares a reciprocal and systematic
relationship with other legal requirements and legal effects. To
express this relation properly, it is desirable to formalize each
legal requirement as a unit. It is to be noted in the formalizing
that in the legal practice each factor describes the various social
relations ruled by law in natural language. The formalized unit
must exactly describe such a variety of the world. And the expression in natural language must always correspond to the description
of the logical formalization with a high degree of regularity.
    In order to realize the formalization easily and exactly, a
formula of compound predicate logic by PROLOG was devised. The
legal effect of a legal norm sentence(head of PROLOG), for example,
would appear as in (1) of Fig. 2.

Fig. 2.
(1) Compound Predicate Logic Formula by PROLOG:
become_effective(ID1,T0,legal_act(ID2,M12,
contract(ID3,M2,M3,M4,Sale),
content(ID4,Have(ID5,T1,M5,M6 (ID7,T2,P1,M7,M8,H1,purchase-
price(ID8,M10,K3,Thing))))))).

(2) Predicate Logic Formula:

$\forall$ID1, $\forall$ID2, $\forall$ID3, $\forall$ID4, $\forall$ID5, $\forall$ID6, $\forall$ID7, $\forall$ID8, $\forall$T0, $\forall$T1, $\forall$T2,
$\forall$P1, $\forall$M1, $\forall$M2, $\forall$M3, $\forall$M4, $\forall$M5, $\forall$M6, $\forall$M7, $\forall$M8, $\forall$M10, $\forall$K3, $\forall$H1(
become_effective(ID1,T0,ID2)&
legal_act(ID2,M1,ID3,ID4)&
contract(ID3,M2,M3,M4,Sale)&
content(ID4,ID5)&
have(ID5,T1,M5,M6,ID6)&
duty(ID6,ID7)&
pay(ID7,T2,P1,M7,M8,H1,ID8,)&
purchase-price(ID8,M10,K3,Thing))

(1') Compound Predicate Logic Formula by PROLOG:
become_effective(id1,1986-5-1,legal_act(id2,fuji_corporation_and
mishima_yoko,contract(id3,fuji_corporation,mishima_
yoko,M4,sale),content(id4,have(id5,
1986_6_1,mishima_yoko,fuji_corporation,duty(id6,pay(id7,1986-6-10,
office(id6_1,fuji_corporation),mishima_yoko,fuji_corporation,
without_delay,purchase_price(id9,M10,¥370,000,english_conversation_
teaching_materials(id10,with(id11,advantage(id12,content(id13,can
(14,M11,go(id15,T3,P2,M12,M13,cheaply,overseas_travel)))))))))))))).

(3) Simple Natural Language Expression:
"On May 1 1986(Fuji Corporation and Mishima Yoko establish((On June
1 1986 to Fuji Corporation Mishima Yoko(On May 10 1986 at the office of Fuji Corporation to Fuji Corporation Mishima Yoko Without
delay(to Fuji Corporation ¥370,000(purchase-price of English conversation teaching materials with advantage of the content to go
overseas travel cheaply)pay)duty)have)content (of sale between
mishima yoko and Fuji Corporation)of contract)of legal act)effect
has come into existence."

(4) Daily Parlance:
"On June 10 1986, at the office of Fuji Corporation, between Mishima Yoko and Fuji Corporation established contract of sale that Mishima Yoko pays to Fuji Corporation the purchase-price of English conversation teaching materials with advantage to go overseas travel cheaply."

In Figure 2, compound predicate logic formula(1) is the expressing form of predicate logic formula(2) by PROLOG. The formula(1') was obtained as the result of a unification of case. And it also corresponds to (simple)natural language expression(3). It can be put into a daily parlance(4) and has the specified logical structure of the legal meaning.

As shown in the correspondence of (1) and (2), the formula of compound predicate logic by PROLOG expresses the legal effect and legal requirement factors ---that compose legal norm sentences --- in the whole form as a compound sentence, logical conjunction of the component proposition, by dealing with slot of frame or case of case grammar as argument of logic. This style enables us to reconstruct the systematic relevance of legal rules with logical precision. We are able to analyze and express precisely the inner structure of each legal requirement factor of the legal rules. And by allocating a certain postpositional particles(as Japanese is a postpositional language rather than a prepositional language, which is to say the particles are placed after nouns rather before) to each argument, it is possible to put PROLOG sentences automatically into simple natural languages or conversely to put simple natural language(written according to the manual) into sentences understood by PROLOG automatically.

When we express the world of legal knowledge in the system, we do so in order to formalize natural linguistic expression of legal rules as it is. We have taken great pains to do so. It would be desirable to translate legal norm sentences into the language on the system within the structure of the natural language, and to change them according to logical inference rules and then in the same way retranslate the results into natural language as output. Thus, it is possible to prove a given legal conclusion as the output for the legal deduction from the given prepositions. As legal reasoning is logical proof, the legal judgement as the conclusion must be something indicated as a logical consequence following from the proposition, which is held to be currently valid. From the point of view of the mission of a legal expert system, it is important to show the conclusion to be valid, and the process to be valid as well.

3. THE CHARACTERISTICS OF LEGAL KNOWLEDGE

3.1 Open-Ended World Knowledge

Knowledge in the legal world is essentially open-ended. That is, in the world it is impossible to regard a particular knowledge set as being always valid. This is so because of various factors, for example the increase or decrease in legal knowledge, as follows:
1) law   : laws(legal norms) are constantly being established or abolished.
2) theory   : valid knowledge is different according to theory.
3) contract : a contract is defined such that a law can be established as being valid only between the contracting parties(that is, "Prinzip der Privatautonomie").
This means that the knowledge set particular only to the parties is added to the common knowledge set.

Since a knowledge set increases or decreases according to various factors, one should regard as the unit of knowledge an article of law which is considered a unit of increase or decrease of legal knowledge. However, such knowledge is closely interrelated, so it is necessary to set up a knowledge structure which is minimally influenced by the increase or decrease of knowledge.

3.2 The Characteristics of Legal Rules

When the knowledge, which is regarded as a unit by lawyers, is formalized into logical formulae, the legal rules will not always take a form of set of logical formulas. This can be explained as follows:

a) Enumeration and Exemplification

Enumeration and exemplification are included in legal rules. Suppose the formulas below represent:

A → P   B → P

When these rules are in enumeration, the logical meaning is:

A or B ← → P   and

$^-$P can be deduced from $^-$A and $^-$B

On the other hand, in exemplification, the logical meaning is:

A or B → P

b) Priority of Legal Rules

In application of law, one rule is prior to the other, there being several legal rules applicable. In this case the prior rule is applied with priority. This is called, "Priority of Rule" in the legal terminology, but there coexist some priorities which should be logically separated from each other. In this paper, "Priority of Application" and "Priority of Ground" are separated.

4. KNOWLEDGE STRUCTURE OF THE SYSTEM

The knowledge structure is called a rule system which is defined in order to represent the characteristics of legal knowledge described in the previous section. The rule system itself is a general knowledge structure and independent of law.

4.1 Rule System

The rule system is expressed in the form : $(R, >_{ap}, >_b)$.   "R" is a set of rules, "$>_{ap}$" and "$>_b$" are binary relations defined on "R", which correspond respectively to priority of application and that of ground.

A rule is expressed in the form of < application condition, rule type, rule body>. The rule body is a Horn clause.

4.2 Rule Type

There are four kinds of rule types: Combination of Positive(P-type)/ Negative(N-type) and Exclusive(E-type)/ Inclusive(I-type).

When rule body has the form $(P→Q)$ and the rule exists by itself, each rule type means:
PE-type: if and only if P, then Q;
PI-type: if P, then Q; NE-type: if and only if P, then not Q; NI-type: if P, then not Q.

	P-type	N-type
E-type	PE-type	NE-type
I-type	PI-type	NI-type

4.3 Application Condition and Priority of Application

To formalize priority of application, it is necessary to provide each rule with application condition. The application condition describes in what case a rule can be applied. Priority of application is a binary relation between rules. When a rule of E-type has priority, the rule excludes non-prior rules, and when a rule of I-type has priority, the rule is added to the non-prior rules.

Here we give the following example:
Rule A : Declaration of intention becomes effective at the time of its arrival.
Rule B : Declaration of intention to accept becomes effective at the time of the dispatch.
In this case, the application conditions are as follows:
The application condition of rule A : effectiveness of declaration of intention.
The application condition of rule B : effectiveness of declaration of intention to accept.
Rule A and rule B have a form of PE-type, and rule B $>_{ap}$ rule A. Thus, in determining the time when the declaration of intention to accept becomes effective, it is possible to apply rule A and rule B. However, only rule B can be applied in this case because rule B is an E-type rule, and hence prior to rule A.

4.4 Priority of Ground

Priority of ground is also a kind of priority of rule. It is a binary relation between positive and negative rules, and it plays a role in deciding which conclusion of rules is prior when the proof of both rules is successful and the conclusions are inconsistent. The following's an example:
Rule A : Birds fly.   Rule B : Penguins do not fly.
Both rules are applicable to a penguin and the conclusions are inconsistent.   In this case, the conclusion that "penguins do not fly" is prior because rule B is prior to rule A.

4.5 The Semantics of the Rule System

The Semantics of rule system(R, $>_{ap}$, $>_b$) is expressed by way of determining the truth value of a given proposition G.
1) Selection of applicable rules: A rule set R_1 in which rules are applicable(i.e. when application conditions are satisfied) to the given proposition G is selected from rule set R.
2) Exclusion of rules by priority of application: a)when R_1 involves a rule of PE-type, the maximum rule(MaxPE) of application is selected from all the PE-type rules in R_1. Let R_2 be a set of rules which excludes all the rules(P-type, N-type) posterior to MaxPE from R_1. If R_1 includes no PE-type rules, $R_2 = R_1$.
b)when R_2 involves a rule of NE-type, the maximum rule(MaxNE) of application is selected from all the rules of NE-type in R_2. Let R_3 be a set of rules which excludes all the negative rules(N-type) posterior from MaxNE in R_2. If R_2 involves no NE-type rules, $R_3 = R_2$.
3) Decision Making Procedure: Rule set(R_3) is divided into a set of positive rules(R^P) and negative rules(R^N). Let R_P be a rule set in R^P which can prove the proposition G, and likewise R_N in R^N.
a) If $R_P \neq \phi$, $R_N = \phi$, then G$\rightarrow$true.
b) If $R_P = \phi$, $R_N = \phi$, then, if R^P involves PE-type rules, G $\rightarrow$ false, regarding rules of R^P as enumeration; if R^P involves no PE-type rules, G $\rightarrow$ indeterminate, regarding rules of R^P as exemplification.
c) If $R_P = \phi$, $R_N \neq \phi$, then G$\rightarrow$false.
d) If $R_P \neq \phi$, $R_N \neq \phi$,
   If $\exists r_P \in R_P \ \forall r_N \in R_N \ r_P >_b r_N$, then G$\rightarrow$true;
   If $\exists r_N \in R_P \ \forall r_P \in R_P \ r_N >_b r_P$, then G$\rightarrow$true.
In the other cases the knowledge structure is not well-defined.

4.6 Rule System and the Characteristics of Legal Knowledge

We explain the correspondence of rule system to the characteristics of legal knowledge.
1)Since a rule system consists of a rule set and binary relations defined on rule set, increasing or decreasing rules means an

increase or decrease in the relevant binary relations and thus affects nothing else.

2)To separate enumeration from exemplification it is assumed that in the former the main rules are E-type and the rest are I-type. In the latter, all the rules are I-type. This separation is made so that in adding exemplifying rules it is not necessary to know whether existing rules are in enumeration or in exemplification.

3)Priority of rules means priority of application and that of ground.

4.7 Method to Introduce Priority of Rules

In introducing a binary relation of priority of application or of ground into a rule set, it is not practical to enumerate binary relation between rules. In the legal field, the following method is used. Priority of application and ground are commonly introduced as priority of rules.

a)Direct Explicit Method

An article of law provides the priority to the other articles in itself: "when·····, ·····, in spite of the provision of the article."

b)Comparative Method of the Character of Rules

For example, "An enforceable law is prior to an adoptive law," "A special law is prior to a general law." In the former, the priority is decided according to whether the rule is enforceable or adoptive. In the latter, according to whether the rule is special or general.

c)Comparative Method of Rule Set

For example, "A written law is prior to an unwritten law." The priority of a rule depends on the priority of the rule set to which the rule belongs.

d)Method to Give a Character to the Rule Itself

For example, "·····except as otherwise provided by other laws." In this case, the rule itself shows that it has the least priority.

5. FUNCTION OF LES-2 SYSTEM

5.1 Architecture of the System

The architecture of this system is shown in Figure 3. The system is provided with a knowledge base of legal rules, inference engines of the substantial and the procedural laws, an explanation module, and a suit game module.

5.2 Knowledge Base

This system has substantial and procedural rules as legal knowledge.

5.2.1 Substantial Law Rules

Substantial law rules are expressed in the clause below:
rule(ID,source, theory,priority_ data,rule_type, application_ condition,rule_ body).

The argument of rule has the following meaning.

1)ID is an identifier of the rule.

2)Source means the

Fig. 3.

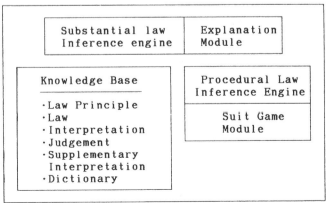

Substantial law Inference engine

Explanation Module

Knowledge Base

·Law Principle
·Law
·Interpretation
·Judgement
·Supplementary Interpretation
·Dictionary

Procedural Law Inference Engine

Suit Game Module

name of law from which the rule,is derived.
3)Theory is the person's name who asserts the rule.
4)Priority data, which is used to decide priority between rules, in
volves other information, such as the name of the law.
5)Rule type and application condition are the same as described in
section 4.
6)The rule body means a legal rule itself. The rule body is
expressed as follows.
     "A contract is established when the offer and the acceptance
both become effective, except in those cases where the offer has become ineffective." rule(id,_,_,p(civil_law,···),PE-TYPE,
established(···,contract),
established(···,contract)←
become_effective(···,offer),become_effective(···,acceptance),not(bec
ome_ineffective(···,offer))).
     A "not" used in the rule body means not only logical negation
but also expresses the distribution of responsibility of assertion
in inference of procedural law. Thus, if the rule body is expressed
in the formula: G: ⁻A,B,not(C)., it is expressed in the logical
formula: A & B & ⁻C → G, in inferring in substantial law and the
responsibilities of assertion and proof are distributed in the
formula: (A,B) and (C), in inferring in procedural law.

5.2.2 Procedural Law Rule

     Procedural law rules are ones used for deciding the truth
values of the propositions in procedural law, that is, the asserted
propositions of procedural law and fact, and are high order rules.
The example is as follows(the first argument is a procedural rule
body, and the second is the explanatory sentence):
   procedural_rule((judicial_confession(P):-
        main_fact(P),subsumption(P),assertion(plaintiff,P),
        assertion(defendant,P)),the_accordance_of_the
asserted_propositions_of_both_parties_becomes_judicial_confession).
        procedural_rule(
        (base_of_suit(P):-
        judicial_confession(P)),the_confessed_pro_
        positions_comes_the_ground_of_judgement_
        as_the_truth_of_suit).

5.3 Substantial Law Inference Engine and Explanation Module

     Substantial law inference engine provides the given case with a
conclusion of the legal judgement(or truth value of suit of the
proposition), and realizes the subset of the inference described in
section "4.5 The semantics of the Rule System."
     The inference is backward reasoning with priority control
added. It resolves the goal by the following procedure, given the
goal G.
1)It extracts the rule set R_3 used to resolve the goal G according
to the procedure of "1) extraction of applicable rules" and "2) exclusion of the other rules by priority of application" in section
4.5. In this procedure, "A special law is prior to a general law"
and "An enforceable law is prior to an adoptive law" appear as legal
knowledge in deciding the priority of application of rules.
2)It divides the rule set R_3 into a positive rule set R^P and a negative one R^N.
3)It resolves the goal G by the positive rule set R^P and gets the
solution G_i. The rule used to get G_i is R_i ($R_i \in R^P$).
4)It determines whether the goal can be resolved by the negative
rule set R^N or not. Comparing the priority of ground of the all
rules ($R_j \in R^N$) resolving G_i with that of rules R_i or R_j which
derived G_i, if R_i is prior to all the R_js which belong to R^N, and

it resolves G_i, then G_i is the solution for the goal G.
An explanation module is the one to explain this inference process, and it enables a user to traverse the "proof tree" of inference.

5.4 Procedural Law Inference Engine
Procedural law inference aims to infer a conclusion(judgement) of procedural law, putting in the argument or evidence of the parties and gives truth value to the procedural law propositions. A higher order rule is used for expressing the truth value. The distribution of responsibility of assertion and proof is processed and determined by an inference engine according to an expression form of substantial law rules. Moreover, the process structure of suit and the flow are also built into the inference engine.

5.5 Suit Game Module
A suit game module can simulate a legal case. Using a procedural law inference engine, it infers the condition of suit action(here, assertion and plea) of litigants(plaintiff, defendant) and the weight of evidence in civil action. Furthermore, it models the interlocutory judgement according to the proceeding of the suit and finally the conclusion of the definitive judgement.

6. The DEMONSTRATION OF THE LES-2 SYSTEM

6.1 The Demonstration of Inference of Substantial Law
In the inference of substantial law, a case is, first, put into the system from the file(it is made with the editor using simple natural language). As the second step, the goal, the goal of the legal judgement, is put in using simple natural language. Then, the system starts to run for the goal, being implemented with necessary data by Q & A between the user and the machine.
In Figure 4 below, this Q & A is described.
a)[5]: As it is short of the data of "Offer's become effective" to reach the goal, the system questions the user.
b)[6]: The system questions the time of the arrival of the offer, as the rule of "Declaration of intention's become effective"(Art.97I, Civil Law) is applied to solve "Offer's become effective".
c)[7]: The goal has been solved. Here, the system does not question the time of the arrival of the acceptance to solve the goal, while acceptance is also declaration of intention. This is because the system applies the special rule(Art.526I, Civil Law) according to the meta rule that a special law is prior to a general law. That is, the system performs the priority control to apply of the rules, so that it reasoned by applying the same article.

6.2 The Demonstration of Simulation on the Civil Procedural Law
To simulate the suit in inference on the civil procedural law, first of all the user puts in the object of the claim:"The defendant should pay the money ...to the plaintiff," and the cause of the claim. Then the plaintiff and the defendant can put in their assertions. The user may output the interim conclusion on the point of civil procedural law with the comment thereof, by putting in the judge command at a certain point.
Figure 5 shows the dialog between the user and the computer. Input is done using the "simple natural language translation method"(see,[1]). This method can automatically translate natural language which is input with parenthese "(   )"and space according to the manual into PROLOG sentences. From the demonstration step[2], it is expressed in ordinary natural language.
a) [1]: Input of the object and the cause of the claim in the

complaint.
 b) [2]: Input of the pleadings
    [3]: Input of the fact freely asserted
 c) [4]: Example of judge report of judge command.
          The object of the claim and pleading, the
          cause of the claim, the plea, and the conclusion
          of the system are described in order.   Here is shown only
the last one.

Fig. 4.
【 The content of the input data is enclosed in quotation marks, i.e.
"   "】
Example of question & answer in inference on the substantial law.
[1]Input of case file:
      "On May 10 1986, Fuji Corporation sent to Mishima Yoko a letter
stating that they wanted to sell her English conversation teaching
materials and in return for her buying said materials Fuji would
provide certain travel discount for her.   On June 1 1986, Mishima
Yoko mailed the notice stating that she wanted to buy the English
conversation teaching materials.   The notice reached the letter box
of Fuji Corporation."
[2]Setting up of the goal to be solved:
      "(contract) has been established"
[3]Start of inference:
[4]Q(uestion) and A(nswer):
[5]Q: Is there the fact that the intention of offer of the sale with
Mishima Yoko reached at the time of X ?
      A: "y"
[6]Q: Put in the content of X.
      A: "May 13 1986"
[7]Conclusion of inference:
      From the present case has been proved: the legal act of the
contract of sale has become effective;
on June 1 1986, to Mishima Yoko, Fuji Corporation has a duty to
transfer the right of property of English conversation teaching
material with advantage to go overseas travel cheaply, and to Fuji
Corporation, Mishima Yoko has duty to pay the purchase-price of
¥370,000.

Fig. 5.
[1]Put in the content of the complaint:
    Name of the party:
        plaintiff: "Fuji_Corporation";   defendant: "Mishima_Yoko"
Object of the claim:
        "Mishima_Yoko   should_pay purchase-price_of_¥370,000   to_
Fuji_Corporation"
    Cause of the claim:
        "(contract   of(sale   of(content   of(on_June_1_1986
to_go_mishima_yoko   fuji_corporation(has(duty to(transfer(property
of(english_conversation_teaching_material)))))),
to_fuji_corporation mishima_yoko(has(duty to(pay(purchase_price
¥370,000)))))))))has_become_effective"
[2]Put in the content of the pleadings:
1. Approve or not approve the assertion of the plaintiff:
        The assertion of the plaintiff 1 [·····] : "argue"
        The assertion of the plaintiff 2 [·····] : "approve"
2. Put in the new assertion of the defendant:
        "declaration and intention in_declaration_of_intention
        were_inconsistent"(abbreviated)
[3]Assertion mode: Put in the additional assertion:
        "·····(abbreviated)"

[4]Example of judgement report.
The conclusion of the judgement from the object of the plaintiff and the plea of the defendant:
From the argument and the examination of evidence, the first cause of claim of the plaintiff and the first plea of the defendant are approved, and the plaintiff will win the suit.

7. CONCLUSION

The central feature of this research is that the project was completed by combined work of experts, such as jurists and knowledge and information scientists. Through this cooperation, we did not always make ourselves understood because we work in different research areas. However, the cooperation provided the prime result that as much as jurists who analyze law as well as knowledge and information, scientists who try to realize the system technologically.

In constructing the system, we developed the knowledge processing equal to the structure of law and legal reasoning, for example, the priority control of application of rules. There are many problems remaining. We could indicate the restricted number of the rules above all, at most 150 or so, which are selected from the general provisions and claim(contract) of civil law and a part of civil procedural law. However, our efforts were brought into focus of such function as the system may be applicable to all laws in private law area. Of course, it is necessary to analyze and systematize legal rules more deeply and increase the number of rules for the system as a legal expert system to work in the field of law. As for the interface, we used simple natural language translation to input and output the data, but have much expectation for the study of natural language processing in the near future.

This system has been developed with an eye towards legal artificial intelligence, and therefore there must be further research done in order to realize a system for practical use. However, we think that the system could show a base for legal artificial intelligence. Moreover, the system is provided with the system structure which works as legal education developing system or a practical system in other areas. Based on the result and problems obtained in the LES-2 system, we are determined to seek ways of solving the remaining problems.

ACKNOWLEDGMENT

This study could be performed by integrating researches with various problems. The researches could not be realized without many supporters. This study was financially greatly supported by Grants in Aid for Scientific Research of 1985 and 1986, Ministry of Education, Culture and Science, Japan as well as by Grants in Commission Research of 1985, ICOT. For having made this study possible, for having provided the information on which it is based, we are greatly indebted to Dr. Koichi Furukawa(Chief, Second Research Laboratory, Research Center,ICOT)as well as the researchers of ICOT, Mr. Masahiro Yamamoto(Manager, Computer System Research Laboratory, C&C Systems Research Laboratories, NEC Corporation), Mr. Takuji Ikeda(Manager, Police and Justice Sales Department, EDP National Government Systems Division, NEC Corporation), fellows of Meiji Gakuin University and the members of LESA.

REFERENCES

Cory H T, Hammond P, Kowalski R A, Kriwaczek F and Sergot M J(1985)

The British Nationality Act as a Logic Program. Depart. of Computing, Imperial College, Univ. of London

Ikeda J (1984) Interpretation and Application of Law by Artificial Intelligence Language. Nikkei Computer 1984.7.9: 197-209; 1984. 7.23: 179-190

Ikeda M, Tanaka H (1985) Expert System of Copy-right Law. Proceedings of Japan Society for Software Science and Technology, pp.1ff

McCarty L T (1980) The TAXMAN Project: Towards a Cognitive Theory of Legal Argument. in: Niblett T B (ed.) Computer Science Logic and Legal Language, Cambridge University Press, Cambridge, 23-43

McCarty L T (1980) Some Notes on the MAP Formalism of TAXMAN II, With Applications to Eisner V. Macomber. Technical Report LRP-TR-6, Laboratory for Computer Science Research, Rutgers University

Nitta K, et al.(1985)Problem Solving Function of Expert System of Industrial Property Law. Proceedings of the Logic Programming Conference'85

Nitta K (1985) A Knowledge Representation and Inference System for Procedural Law KRIP/L. Proceedings of Japan Society for Software Science and Technology, pp. 65ff

Ohta S (1983) The Base of Proof Theory in Civil Action. Kohbundo, Tokyo

Yoshino H (1981) Die Logische Struktur der Argumentation bei der Juristischen Entscheidung. in: Arnio A,u.a.(Hrsg.), Methodologie und Erkenntnistheorie der juristischen Argumentation, Rechtstheorie Beif. 2, S. 233ff

Yoshino H (1984) An application of Computers to Reasoning in the Judicial Process. Law and Computers No.3; pp. 77ff.

Yoshino H (1986) A Possibility of Legal Expert System. ICOT Commission Research Report'86

Yoshino H (1986) Legal Expert System as A Legal Reasoning. 86-IS-11 Proceedings of Japan Society for Software Science and Technology Vol.86, No.43

A Prototype Software Simulator for FGHC

Y. OHARA, S. TORII, E. ONO, M. KISHISHITA, J. TANAKA*, T. MIYAZAKI*

FUJITSU LIMITED
1015 Kamikodanaka Nakahara-Ku, Kawasaki 211, Japan

* INSTITUTE FOR NEW GENERATION COMPUTER TECHNOLOGY
  Mita-Kokusai-Building 21FL. 1-4-28, Mita,Minato-Ku,Tokyo 108, Japan

Abstract

We have implemented a prototype software simulator for FGHC : Flat
Guarded Horn Clauses. This simulator executes a pre-processed FGHC
program in a distributed environment. In this paper, we describe the
distributed computation model and its prototype software simulator.
The evaluation results of sample programs using the simulator are
also presented.

Introduction

GHC (Guarded Horn Clauses)(Ueda 1985) is a logic programming language
for parallel execution. Though GHC provides the descriptive power of
efficient parallel execution of programs, the parallel execution
image of GHC is still not clear. This paper reports on our attempt to
clarify this issue, assuming a distributed computer architecture.
The organization of this paper is as follows :
Section 1 briefly outlines the underlying language, FGHC. Though FGHC
is a subset of GHC, it is still powerful enough for practical
applications. Section 2 describes a distributed computation model in
which FGHC programs will be executed. Section 3 describes several
implementing algorithms. Goal distribution, inter-PE communication,
and distributed unification are described to execute FGHC programs in
distributed computation model. The more detailed implementing
information, such as execution code, compiler construction, is given
in Section 4. Section 5 gives simulation results from two sample
programs listed at the end of this paper, and evaluates these from
the viewpoints of the "effect of distributed execution" and the
"relation between input data and effect of goal distribution".

1   Parallel logic programming language FGHC

A GHC program is defined by a set of predicates which are Horn clauses
with guards. Goals can be executed in parallel and a guard provides
the synchronization mechanism between goals. In contrast to GHC, FGHC
allows only system predicates in guard, and sequentiality of
evaluation is added considering practical implementation.
An FGHC clause has the following format.

```
H(Arg1,Arg2,···,Argk) :- G1,G2,···,Gm | B1,B2,···,Bn.
     head part            guard part       body part
            passive part              active part
```

An FGHC clause consists of three parts: head part, guard part, and body part. The head and guard part are called the "passive part", since these parts do not instantiate variables. The body part is called the "active part", since we can instantiate variables in this part.
The features of FGHC and its evaluation rules can be summarized as follows:

① Only system predicates are allowed as goals in the guard part.
② The passive part is executed sequentially. First, head unification is executed sequentially from left to right, then the guard part is executed sequentially.
③ Suspension occurs when unification in the passive part tries to instantiate global variables, i.e., the passive part never exports the binding to the outer world.
④ The passive part of each candidate clause is tested sequentially. If a passive part of some candidate clause fails or suspends, next candidate clause will be tested. When none of the candidate clauses succeed and there exist more than one suspended clause, that goal is suspended.
⑤ A suspended goal is resumed when the variable which causes the suspension is instantiated.

2   The distributed computation model

To examine how FGHC can be executed efficiently in a distributed environment, we need to establish the distributed computation model first.
The distributed computation model has been developed. Fig. 1 shows the overall structure of our distributed computation model. This model has the following features.

· Each Processing Element (PE) consists of an FGHC processing system, scheduling queue, variable management table, and input/output channels. PEs are connected with each other by a grid network.
· Inter-PE communication is done via message exchange on the network. Each message placed on each output channel is sent to the corresponding PE according to the address information in it.
· Each PE runs in parallel, and goals on the scheduling queue are processed one by one.
· Each PE has its local memory. It has no global memory nor global address space. Since each PE has its own address space, a variable in another PE is referenced via message exchange. Variables shared by PEs are managed with the variable management table.
· Each PE contains the identical program. Initially, goal is put into one PE, this goal automatically starts its computation. Each PE executes goals which are sent from other PEs besides processing local goals.

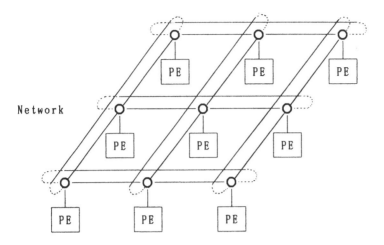

Fig. 1.   Distributed Computation Model

3   An FGHC software simulator

We have implemented the FGHC distributed software simulator based on
the Murakami's work (Murakami 1985).
Our software simulator has the following features.

①   A goal allocation schema is added to FGHC programs.
②   The simulator consists of the pre-processing compiler part which
     translates FGHC programs into internal execution code, and the
     execution part which simulates its distributed execution based on
     the code.
③   Prolog is adopted as the execution code. Some special "system"
     predicates are added for distributed unification.
④   It can perform various simulations by varying the goal scheduling
     process, trace output level, the number of PEs, and so on.

3.1   Goal distribution

We added "pragma" (Shapiro 1984) to FGHC for distributed
implementation. The goal allocation schema in the distributed
environment is specified by "pragma". Pragma can be added to the body
part goals in FGHC clauses. Our "pragma" has the following format.

$$\text{throw (Goal , } \begin{bmatrix} up \\ down \\ left \\ right \end{bmatrix} \text{)}$$

Consider the case where the goal "throw (f(X),right), g(X)" is
executed in PE#i. Here, we assume that the right neighbor of PE#i is
PE#j. This situation is shown in Fig. 2. In this case, the variable X
must be shared between PE#i and PE#j. Since our distributed
implementation model does not have global address space, shared
variables among PEs need some mechanism to realize variable sharing.

Therefore, we have adopted the following strategy :
The sender PE "PE#i" transforms the variable X into the form "$VAR(i, n)" where i is the ID number of sender PE and n is a newly generated number. This relation " [X, $VAR(i,n), _] " is registered on the variable management table in PE#i. The transformed goal "f($VAR(i,n))" is sent to PE#j on the network (Fig. 2 (1)).
The receiver PE "PE#j" generates a new local variable X' from the form "$VAR(i,n)" and registers this correspondence on its variable management table in the form " [X', $VAR(i,n), F] ", where F is "on-asking flag". At the same time, the variable in the received goal is replaced by "$CHA(X',F)". Here, "$CHA(X',F)" is called a "channel-variable" (Fig. 2 (2)).
When the channel-variable "$CHA(X',F)" is referenced, PE#j looks up its variable management table and finds that X' is actually "$VAR(i, n)". Then PE#i is asked for its value. When PE#i receives this request, PE#i also looks up its variable management table and finds that "$VAR(i,n)" is actually X. Therefore the value of X is requested (Fig. 2 (3)).

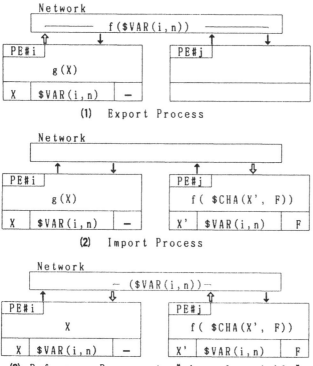

(1) Export Process

(2) Import Process

(3) Reference Process to "channel-variable"

Fig. 2. Goal Distribution

3. 2   Inter-PE communication

Communication between PEs is one of the most important issues in realizing distributed computation. We have provided the following five "system" predicates:

① send＿goal(PE-ID, Goal)
Send "Goal" to the PE specified by "PE-ID". The pragma "throw" is transformed into this form.

② get ＿value(C ＿Var, Result)
Request the value of "C ＿Var". The value is returned to "Result" by "reply ＿ result" message. This message is used in executing passive part of the source program.

③ unify(C ＿Var, Value, Result)
Request the unification of "C ＿Var" and "Value" to the PE to which "C＿Var" belongs. "Value" must have been instantiated at execution time. The computation result is returned to "Result" by a "reply ＿result" message. This message is used in executing the active part of the source program.

④ unify ＿channels(C＿ Var1, C＿ Var2, Result)
Request the unification of "C ＿Var1" and "C＿Var2" to the PE to which "C ＿Var1" belongs. The computation result is returned to "Result" by a "reply ＿ result" message. This message is used in executing the active part of the source program.

⑤ reply ＿result(Result, Value)
Return the unification result or computation result to "Result". "Value" must have been instantiated at execution time.

3.3 Distributed unification

We have introduced the concept of channel variables in Section 3.1. The "channel-variable" is used to realize distributed unification. The distributed unification algorithm can be summarized as follows:

① Unification in the passive part

We cannot instantiate a global variable before the clause is committed, only the values of global variables can be referenced. When unification with the channel variable is attempted, it issues the "get＿value" message and unification is suspended until the value is returned by a "reply ＿result" message.

② Unification in the active part

In the active part, there is no regulation as in the passive part. Variables can be instantiated to values.

(a) Unification between a variable and a channel variable
If the variable is uninstantiated, it is instantiated to the channel variable. If the variable has already been instantiated, a "unify" message is sent to the PE which the channel variable points to. Unification is resumed when the value is returned by a "reply ＿ result" message.

(b) Unification between two channel variables
Unification between two channel variables invokes the "unify＿ channels" message. This message is sent to the PE to which the first channel-variable belongs. Then this message is processed as exactly the same as in (a).

4 Implementing of software simulator

Based on the FGHC distributed model and its execution image, we have implemented the FGHC software simulator in Prolog on FACOM M380. The simulator is 2K steps long and took 10 person-months to complete it, including the detailed design and the debugging.

4.1 Execution code

Our software simulator simulates the execution of pre-processed FGHC programs in a distributed environment.
We have adopted Prolog as the execution code of our software simulator because of its similarity to FGHC and its ease of implementation.
In this Section, we explain our execution code by showing the example of predicate "part" in the program "quick-sort".(Full program for "quick-sort" is shown at the end of this paper as an appendix.)

```
part( [X |Xs] ,A,S,L0) :-  A<=X  |  L0 = [X |L1] , part(Xs,A,S,L1).

part( [X |Xs] ,A,S0,L) :-  A> X  |  S0 = [X |S1] , part(Xs,A,S1,L).

part( [] , _,S,L) :-  true  | S= [] , L= [] .
```

In executing an FGHC program, it is necessary to handle the suspension of goals and the unification with a channel variable. Since Prolog unification is not applicable in this case, we must generate execution code in which FGHC's unification is performed explicitly.
The above program is translated into the following execution code.

```
      ①   ②              ③   ④
part(1, ∂(A1,A2,A3,A4), R, ['∂s'(ulist(A4,X,L1)),
                           '∂'(part(Xs,A2,A3,L1)) | Bt] ,Bt) :-
      ⑤ ulist(A1,X,Xs,R1),(not(R1==succeed),R=R1;
      ⑥ '<='(A2,X,R)), !.

part(2, ∂(A1,A2,A3,A4), R, ['∂s'(ulist(A3,X,S1)),
                           '∂'(part(Xs,A2,S1,A4)) | Bt] ,Bt) :-
      ulist(A1,X,Xs,R1),(not(R1==succeed),R=R1;
      '>'(A2,X,R)), !.

part(3, ∂(A1,A2,A3,A4), R, ['∂s'(unil(A3)), '∂s'(unil(A4)) | Bt] ,Bt) :-
      unil(A1,R), !.
```

① : A candidate clause number which is used to execute the passive part of each candidate clause sequentially.
② : A sequence of variables which corresponds to formal arguments of the head part.
For example, a sequence of arguments "([X |Xs] ,A,S,L0)" in the first clause of the original source program is translated into the sequence of execution code "∂(A1,A2,A3,A4)".
③ : A field on which execution result of the candidate clause is kept.
④ : A sequence of pre-processed body part goals which are represented by the D-list.
For example, a sequence of body part goals " L0= [X |L1] , part(Xs,A,S,L1)" in the first clause of the original program is translated into a sequence of the execution codes " '∂s'(ulist(A4, X,L1)), '∂'(part(Xs,A2,A3,L1))". Here, the goal prefixed by '∂s'

represents the system predicate call; the other represents the user-defined predicate call. The goal `"'as'(ulist(A4,X,L1))"` represents the system predicate call which unifies between `"A4"` and `" [X | L1] "`.

⑤ : In relate to non-variable formal arguments of a clause, they are unified with the corresponding structures. If this unification succeeds, it proceeds to execute the guard part. If it fails or suspends, the computation result will be kept on ③ and the execution of the clause terminates.

Here, head unification code `"ulist(A1,X,Xs,R1)"` is generated for the argument `" [X | Xs] "` of the first clause in the original program. This means that `"A1"` and `" [X | Xs] "` will be unified and the result will be kept on R1.

⑥ : In FGHC, goals in the guard part are executed sequentially from left to right. If one of the goals fails or suspends, the subsequent goals are not executed. If all goals in the guard part succeed, that clause will be committed. Therefore, for each goal in a guard part, execution code is generated which keeps the execution result on ③.

In this case, the guard part goal `"A<=X "` of the first clause in the original program is translated into the execution code `"'<='(A2,X,R)"`. This code means that the comparison result between `"A2"` and `"X"` is kept on R.

4.2   FGHC compiler

The compiler translates an FGHC program into execution code. The techniques used in (Ueda 1985) has been applied to our compiler. The program compilation is performed as follows:
Each clause in the source program is separated into a head part, guard part, and body part. Each part is separated into a sequence of unification goals and a sequence of other goals, each of which is represented in a D-list. Then, each goal in the D-list is compiled separately and combined in execution code.

4.3   Simulation algorithm

As shown in Fig. 3, the simulator has a PE management queue which schedules PE execution, and each PE has one scheduling queue which schedules goal execution.
Each PE in the PE management queue is executed in turn until there are no goals left to be executed. The PE processes only the leftmost goal inside its scheduling queue. Candidate clauses of the goal are tested sequentially according to the candidate clause number. The clause which has succeed first will be committed. The body part goals which are represented with the D-list, are enqueued to its scheduling queue. System messages which are issued during goal execution for the inter-PE variable reference are enqueued to its output channel.
In the following discussion, we call the 1-cycle execution of the PE management queue "1 cycle time". In our distributed implementation model, this roughly corresponds to the time it takes each PE to execute one goal in parallel.

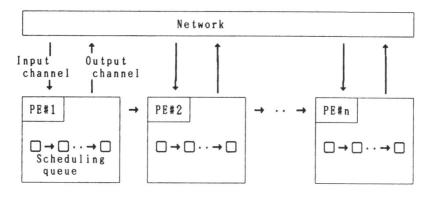

PE Management Queue

Fig. 3.   Structure of Software Simulator

5 Simulation results and its evaluations

We have simulated two FGHC programs, a "matrix multiplication" program and a "quick-sort" program listed at the end of this paper, to compare execution on one PE and distributed execution on nine PEs. The "matrix multiplication" program is executed according to the size of input data. The followings are the mesured items and their meanings.

① Execution time (cycle time) : The total cycle time in which goals are executed.
② The total number of executed goals : The total number of goals which are executed. (Including suspended goals.)
③ Amount of inter-PE communications (number of messages) : The total number of messages on network. (In sequential execution, the amount is 0.)
④ Number of suspended goals (number of goals) : The total number of suspended goals.
⑤ The waiting time for resuming (cycle time / number of goals) : Dividing the cycle time for goals between suspended and resuming by the number of suspended goals, i.e., the average cycle time that suspended goals cost for resuming their execution.

Table 1 lists the simulation results in the case where the input data is a 3×3 matrix. Table 2 shows the simulation result in the case where the input data is a list of 11 elements. In these tables, **(a)** represents the simulation result in the case where goals with "pragma" are executed before the others. **(b)** represents the simulation result in the case where goals with "pragma" are executed after the others.

Table 1. Simulation Result for
"matrix multiplication"
Program

Table 2. Simulation Result
for "quick-sort"
Program

Programs	Matrix multiplication			Quick-sort		
PE Items	1 P E	9 P E s		1 P E	9 P E s	
		(a)	(b)		(a)	(b)
Execution time	1 4 0	2 6	8 7	1 1 5	6 3	6 8
The total number of executed goals	1 4 0	1 4 0	1 4 0	1 1 5	1 4 6	1 1 5
Amount of communications	0	3 6	3 6	0	7 6	3 4
Number of suspended goals	0	0	0	0	3 1	0
The waiting time for resuming	0	0	0	0	5. 3	0

Fig. 4 shows how the input data size affects the effect of goal
distribution. The input data size is varied from 2×2 to 9×9 matrix.
In this figure, we define "problem size" and "effect of goal
distribution" as follows : the "problem size" is the cost of
executing the problems sequentially ; the "effect of goal
distribution" is the ratio of sequential execution time to distributed
execution time. For example, in the case of the 3×3 matrix, Table 1
shows that problem size is 140 cycles. The effect of goal distribution
is 5.4. The value is obtained by dividing the cost "140" in
sequential execution by the cost "26" in distributed execution.

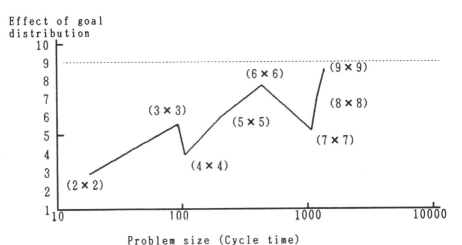

Fig. 4.   The Relation between Problem Size and
Effect of Goal Distribution

(1) Effect of distributed execution

Judging from the simulation result, the execution cost for distributed execution is less than that in sequential execution. Therefore, it is clear that distributed execution has a beneficial effect on execution cost. However, in the case of the "quick-sort" program efficiency is low. This result may come from the fact that problem size of "quick-sort" is too small to be executed on all the PEs in parallel. In this respect, we know that the effect of goal distribution depends on its input data. If we had simulated the "quick-sort" program using more input data, we might have obtained different results.
Many primitive messages were issued in both "matrix multiplication" and "quick-sort". Especially, in the latter program, many goals are suspended during their execution. In that case, communication will burden the interconnection network and increase the total execution cost. Since it is difficult to deal with the increase of inter-PE communication on the software level, it would be better to deal with it in firmware or hardware.
We varied the timing of goal distribution in the simulation of distributed execution. In the case of "matrix multiplication", it became clear that execution of goals with "pragma" before the other goals affects the effect of goal distribution. On the other hand, in the case of "quick-sort", no such effect was found. In the latter program, the distributed goal needs data which is generated by the other goals. When such a goal is distributed and the necessary value is not determined, the goal suspends its execution and issues a primitive message asking for the value. As a result, total inter-PE communication increases and much time is spent waiting for resuming the goal. This is why the effect of goal distribution does not appear in the "quick-sort".

(2) The relation between input data size and effect of goal distribution

In general, it seems that the goal distribution effect approaches the ideal state with the increase of problem size. However, when the input data is a 4×4 matrix or a 7×7 matrix, the effect decreases. This situation can be explained as follows. Since nine PEs are arranged in a square and the simple "pragma" strategy is adopted, the burden of goal execution is concentrated in some specific PE. To solve this problem, we must investigate a higher level strategy of goal distribution.

Concluding remarks

We have implemented the software simulator to clarify the execution image of FGHC and evaluate how it can be executed efficiently. We evaluated two FGHC programs using the simulator. In this evaluation, it became clear that distributed processing is indeed effective and "pragma" is very important.
The evaluation of our FGHC software simulator must be continued based on these results.
Many problems were revealed by the evaluation. They are as follows.

① We must test many FGHC programs. In order to clarify the image of an effective distributed execution, various simulations varying the number of PEs are necessary.
② We must examine the goal execution strategy. We need to examine

various scheduling strategies, e.g., breadth-first and depth-first, to obtain the strategy suited to distributed execution.

③ We must find a better pragma strategy. Current pragma only treats the goal distribution to four directions (up,down,left,and right). Therefore, many goals may gather at one specific PE.

④ Investigation of the parallel programming paradigm is necessary. Since the present programming paradigm is just built on the sequential machine, it would not be suitable for the distributed environment. We must develop the programming paradigm which suits FGHC programming in the distributed environment.

References

Miyazaki T, Taki K (1986) Flat GHC Implementation on Multi-PSI. The Logic Programming Conference '86, pp.83-92 (in Japanese)

Murakami K (1986) The Study of Unifier on Parallel Inference Machine, Tasking Group of Computer System, The Institute of Electronics and Communication Engineers of Japan (in Japanese)

Shapiro E Y (1984) Systolic Programming. A Paradigm of Parallel Processing, Proceedings of the International Conference on Fifth Generation on Computer Systems '84, pp.458-470

Ueda K (1985) Guarded Horn Clauses. ICOT Technical Report TR-103, Institute for New Generation Computer Technology, Tokyo

Ueda K, Chikayama T (1985) Concurrent Prolog Compiler on Top of Prolog, In Proc. 1985 Symp. on Logic Programming, IEEE Computer Society, pp. 119-126

Sample programs

1 "Quick-sort" program

```
  ?- qsort ( [12,6,43,2,9,76,5,32,1,0,99] ,R).

qsort( Xs, Ys) :- true | qsort1(Xs, Ys,  [] ) .
qsort1( [ X | Xs] , Ys0, Ys2) :- true |
        part(Xs, X, S, L),
        throw(qsort1(S, Ys0, [ X | Ys1 ] ), up),  *1
        throw(qsort1(L, Ys1, Ys2), right).    *1
qsort1( [] , Ys, 0 ) :- true  | 0  = Ys .
part( [ X | Xs] , A, S, L0 ) :- A <= X  |
        L0 = [ X | L1] , part(Xs, A, S, L1 ) .
part( [ X | Xs] , A, S0, L ) :- A > X  |
        S0 = [ X | S1] , part(Xs, A, S1, L ) .
part( [] , _ , S, L ) :- true  | S = [] , L = [] .
```

*1 In the one PE execution, we simulated this program without "pragma" ('throw').

2 "Matrix multiplication" program

```
  ?- mm( [ [1,1,1 ] , [2,2,2 ] , [3,3,3 ] ] ,
          [ [1,1,1 ] , [2,2,2 ] , [3,3,3 ] ] , A ).*1
mm( [] , _ , Zs ) :- true   |   Zs = [] .
mm( [ Xi | Mx ] , My, Mz ) :- true   |
        vm( Xi, My, Zi ),
        Mz = [ Zi | Mz2] ,
        throw ( mm( Mx, My, Mz2 ), up).            *2
vm( [] , _ , Z ) :- true   |   Z = [] .
vm( Xi, [ Yj | My] , Zi ) :- true   |
        ip( Xi, Yj, Zij ),
        Zi = [ Zij | Mi2] ,
        throw ( vm( Xi, My, Mi2 ), right).         *2
ip( Xi, Yj, Zij ) :- true   | ip2( Xi, Yj, 0, Zij) .
ip2( [ Xik | Xi] , [ Yjk | Yj] , Sum, Zij ) :- true   |
        Sum2 := (Xik * Yjk ) + Sum,
        ip2( Xi, Yj, Sum2, Zij ) .
ip2( [] , [] , Sum, Zij) :- true |   Sum = Zij .
```

*1 In the simulation of various sizes of input data, we changed this call of top level.

*2 In execution on one PE, we simulated this program with out "pragma" ('throw').

A Foundation of Reasoning by Analogy:
Analogical Union of Logic Programs

Makoto Haraguchi and Setsuo Arikawa

Research Institute of Fundamental Information Science
Kyushu University 33, Fukuoka 812, Japan

Abstract

This paper presents a theoretical foundation of reasoning by analogy
between logic programs.   We give a formal definition of reasoning by
analogy in terms of logic programming.   We also introduce a notion of
analogical union of logic programs by which we characterize the
reasoning.   Then we can regard the reasoning as a deduction from the
analogical union.   Based on this characterization, we present a general
framework which is useful for discussing various requirements of
analogies.

1.   Introduction

By some analogy between two or more domains, we often reason some unknown
knowledge to solve problems concerning the domains.   The reasoned facts
are not always true.   However the analogy gives an evidence that the fact
may be true.   Generally we need enough knowledge of domains to perceive a
suggestive analogy.   Hence the power of reasoning by analogy depends on
the amount of knowledge about the domains and also depends on the power
of deducing knowledges.   From this viewpoint, we present in this paper a
formalism of reasoning by analogy in terms of deduction.   Among many
possible systems of deduction, we take a logic programming system based
on Horn logic, since we now have a powerful computer system to perform it.

The first problem is to define the notion of analogy in formalizing the
reasoning by analogy.   Generally an analogy is a partial likeness of
domains to each other, and such analogous domains can be regarded as
identical in some respects.   More exactly, the two analogous domains have
their portions that are viewed identical.   To determine if two different
domains have such identical portions, we need a correspondence between
the domains.   Hence, in formalizing the notion of analogy, we need
(1)   a representation language for describing the domains,
(2)   an interpretation i.e. semantics of the representation,
(3)   a definition of possible correspondences between the
domains, and
(4)   a notion to precisely state the identical portions under the
possible correspondence.

Following the works by Polya (1954), Gentner (1982) and Winston (1980,
1983), we define a formal analogy as a relation of terms with an

identification of facts. We choose as the domains logic programs which are finite sets of definite clauses. A program is interpreted as its least Herbrand model. Then the correspondence between the domains is a relation of terms which satisfies the following axiom:

$$f(X_1, \ldots, X_n) \sim f(Y_1, \ldots, Y_n) \leftarrow X_1 \sim Y_1, \ldots, X_n \sim Y_n,$$

for each n-ary function symbol f (n $\geq$ 1), where $\sim$ is a predicate symbol to denote the relation of terms, and the terms denote elements in the domains. Then our formal analogy consists of the relation of terms and a set of facts (ground atoms) which are identical up to $\sim$. This definition of formal analogy is conceptually based on Polya's clarified analogy (Polya 1954): "Two systems are analogous if they agree in clearly definable relations of their respective parts", where the systems and the parts correspond to logic programs and terms, respectively.

The second problem is to define the reasoning by analogy. For this purpose, we consider the Winston's analogy-based reasoning (Winston 1983), in which "similar" reasons are assumed to lead to "similar" effects. We introduce a notion of rule transformation to deal with the reasoning in the framework of deduction. In fact, we can formally define the reasoning by analogy in terms of logic programming with the function of transforming rules. Then we precisely define the set of ground atoms which are reasoned by analogy.

Since we formalize the reasoning by analogy in terms of deduction, it has naturally some logical aspects. The third problem is to characterize the reasoning in terms of deduction. For this purpose, we introduce the notion of analogical union of logic programs. The analogical union of programs P_1 and P_2 is itself a logic program which has copies of P_1 and P_2. It also has some definite clauses concerning the predicate $\sim$. Then we show that ground atoms are reasoned by analogy iff they are logical consequences of the analogical union.

According to the previous studies of analogy, some semantic constraints are often required to the relation denoted by $\sim$. Such semantic constraints can be represented by using some additional axioms for $\sim$. As an example of such a constraint, we can consider the analogy as a partial identity (Haraguchi and Arikawa 1986). Then the constraints for $\sim$ can be represented by a first order theory. Actually the analogy is a model for the theory. Based on this observation, we give a general framework of reasoning by analogy which enables us to deal with various constraints for the analogy.

2. Reasoning Based on Formal Analogy

We define in this section a notion of formal analogy and the reasoning by it. Since we assume that each domain is represented by a logic program, we first give some necessary definitions concerning logic programs. A definite clause is a clause of the form

$$A \leftarrow B_1, \ldots, B_n \qquad (n \geq 0),$$

where A and B_j are positive literals. We call the definite clause a rule. A logic program is a finite set of rules, and is simply called a program. Since a program P is a set of clauses, any model for P can be considered as the corresponding Herbrand model. Every Herbrand model for P has the same domain $U(P)$ called the Herbrand universe, and the same meaning of function symbol appearing in P. $U(P)$ is defined to be the set of all ground terms whose symbols appear in P. The meaning of n-ary function symbol f is defined to be a function $I_f : U(P)^n \rightarrow U(P)$, where $I_f(t_1,\ldots,t_n) = f(t_1,\ldots,t_n)$. We also need the notion of Herbrand base. The Herbrand base $B(P)$ of a program P is defined as

$$B(P) = \{ p(t_1,\ldots,t_n) \mid p \text{ is an n-ary predicate symbol}$$
$$\text{in P, and } t_j \in U(P)\}.$$

An element in $B(P)$ is called a ground atom. Then each Herbrand model (interpretation) is specified by a subset of $B(P)$. By the model intersection property (Apt and Emden 1982), the intersection of all Herbrand models for P is also a model for P, which is called the least model for P, and is denoted by $M(P)$.

<u>Proposition 2.1</u>. (Apt and Emden 1982, Lloyd 1984)) $M(P)$ is the set of all ground atoms which are logical consequences of P.

From Proposition 2.1, we take $M(P)$ as the formal meaning of P, and call an element in $M(P)$ a fact. In what follows, we consider only the Herbrand models, and simply call them models.

We define the correspondences of analogy by a pairing of elements in domains.

<u>Definition 2.1</u>. Let P_1 and P_2 be logic programs. We call a finite subset of $U(P_1) \times U(P_2)$ a pairing of terms. For a pairing ϕ, we define the set ϕ^+ to be the smallest set that satisfies the following conditions:

$$\phi \subseteq \phi^+ , \tag{2.1}$$
$$\text{if } \langle t_1, t'_1 \rangle,\ldots,\langle t_n, t'_n \rangle \in \phi^+ , \text{ then}$$
$$\langle f(t_1,\ldots,t_n), f(t'_1,\ldots,t'_n) \rangle \in \phi^+ , \tag{2.2}$$

where f is a function symbol appearing in both P_1 and P_2.

As mentioned in the introduction, we need a notion to make clear the identical portions of domains under ϕ.

<u>Definition 2.2</u>. For a pairing ϕ, two ground atoms $\alpha \in B(P_1)$ and $\alpha' \in B(P_2)$ are said to be identified by ϕ, denoted by $\alpha \phi \alpha'$, if α and α' are compatible, that is, they are written as

$$\alpha = p(t_1,\ldots,t_n), \quad \alpha' = p(t'_1,\ldots,t'_n),$$

for some predicate symbol p, and α and α' are syntactically the same up to the pairing ϕ, i.e. $\langle t_i, t'_i \rangle \in \phi^+$.

Since our domains we are considering are the least models $M(P_1)$ and $M(P_2)$, ϕ determines a relation $ID(P_1,P_2;\phi)$ of facts as follows:

$$ID(P_1,P_2;\phi) = \{ \langle \alpha, \alpha' \rangle \mid \alpha \in M(P_1), \alpha' \in M(P_2), \alpha \phi \alpha' \}.$$

When we say that a pairing ϕ is an analogy, we generally require some constraints for ϕ. However, first we consider that the set $ID(P_1,P_2;\phi)$ represents the identical portions of domains which can be viewed the same under the pairing ϕ. Now the reasoning by analogy is stated as follows:

Assume that, in P_1, the premises $\beta_1, \ldots, \beta_n$ logically imply a fact α. Assume also that the analogous premises $\beta_1', \ldots, \beta_n'$ hold in P_2. Then we reason an atom α' in P_1 such that α and α' are analogous.

The reasoning above is conceptually due to Winston's analogy-based reasoning (Winston 1983) based on the causal structures of domains. Since our analogy between $M(P_1)$ and $M(P_2)$ is a pairing ϕ with $ID(P_1, P_2; \phi)$, we can restate the statement as follows:

Let $\beta_1, \ldots, \beta_n$ in $M(P_1)$ logically imply α in P_1, and assume that there exist $\beta_1', \ldots, \beta_n'$ in $M(P_2)$ such that $\beta_j \phi \beta_j'$ for all j. Then we reason an atom α' in $B(P_2)$ such that $\alpha \phi \alpha'$.

The reasoned ground atom α' may not a logical consequence of P_2. Hence the reasoning is beyond a deduction. Our goal is to describe the reasoning in terms of deduction. For this purpose, we need the following definition:

<u>Definition 2.3</u>. Let
$$R_1 = (\alpha \leftarrow \beta_1, \ldots, \beta_n), \quad R_2 = (\alpha' \leftarrow \beta_1', \ldots, \beta_n')$$
be two ground rules ($n \geq 1$) whose symbols appear in P_1 and P_2, respectively. Let ϕ and I_j be a pairing and an Herbrand interpretation of P_j, respectively. Then the rules R_1 and R_2 are called ϕ-analogous w.r.t. I_1 and I_2, if $\beta_j \in I_1$, $\beta_j' \in I_2$, $\alpha \phi \alpha'$, and $\beta_j \phi \beta_j'$. In this case, R_1 (R_2) is called a ϕ-analogue of R_2 (R_1) w.r.t. I_1 and I_2. Moreover we call the conversion of R_1 into R_2, or R_2 into R_1, a transformation of rules.

In what follows, we represent the transformation by the following schema:

$$\frac{\alpha \leftarrow \beta_1, \ldots, \beta_n}{\alpha' \leftarrow \beta_1', \ldots, \beta_n'} \quad (\phi, I_1, I_2)$$

where $\alpha \phi \alpha'$, $\beta_j \phi \beta_j'$, $\beta_j \in I_1$, $\beta_j' \in I_2$ and the dotted line shows that the upper rule is transformed into the lower rule. By using the schema, we can represent the reasoning by analogy as follows:

$$\frac{\dfrac{A \leftarrow B_1, \ldots, B_n}{\alpha \leftarrow \beta_1, \ldots, \beta_n} \quad (\theta)}{\dfrac{\alpha' \leftarrow \beta_1', \ldots, \beta_n' \qquad \beta_1', \ldots, \beta_n'}{\alpha'}} \quad (\phi, M(P_1), M(P_2))$$

where $A \leftarrow B_1, \ldots, B_n$ is a rule in P_1, θ is a ground substitution to get a logically true ground rule $\alpha \leftarrow \beta_1, \ldots, \beta_n$, and the second real line shows the modus ponens. Thus the reasoning by analogy is a combination of the usual deductions and the rule transformations. This schema is said to be basic.

In general, reasoning is a process of application of inference rules. Thus it is natural to consider a process in which the rule transformation and modus ponens are applied successively. For instance, consider an example below:

Example 2.1. Let P_1 and P_2 be the following programs:

$$P_1 = \{ \; p(a,b) \; ,$$
$$q(b) \; ,$$
$$r(b) \; ,$$
$$s(b) \leftarrow q(b), \; r(b)\} \; ,$$
$$P_2 = \{ \; p(a',b') \; ,$$
$$r(b') \; \}.$$

Then we have the following basic schema:

$$\frac{q(b) \; \leftarrow \; p(a,b)}{\frac{p(a',b') \quad q(b') \leftarrow p(a',b')}{q(b')}} \quad (\phi \; ,M(P_1),M(P_2))$$

where $\phi = \{ \; \langle a,a' \rangle, \; \langle b,b' \rangle \; \}$. Although $q(b')$ is not a logical consequence of P_2, we use $q(b')$, as if it is a fact, to derive some additional ground atoms. In fact, we can derive $s(b')$, since

$$\frac{s(b) \leftarrow q(b), \; r(b)}{\frac{s(b') \leftarrow q(b'), \; r(b')}{s(b')}} \quad \frac{(\phi \; ,M(P_1),M(P_2) \cup \{q(b')\})}{q(b'), \; r(b')}$$

is a basic schema. Thus the successive use of the basic schemata monotonically extend the models for P_2.

Definition 2.4. For a given pairing ϕ , we define a set $M_i(*)$ for $i=1,2$ as follows:

$$M_i(*) = \cup_n M_i(n),$$
$$M_i(0) = M(P_i) = \{ \alpha \in B(P_i) \mid \; P_i \vdash \alpha \; \},$$
$$M_i(n+1) = \{ \alpha \in B(P_i) \mid R_i(n) \cup M_i(n) \cup P_i \vdash \alpha \; \},$$

where $S \vdash \gamma$ denotes that γ is a logical consequence of S, $R_i(n)$ is the set of all ground rules that are ϕ-analogues of ground instances of rules in P_j ($j \neq i$) with respect to $M_j(n)$ and $M_i(n)$.

The following proposition asserts that our extension of the least model $M(P_i)$ to $M_i(*)$ is admissible.

Proposition 2.2. For each i, $M_i(*)$ is an Herbrand model for P_i.

To prove this proposition, we need an operator concerning the fixpoint semantics of logic programs (Apt and Emden 1982, Lloyd 1984). Let P and Pow(S) be a possibly infinite set of rules and the power set of a set S, respectively. Then we define an operator

$$T(P) : Pow(B(P)) \rightarrow Pow(B(P))$$

as follows: For a set $I \subseteq B(P)$, $\alpha \in T(P)(I)$ iff there exists a rule $A \leftarrow B_1, \ldots, B_n$ $(n \geq 0)$ in P and a ground substitution θ such that $A\theta = \alpha$ and $B_j\theta \in I$ for all j.

Proposition 2.3. (Apt and Emden 1982) For a logic program P and an Herbrand interpretation I of P, the following conditions are equivalent:

    (1)   I is a model for P.

    (2) $T(P)(I) \subseteq I$.

    (3) $T(\{C\})(I) \subseteq I$ for any rule C in P.

Proof of Proposition 2.2. Let $A \leftarrow B_1, \ldots, B_n$ be a rule in P_i and θ be a ground substitution such that $B_j\theta \in M_i(*)$. Since $M_i(*) = \cup M_i(n)$, there exists a natural number N such that $B_j\theta \in M_i(N)$. Hence $M_i(N) \cup P_i \vdash A\theta$, and hence $A\theta \in M_i(N+1) \subseteq M_i(*)$. Therefore we have $T(P_i)(M_i(*)) \subseteq M_i(*)$. Thus, from Proposition 2.3, $M_i(*)$ is a model for P_i. $\square$

From this proposition, the extension $M_i(*)$ of $M(P_i)$ is admissible in the sense that $M_i(*)$ is a model for P_i. In the next section, we give a more logical characterization of $M_i(*)$.

3.   Analogical Union of Logic Programs

In this section, we introduce a notion of analogical union, and study a logical aspects of reasoning by analogy. Because the transformation of rules are used in derivation, the ground atoms in $M_i(*)$ are not always logical consequences of P_i. However the relation ϕ^+ of terms gives a correspondence between Herbrand universes, and the transformation is carried out according to this correspondence. We specify both ϕ^+ and the transformation by logic programs.

We need a predicate symbol $\sim$ to denote the correspondence defined by ϕ^+, and we also need the following rules:

    (1) $t \sim t'$, for each pair $\langle t, t' \rangle$ in ϕ

    (2) $f(X_1, \ldots, X_n) \sim f(Y_1, \ldots, Y_n) \leftarrow X_1 \sim Y_1, \ldots, X_n \sim Y_n$,

for each function symbol appearing in both P_1 and P_2. The set of these rules is denoted by PAIR(ϕ). Then we can easily prove

<u>Proposition 3.1</u>. For a pairing ϕ, $\langle t,t'\rangle \in \phi^+$ iff PAIR(ϕ) $\vdash$ t $\sim$ t'.

The notion of analogical union of two logic programs is used to justify the transformation of rules. Conceptually it corresponds to the notion of completion of a logic program, which was introduced to justify the negation as failure rule (Clark 1978). The analogical union of P_1 and P_2 is itself a logic program which has copies of P_i and some additional definite clauses. Each predicate symbol in the copy of P_i has a suffix i which shows that it comes from P_i. For simplicity, we replace each predicate symbol p in P_i by p_i. The transformation of rules is now specified by definite clauses which have the predicate symbol $\sim$ in their bodies. Formally, we associate a rule

$$p(t_1,\ldots t_n) \leftarrow \ldots, q(s_1,\ldots s_k),\ldots$$

in P_1 with the following clause:

$$p_2(W_1,\ldots,W_n) \leftarrow \qquad \ldots$$
$$t_1 \sim W_1,\ldots, t_n \sim W_n,$$
$$s_1 \sim V_1,\ldots, s_k \sim V_k$$
$$q_1(s_1,\ldots,s_k),$$
$$q_2(V_1,\ldots,V_k),$$
$$\ldots \quad .$$

Similarly we associate a rule

$$p(t_1,\ldots,t_n) \leftarrow \ldots, q(s_1,\ldots,s_k), \ldots$$

in P_2 with

$$p_1(W_1,\ldots,W_n) \leftarrow \qquad \ldots$$
$$W_1 \sim t_1,\ldots, W_n \sim t_n,$$
$$V_1 \sim s_1,\ldots, V_k \sim s_k,$$
$$q_2(s_1,\ldots,s_k),$$
$$q_1(V_1,\ldots,V_k),$$
$$\ldots$$

In both cases W_i and V_j are the newly introduced variables not in P_1 or P_2.

<u>Definition 3.1</u>. Let P_1 and P_2 be logic programs. Let ϕ be a pairing. The analogical union of P_1 and P_2, denoted by $P_1 \phi P_2$, is the collection of definite clauses which are associated with each rule in P_i (i=1,2) together with PAIR(ϕ).

Example 3.1. Let

$$P_1 = \{ \ p(a,b) \ ,$$
$$p(f(X),b) \leftarrow p(X,b) \ \},$$

$$P_2 = \{ \ p(f(c),d). \ \}, $$
$$\phi = \{ \ \langle a,f(c)\rangle, \ \langle b,d\rangle \ \}.$$

Then the analogical union $P_1 \phi P_2$ is

$\{ \ p_1(a,b) \ ,$

$\quad p_1(f(X),b) \leftarrow p_1(X,b),$

$\quad p_2(W_1,W_2) \leftarrow f(X) \sim W_1, \ b \sim W_2,$

$\qquad\qquad\qquad p_1(X,b),$

$\qquad\qquad\qquad p_2(V_1,V_2),$

$\quad p_2(f(c),d) \ ,$

$\quad a \sim f(c) \ ,$

$\quad b \sim d \ ,$

$\quad f(X) \sim f(Y) \leftarrow X \sim Y \ \}.$

The reasoning we have defined in Section 2 is now characterized by the least Herbrand models for the analogical union.

<u>Theorem 3.1</u>. $M(P_1 \phi P_2) = M'_1(*) \cup M'_2(*) \cup \phi'^+,$
where

$\quad M'_i(*) = \{ p_i(t_1, \ldots, t_n) \mid p(t_1, \ldots, t_n) \in M_i(*) \},$

$\quad \phi'^+ = \{ \ s \sim t \mid PAIR(\phi) \vdash s \sim t \ \}.$

In what follows, we can identify $M_i(*)$ with $M'_i(*)$, and also identify ϕ^+ with ϕ'^+ according to Proposition 3.1.

<u>Proof of Theorem 3.1</u>.   First we show that $M(P_1 \phi P_2) \subseteq M_1(*) \cup M_2(*) \cup \phi^+$. Let $M(*)$ denote $M_1(*) \cup M_2(*) \cup \phi^+$. Since $M(P_1 \phi P_2)$ is the least model, it suffices to prove that $M(*)$ is a model for $P_1 \phi P_2$. We assume, for the sake of simplicity, that each rule in P_i is an assertion of facts or has a single literal in the body. Suppose that

$\quad C_0 : p_2(W_1, \ldots, W_n) \leftarrow$

$\qquad\qquad t_1 \sim W_1, \ \ldots, \ t_n \sim W_n, \ s_1 \sim V_1, \ \ldots, \ s_k \sim V_m,$

$\qquad\qquad q_1(s_1, \ldots, s_m), \ q_2(V_1, \ldots, V_m)$

is in $P_1 \phi P_2$. From the definition of analogical union, the rule

$\qquad\qquad C_1 : p_1(t_1, \ldots, t_n) \leftarrow q_1(s_1, \ldots, s_m)$

should be in P_1, and the variables W_j and V_k are not in C_1. Let θ be a ground substitution such that $t_j\theta \sim W_j\theta$ for all j, $s_i\theta \sim V_i\theta$ for all i, and $q_1(s_1\theta, \ldots, s_m\theta), q_2(V_1\theta, \ldots, V_m\theta) \in$ in $M(*)$. Clearly $t_j\theta \sim W_j\theta$ and $s_i\theta \sim V_i\theta$ are in ϕ^+, and $q_1(s_1\theta, \ldots, s_m\theta) \in M_1(*),$ $q_2(V_1\theta, \ldots, V_m\theta) \in M_2(*)$. Hence there exists a natural number N such that $q_1(s_1\theta, \ldots, s_m\theta) \in M_1(N)$ and $q_2(V_1\theta, \ldots, V_m\theta) \in M_2(N)$. Therefore the rule

$\qquad\qquad C_2 : p_2(W_1\theta, \ldots, W_n\theta) \leftarrow q_2(V_1\theta, \ldots, V_m\theta)$

is a ϕ -analogue of
$$p_1(t_1\theta ,\ldots,t_n\theta) \leftarrow q_1(s_1\theta ,\ldots,s_m\theta),$$
which is an instance of rule C_1 in P_1 with respect to $M_1(N)$ and $M_2(N)$.
Thus $C_2 \in R_2(N)$ (see Definition 2.4) and therefore
$$R_2(N) \cup M_2(N) \vdash p(W_1\theta ,\ldots,W_n\theta),$$
which implies
$$p(W_1\theta ,\ldots,W_n\theta) \in M_2(N+1) \subseteq M_2(*).$$
Hence we have
$$T(\{C_0\})(M(*)) \subseteq M(*).$$
For a rule in $P_1\phi P_2$ with $p_1(X_1,\ldots,X_k)$ as its head, we can give a completely similar proof. For a rule C in $P_i \subseteq P_1\phi P_2$, we have already proved in Proposition 2.2 that $T(\{C\})(M(*)) \subseteq M(*)$. Hence, by Proposition 2.3, $M(*)$ is a model for $P_1\phi P_2$.

Conversely we show that $M(*) = M_1(*) \cup M_2(*) \cup \phi^+ \subseteq M(P_1\phi P_2)$. From Proposition 3.1 and the definition of $P_1\phi P_2$, it suffices to prove that $M_1(*) \cup M_2(*) = \cup_n (M_1(n) \cup M_2(n)) \subseteq M(P_1\phi P_2)$. We prove that $M_i(n) \subseteq M(P_1\phi P_2)$ for $i=1,2$, by an induction on n. Suppose first that $n=0$. Then $M_i(0) = M(P_i)$. So the result is trivial. Now suppose that, for some $n > 0$, $M_i(n) \subseteq M(P_1\phi P_2)$ holds for $i=1,2$. By the definition, $M_2(n+1) = M(P_2(n))$, where $P_2(n) = R_2(n) \cup M_2(n) \cup P_2$. Since $M(P_2(n))$ is the least model for $P_2(n)$, we show that
$$M_2(n+1) = M(P_2(n)) \subseteq M(P_1\phi P_2)$$
by proving that $M(P_1\phi P_2)$ is a model for $P_2(n)$. It suffices to verify that $T(\{C\})(M(P_1\phi P_2)) \subseteq M(P_1\phi P_2)$ for each C in $P_2(n)$.
Case 1: $C \in M_2(n) \subseteq P_2(n)$. By the induction hypothesis and the fact that C is a ground atom, we have
$$T(\{C\})(M(P_1\phi P_2)) = \{C\} \subseteq M_2(n) \subseteq M(P_1\phi P_2).$$
Case 2: $C \in P_2 \subseteq P_2(n)$. Since $P_2 \subseteq P_1\phi P_2$, the result is trivial.
Case 3: $C = (\alpha' \leftarrow \beta'_1,\ldots,\beta'_k) \in R_2(n) \subseteq P_2(n)$. By the definition of $R_2(n)$, there exists a rule $C_1 : A \leftarrow B_1,\ldots,B_k$ in P_1 and a ground substitution θ such that $B_1\theta ,\ldots,B_k\theta \in M_1(n)$, $\beta'_1,\ldots,\beta'_k \in M_2(n)$ and $A\theta \sim \alpha'$, $B_j\theta \sim \beta'_j$ for all j. Since $M_2(n) \subseteq M(P_1\phi P_2)$, we have $T(\{C\})(M(P_1\phi P_2)) = \{ \alpha' \}$. For the sake of simplicity, we assume that $k=1$, and write C and C_1 as follows:
$$C_1 : p_1(s) \leftarrow q_1(t),$$
$$C : p_2(s') \leftarrow q_2(t'),$$
where $\alpha'=p(s')$, $s\theta \sim s'$, $t\theta \sim t'$, $q_1(t\theta)\in M_1(n)$ and $q_2(t') \in M_2(n)$. From the definition, $P_1\phi P_2$ contains
$$C_2 : p_2(W) \leftarrow s \sim W, t \sim V, q_1(t), q_2(V),$$
where the variables W and V never appear in s nor in t. Let
$$\sigma = \theta \cup (W \leftarrow s', V \leftarrow t').$$

Then, by the induction hypothesis, we have
$$q_1(t\sigma) = q_1(t\theta) \in M_1(n) \subseteq M(P_1 \phi P_2),$$
$$q_2(V\sigma) = q_2(t') \in M_2(n) \subseteq M(P_1 \phi P_2).$$
Hence, by the definition of $T(\{C_2\})$, we have
$$\alpha' = p_2(s') = p_2(W\sigma) \in T(\{C_2\})(M(P_1 \phi P_2)).$$
Since $C_2 \in P_1 \phi P_2$, this implies that $\alpha' \in M(P_1 \phi P_2)$. As a result, we have proved that $M_2(n+1) \subseteq M(P_1 \phi P_2)$. $M_1(n+1) \subseteq M(P_1 \phi P_2)$ is similarly proved. Hence we have $M_1(n) \cup M_2(n) \subseteq M(P_1 \phi P_2)$ for all n. This completes the proof. $\square$

4. General Framework of Reasoning by Analogy

Based on the results in the previous sections, we present a general framework of reasoning by analogy. Definition 2.4 formalizes the reasoning by analogy, given some underlying pairing ϕ, and Theorem 3.1 logically characterizes the reasoning in terms of the deducibility from the analogical union.

Hence, once a pairing is detected, the problem of analogy is solved in the framework of deduction. However the problem of analogy detection is still left as an important problem. The problem is to find a pairing which satisfies certain constraints. As discussed before, the constraint required so far was
$$A_0 : f(X_1,\ldots,X_n) \sim f(Y_1,\ldots,Y_n) \leftarrow X_1 \sim Y_1, \ldots, X_n \sim Y_n.$$
Gentner (1982) required that a possible pairing of analogy be one-to-one.

<u>Definition 4.1</u>. (Haraguchi and Arikawa 1986) For programs P_1 and P_2, a pairing ϕ is called a partial identity if ϕ^+ is a one-to-one relation of terms.

If we require that ϕ be a partial identity, we need the following new axioms:
$$A_1 : X =_1 Y \leftarrow X \sim Z, Y \sim Z,$$
$$A_2 : X =_2 Y \leftarrow Z \sim X, Z \sim Y,$$
where $=_i$ is a predicate symbol to denote the identity relation on each Herbrand universe $U(P_i)$. Due to Clark (1978), the following theory, denoted by EQ_i, is sufficient for $=_i$ to denote the identity relation:

1. $c \neq_i d$, for all pairs of distinct constants c, d in P_i.
2. $f(X_1,\ldots,X_n) \neq_i g(Y_1,\ldots,Y_m)$, for all pairs of distinct function symbols f, g in P_i.

3. $f(X_1, \ldots, X_n) \neq_i c$, for all pairs of constant c and function f in P_i.

4. $t[X] \neq_i X$, for each non-variable term $t[X]$ in P_i.

5. $X_j =_i Y_j \leftarrow f(X_1, \ldots, X_n) =_i f(Y_1, \ldots, Y_n)$, for each function f in P_i.

6. $X =_i X$.

7. $f(X_1, \ldots, X_n) =_i f(Y_1, \ldots, Y_n) \leftarrow X_1 =_i Y_1, \ldots, X_n =_i Y_n$, for each function f in P_i.

8. $p(Y_1, \ldots, Y_n) \leftarrow X_1 =_i Y_1, \ldots, X_n =_i Y_n, p(X_1, \ldots, X_n)$, for each predicate p in P_i.

Then the constraint for ϕ is now written as the following theory $CT(\phi)$:

$$CT(\phi) = EQ_1 \cup EQ_2 \cup \{A_0, A_1, A_2\} \cup \phi.$$

Then it is clear that ϕ is a partial identity iff $CT(\phi)$ is consistent. It should be noted that a model for $CT(\phi)$ can define a partial identity. In other words, the analogy we desire is a model for the theory $CT(\phi)$. Based on this fact, we give a general framework of the reasoning by analogy.

<u>Problem of analogy detection</u>: Given P_1 and P_2, find a pairing ϕ such that $CT(\phi)$ is consistent.

Once the problem above is solved, we go to the next step by using Theorem 3.1:

<u>Problem of reasoning based on the pairing</u>: Given P_1, P_2 and ϕ, deduce some useful information from the analogical union $P_1 \phi P_2$ with respect to ϕ.

The authors have already given an effective solution to the problem of analogy detection, provided that the pairing is a partial identity (Haraguchi and Arikawa 1986). Even when we choose the constraint $CT(\phi)$ other than the partial identity, our framework based on the analogical union is still valid to describe the reasoning by analogy.

5. Concluding Remarks

We have presented a formalism of reasoning by analogy in terms of logic programming based on Horn logic. Since we cannot deal with negative literals in definite clauses, we have not paid any attention to the use of negative information. However it is natural to make use of them in order to reject wrong analogies. Such negative information should be described as formulas, and then added to the theory $CT(\phi)$ so that ϕ

does not define a wrong analogy. Furthermore the search space of possible pairings is reduced if we consider such a theory. From this viewpoint, we are developing another theory of reasoning by analogy in which we can deals with the negative information.

References

Apt, K.R. and van Emden, M.H. (1982): Contribution to the theory of logic programming, JACM, 29, 3, 841-862.

Clark, K.L. (1978): Negation as Failure, in Logic and Databases, H. Gallaire and J. Minker (Eds.), Plenum Press, New York, 293-322.

Gentner, P. (1982): Are scientific analogies metaphors?, in Metaphor: Problems and Perspectives, D.S. Miall (Ed.), The Harvester Press, Sussex, 106-132.

Haraguchi, M. and Arikawa, S. (1985): Analogical reasoning based on the theory of analogy, Res. Rept. Inst. Fund. Inform. Sci. Kyushu Univ., No. 105.

Haraguchi, M. (1986): Analogical reasoning using transformations of rules, Bull. of Infor. Cybernetics, 22.

Haraguchi, M. and Arikawa, S. (1986): A formulation and a realization of analogical reasoning, Journal of JSAI, 1, 1 (in Japanese).

Lloyd, J.W. (1984): Foundations of logic programming, Springer-Verlag.

Polya, G. (1954): Induction and analogy in mathematics, Princeton University Press.

Winston, P.H. (1980): Learning and reasoning by analogy, CACM, 23, 689-703.

Winston, P.H. (1983): Learning new principles from precedents and exercises, Artificial Intelligence, 19, 321-350.

Logic Interface System on Navigational
Database Systems

Makoto Takizawa, Hideaki Itoh+ and Kunihiko Moriya*

Department of Systems and Management Engineering, Tokyo Denki University
+Japan Information Processing Development Center
*Hitachi Software Engineering

Abstract

This paper presents the design and implementation of logic language interface on conventional
network database systems which provide network data structure and navigational data manipulation language. This interface provides users with unified view of various data structures in
logics and inference facilities of theorem proving. Although most researchers try to combine
logic systems like Prolog and relational database systems, we try to augment the conventional
network database system with logic interface, since the network ones have been already mainly
used in database applications. This also can be used as a common interface on heterogeneous
database systems in distributed database systems. We show a refutation procedure which can
reduce the search space by avoiding meaningless backtracking and redundant refutations.

1. Introduction

Recent computer systems provide two types of database management systems, relational
[CODD] and network[CODA73,OLLE] ones, which play a central role of most computer applications.
The relational ones provide non-procedural data manipulation languages (DMLs) like SQL[DATE]
on logical data structures and are used for ad hoc applications like CAD. The network ones
provide navigational DMLs[OLLE] on the mixture of logical and physical data structures, and
have been used for well-formed business applications which require high performance. At
present, high level interfaces on the database systems are required. Relational interface systems which can provide non-procedural languages on the conventional network database systems
have been realized by [TAKI80,DAYA].

Logic languages like Prolog[KOWA] have advantages to the relational model: unified and
recursive treatment of data structure, procedures, queries and integrity constraints. Although
most researchers[CHAN,LID,OHSU etc.] try to combine the relational model and logic languages,
we discuss a pure Prolog interface on the network database system, because they have been
mainly used in database applications and resolution is based on a tuple-at-a-time, navigational access like the DML[OLLE]. In our refutation procedure, record occurrences are accessed
according to sequences implemented in the network database system. Also, we try to reduce the
search space in the resolution by avoiding meaningless backtracking and redundant refutations.

In chapter 2 and 3, we define a formal system of the network database system and semantics of the conventional DML. In chapter 4, 5 and 6, we discuss how to combine a refutation
procedure and navigational data manipulation on the network database.

2. Navigational Database System

First, a navigational model is defined by extracting an essential, logical part of the conventional network model [CODA73,78, OLLE].

2.1 Network Data Structure

A network data structure N is composed of a schema $\underline{N}$, and a database N. $\underline{N}$ is composed of two kinds of types, entity (E-) and function (F-) types. The E-type $\underline{E}$ is a tuple of attributes (@E, A1, ..., Am)(m≥0). @E is an identifier and Ai (i=1,...,m) a data attribute. For an attribute T of $\underline{E}$, let dom(T) denote a domain of T. An E-set for $\underline{E}$ is E ⊆ dom(@E) x dom(A1) x...x dom(Am). Each element e in E is an E-tuple. Let T(e) denote T's value of e. Every E-tuple has different identifier.

If there exists a functional relation from an E-type E1 to E2, an F-type $\underline{F}$ is defined as $\underline{F}$ = (E1, E2). E1 is the domain and E2 the range. An F-set for $\underline{F}$ is F ⊆ E1 x E2. F represents a partial function F: E1 -> E2.

A family of the E-sets and F-sets is a network database N. $\underline{N}$ is represented by a graph whose nodes denote E-types and directed arcs F-types. Fig.1 shows the network schema which represents information on departments (Dep), employees (Emp), and projects (Proj). For example, an arc DE from Emp to Dep indicates an F-type $\underline{DE}$=(Emp,Dep).

```
E-types Dep = (dname)    F-type  DE = (Emp, Dep)
        Emp = (ename)            EP = (Pel, Emp)
        Pel = ()                 PE = (Pel, Proj)
        Proj = (pname)
```

```
--------------- DE -------------- EP ------- PE ---------------
| Dep(dname)  |<-----| Emp(ename) |<-----| Pel |----->| Proj(pname) |
---------------       --------------       -------     ---------------
```

Fig.1 Network Schema.

2.2 Navigational Data Structure and Access Functions

A navigational data structure V is defined by introducing ordering relations on the network data structure N. For an E-set E and an attribute T of $\underline{E}$, an ordered E- (OE-) set E/T is a totally ordered set(tos) (E,<) where for every e and f in E, e<f in E/T if and only if (iff) T(e)≤T(f). e<<f (f is an immediate successor of e) iff e<f and no g in E such that e<g<f.

E%T is a partially ordered set (pos) (E,<) where for every e, f in E, e<f in E%T iff T(e)=T(f) and @E(e)<@E(f). E%T is partitioned into a tos E%T[v]=({e| e∈E and T(e)=v},<) for every d in dom(v). e<<f in E%T is defined like E/T.

For an F-set F of $\underline{F}$=(E1,E2), some attribute T of E1, and e2 in E2, F%T is a pos (F,<) where for f=<e,g> and f'=<e',g> in F, f<f' in F%T iff T(e)≤T(e'). F%T is also partitioned into a tos F%t[e2]=({<e1,e2>| <e1,e2>∈F },<) for every e2 in E2. << in F%T is defined like E/T.

Here, E/@E, E%T, and F%t represent conventional record-type, CALC item T, and set-type whose sort key is T [CODA73], respectively.

There are following access functions for V. Here, E' is a set E U{⊥} where ⊥ means "undefined".

1) topE/T:->E, lastE/T:->E. topE/T() (lastE/T()) gives the greatest (least) element in E/T.
2) nextE/T:E->E', priorE/T:E->E'. For every e in E, nextE/T(e) (priorE/T(e)) gives f such that e<<f (f<<e) in E/T. Here, nextE/T(lastE/T ())=⊥ and priorE/T(topE/T())=⊥.
3) dtopE%T:dom(T)->E', dlastE%T:dom(T)->E'. For every v in dom(T), dtopE%T(v) (dlastE%T(v)) gives the greatest (least) one in E%T[v].

4) $dnextE\%T:E\rightarrow E'$, $dpriorE\%T:E\rightarrow E'$. For every e in E, $dnextE\%T(e)$ $(dpriorE\%T(e))$ gives f such that $e<<f$ $(f<<e)$ in $E\%T$. Here, $dnextE\%T(dlastE\%T())=\downarrow$, $dpriorE\%T(dtopE\%T())=\downarrow$.
5) $ftopF\%T:E2\rightarrow E1'$, $flastF\%T:E2\rightarrow E1'$. For every e2 in E2, $ftopF\%T(e2)$ $(flastF\%T(e2))$ gives e of the greatest (least) $<e,e2>$ in $F\%T[e2]$. If $F\%T[e2]$ is empty, they are $\downarrow$.
6) $fnextF\%T:E1\rightarrow E1'$, $fpriorF\%T:E1\rightarrow E1'$. For every e in E1, $fnextF\%T(e)$ $(fpriorF\%T(e))$ is e' such that $<e,e2>$ $<<(>>)$ $<e',e2>$ in $F\%T$. Here, $fnextF\%T(flastF\%T())=\downarrow$, $fpriorF\%T(ftopF\%T())=\downarrow$.
7) $F:E1\rightarrow E2'$. For every e1 in E1, $F(e1)$ gives e2 in E2 where $<e1,e2>$ in F.

The access functions correspond to DMLs [OLLE]. For example, $ftopF\%T(e)$ is a COBOL DML "find first E2 within F" where the currency[CODA73] indicates the record occurrence e in E1. Also, $ftopE\%T(v)$ means "move v to T in E. find any E".
    A navigational model is a pair of the navigational data structure and access functions, which is an abstract model of the conventional network model.

3.   Network System

    We define a first-order theory called a network system NS for N. NS is a tuple of a network schema $\underline{N}$, network language L, axiom set, and two inference rules, i.e. modus ponens and generalization.

3.1 Network Language

    A network language L for $\underline{N}$ is a first-order, function-free language which includes following three types of predicate symbols:
1) For every E-type $\underline{E}=(@E,A1,...,Am)$ $(m\geq0)$, an $(m+1)$-place E-type predicate symbol E.
2) For every F-type $\underline{F}=(\underline{E1}, \underline{E2})$, two-place F-type predicate symbol F.
3) For every attribute T in $\underline{N}$, one-place T-type predicate symbol T.
In L, variables are written in upper-case letters and constants lower-case letters. Logical connectives && and || represent conjunction and disjunction.
    Here, assume that a constant mapping CM of an interpretation I of L is bijective, i.e. for every individual d in a universe of I, there exists only one constant d such that $CM(d)=d$.

3.2 Axioms

    Let $\underline{E}=(@E,A1,...,Am)$ and $\underline{E1}=(@E1,B1,...,Bn)$ be E-types and $\underline{F}=(E,E1)$ an F-type. Let C be a set $\{d1,...,dq\}$ of constants in L. The non-logical axioms of NS are as follows:

(1)[Completion axioms] For every n-ary predicate symbol P in L, let CP be a set $\{<c1i,...,cni>$ | $P(c1i,...,cni)$ is a ground atom in NS $(i=1,...,s)\}$. A following formula is an axiom.
    $P(X1,...,Xn) \rightarrow ((X1=c11 \&\&...\&\& Xn=cn1) ||...|| (X1=c1s \&\&...\&\& Xn=cns))$.
(2)[Unique name axioms] For every i, j $(i\neq j)$, $(di \neq dj)$.
(3)[Domain closure axiom] $\forall X$ ($X=d1 ||...|| X=dq$).
(4)[Network axioms]
  $\forall K\forall X1...\forall Xm$ ($E(K,X1,...,Xm) \rightarrow @E(K) \&\& A1(X1) \&\&...\&\& Am(Xm)$).
  $\forall K\forall X1...\forall Xm \forall Y1...\forall Ym$ ($E(K,X1,...,Xm) \&\& E(K,Y1,...,Ym) \rightarrow X1=Y1 \&\&...\&\& Xm=Ym$).
  $\forall K\forall K1$ ($F(K,K2) \rightarrow @E(K) \&\& @E1(K1)$).
  $\forall K\forall K1 \exists X1...\exists Xm \exists Y1...\exists Yn(F(K,K1) \rightarrow E(K,X1,...,Xm) \&\& E1(K1,Y1,...,Yn)$).
  $\forall K\forall K1\forall K2(F(K,K1) \&\& F(K,K2) \rightarrow K1=K2$).
    Also, we make a closed world assumption(CWA). An interpretation I which satisfies these

axioms is a network model. It is clear that a network database N is a network model. Since our network system is a first-order theory, it is complete and sound.

3.3. Deductive Network Database System

By restricting wffs in Horn clauses, we define a deductive network database (DNB) to be composed of a fact base (FB) and a rule base (RB). The FB is a set of ground unit clauses, i.e. FB includes $E(k,d1,...,dm)$ for every E-tuple $<k,d1,...,dm>$ in E, and $F(k,k1)$ for every F-tuple $<<k,d1,...,dm>, <k1,e1,...,en>>$ in F. Fig.2 shows a network database for Fig.1 and (1) shows its FB. The RB is a set of rule clauses. (2) indicates an example of the RB for (1). Predicate symbols in heads of the rule clauses never appear in the FB. Queries are represented in goal clauses. For example, a query "find employees Y transitively participated in a project a" is written as ?-Pemp(a, ?Y). Here, Y is a target variable.

FB={1) Dep(1,d), 2) Dep(2,a), 3) Emp(1,a), 4) Emp(2,b), 5) Emp(3,c), 6) Emp(4,d),
    7) Proj(1,dbs), 8) Proj(2,nw),
    9) Pel(1), 10) Pel(2), 11) Pel(3), 12) Pel(4), 13) Pel(5),
    14) DE(1,1), 15) DE(2,1), 16) DE(3,2), 17) DE(4,2),
    18) EP(1,1), 19) EP(2,1), 20) EP(3,2), 21) EP(4,3), 22) EP(5,4),
    23) PE(1,1), 24) PE(3,1), 25) PE(4,1), 26) PE(2,2), 27) PE(5,2) }...(1)

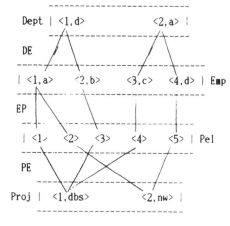

RB = { 28) Projemp(X,Y):-Proj(K,X),PE(L,K),
                        Pel(L,Z),EP(L,M),Emp(M,Y),
       29) Pemp(X,Y):- Projemp(X,Y),
       30) Pemp(X,Y):- Projemp(X,Z), Pemp(Z,Y)}
                        ... (2)

Fig.2   Network Database

4. Refutation Procedure

4.1 Prolog Refutation Procedure

For a goal $H=?-A1,...,Am$, a selected atom Ai by a computation rule R, an input clause $C= A:-B1,...,Bp(p\geq0)$ in a DNB D, and a most general unifier (mgu) θ such that $Ai\theta=A\theta$, $?-(A1, ...,A<i-1>,B1,...,Bp,A<i+1>,...,Am)\theta$ is an SLD resolvent of C and H via R. This is an SLD resolution [KOWA,APT,LLOY]. A linear sequence of SLD resolutions is an SLD deduction. An SLD refutation is an SLD deduction which derives an empty clause □. Let F be an SLD refutation of D U {G} with mgus $\theta1,...,\theta n$. A restriction of a composition $\theta1...\theta n$ on the target variables in G is an answer substitution.

All deductions for D U{G} are represented by an SLD tree as shown in Fig.3, where nodes denote goal clauses, branches indicate input clauses, and selected atoms are underlined. A root-to-leaf path represents a deduction. A path whose leaf is □ is a success path which represents a refutation.

Problem is how to find success paths in the SLD tree. Procedures to do that are refutation procedures. In the Prolog refutation procedure, the computation rule PR selects the right-most atom in a goal clause, input clauses are selected according to a predefined ordering, and the SLD tree is searched in a depth-first manner.

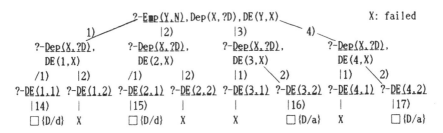

Fig.3 SLD Tree T by the rule PR.

4.2 Improvement of Prolog Refutation Procedure

Let us discuss how to combine the SLD resolution and the accesses to the navigational database V. If input clauses C are facts, E- or F-tuples denoted by C are retrieved from V. Fig.3 shows the SLD tree T by the Prolog rule PR. Fig.4 shows an SLD tree U by another computation rule R. U has less nodes than T. If input clauses are ordered as 1)<2), 14)<15), 16)<17) according to V, answer substitutions for U are obtained by the access function procedure in (3). From this, if atoms are selected according to the sequence in V, the SLD tree can be reduced and all answer substitutions are obtained by accessing navigationally V.

```
     ?-Emp(Y,N),Dep(X,?D),DE(Y,X)          d = topDep/@Dep();
              /1)              | 2)         while ( d ≠ ⊥ )
     ?-Emp(Y,N),DE(Y,1)   ?-Emp(Y,N),DE(Y,2)   { e = ftopDE/@Emp(d);
      / 14)      |15)       /16)      |17)        while ( e ≠ ⊥ )
  ?-Emp(1,N)  ?-Emp(2,N)  ?-Emp(3,N)  ?-Emp(4,N)  { output( dname(d));
      |3)       |4)         |5)        |6)           e = fnextDE/@Emp(e); }
   (1)□{D/d}  (2)□{D/d}  (3)□{D/a}  (4)□{D/a}     d = nextDep/@Dep(d);
                                                }     ... (3)
```

Fig.4 SLD Tree U by the rule R.

Next, let us consider a goal H1=?-A(X,Y),B(X,?N),C(Y,M) with the rule PR, where A, B, C are facts in the FB. H2=?-(B(X,?N),C(Y,M))θ1 and H3=?-C(Y,M)θ1θ2 are resolved in this sequence. θ1 includes bindings for X and Y, and θ2 for N. If H3's resolution fails, by going back to H2, another input clauses for B(X,?N)θ1 with new θ2 are tried to be found in the FB. However, even if any new θ2 is found, H3's resolutions necessarily fail since θ2 includes only a binding for N and H3 still remains unchanged. In this sense, this backtracking is meaningless. If we go back directly to H1 from H3, we may find a refutation since θ1 may include new binding for Y. Hence, if we backtrack to the nearest ancestor which has common variables, meaningless backtracking can be avoided.

Let us consider Fig.4. Refutations (1)-(2) have the same answer substitution {D/d} and (3)-(4) {D/a}. Refutation (2) is redundant in a sense that it has the same answer substitutions as (1). Also, (4) is redundant for (3). Since we purpose to find answer substitutions, redundant refutations have to be avoided. One point is that once a refutation (1) is found, we backtrack directly to the root whose selected atom includes the target variable D. Another input clause 2) is found and new answer substitution {D/a} is found.

5. Similarity Classes

5.1 Definitions

Let SP be a set of SLD deductions for a deductive network database(DNB) D and a goal G via a computation rule R. First, let us define a similarity relation on SP.

$$?-(B1,\ldots,\underline{Bj},\ldots,Bk)\,\theta<i-1> \quad ?-(B'1,\ldots,\underline{B'j'},\ldots,B'k')\,\theta'<i-1>$$

```
        |                                    |
        |  Ci= B:-A1,...,Am                  |  C'i= B':-A'1,...,A'm'
        |   / Bjθ<i-1>σi=Bσi                 |   / B'j'θ'<i-1>σ'i=B'σ'i
        |  /                                 |  /
?-(B1,...,B<j-1>,                    ?-(B'1,...,B'(j'-1),
    A1,...,Am,                          A'1,...,A'm',
    B<j+1>,...,Bk)θi                    B'<j'+1>,...,B'k')θ'i
     a) Ri                                 b) R'i
```

Fig.5 The i-th resolution.

[Definition] Let F and F' be SLD deductions in SP. F and F' are said to be similar iff they satisfy the following conditions:
 1) F and F' have the same length r, $\theta0=\theta'0=\varepsilon$ (identity substitution) and
 2) for every i-th resolution Ri in F and R'i in F' as shown in Fig.5 (i=1,...,r), k=k', j=j'(i.e. Bj=B'j'), m=m', $\theta i=\theta<i-1>\sigma i$, $\theta'i=\theta'<i-1>\sigma'i$, and
    if m=m'=0, B and B' are atoms of a same predicate symbol,
    if m=m'>0, input clauses Ci and C'i are the same rule clause.
Here, Bj is a selected atom at Ri and θi a substitution of Ri. A variable X in Bj such that X θi is ground and $X\theta<i-1>$ is not is said to be instantiated at Ri.

All SLD deductions in Fig.3 are similar. Since the similarity relation is clearly an equivalence relation, SP is partitioned into equivalence classes (called similarity classes), SP1, SP2,... We try to get all answer substitutions by the following two-step procedures:
    1) one to find a similarity class SPi which includes refutations, and
    2) one to find all answer substitutions for SPi.
Problem in 1) is how to find a refutation by avoiding failed deductions.

[Definition] Let A and B be nodes in an SLD tree T. Suppose that B is in a path from the root to A. If P and Q have a common variable X and X is instantiated at B, a backtracking from B to A is said to be meaningful and B a backtrack(BK)-node on X. Otherwise, it is said to be meaningless. A BK-node of B is one which is the nearest to B among BK-nodes on variables in B.

If a meaningless backtracking is avoided, a refutation can be found efficiently.

[Definition] Let θ and θ' be substitutions in refutations F and F', respectively. Let $\theta1$ and $\theta'1$ be substitutions which include all ground bindings for target variables, where there exist $\theta2$ and $\theta'2$ such that $\theta=\theta1\theta2$ and $\theta'=\theta'1\theta'2$. If $\theta1=\theta'1$, F and F' are redundant.

If redundant refutations can be avoided, all answer substitutions for SPi are found by the smaller number of resolutions.

In this paper, we try to generate access function procedures with no meaningless backtracking and less redundant refutations.

5.2 Navigational Tree

We consider how to find a similarity class SPi which includes at least one refutation.

[Definition] For a goal G= ?-A1,...,Am, a goal graph TG is defined as one obtained by constructing
1) a node Ai for every atom Ai (i=1,...,m) in G, and
2) an edge X between Ai and Aj which have a common variable X and both are not F-type.

For example, let us consider a goal clause G= ?-Pel(X,S),EP(X,Y),Emp(Y,?N),PE(X,Z),Proj(Z,P). A goal graph for G is shown in Fig.6.

```
 --------     Z   ------   X   -------   X   ------   Y   -------
| Proj |-------| PE |-------| Pel |-------| EP |--------| Emp |
 --------       ------       -------       ------       -------
```

Fig.6 Goal Graph

[Definition] A navigational tree T for a goal graph TG is an ordered tree obtained by the following procedure:
1) Select a node X where a cost function cost(X) is minimum in TG. Let X be a root. Mark(X) (Mark(X) is a procedure which marks X, all variables in X, and edges whose both ends are already marked).
2) Select an unmarked node Y connected to X by an unmarked edge with minimum cost(Y). Mark(Y).
     If Y is a fact, include Y as X's right-most child in T. Go to 2).
     If Y is a rule, select an input clause C and replace Y with the body of C. Go to 2).
3) [No unmarked edge incident on X] If X is a root,
     if all nodes in TG are already marked, then terminate,
     else select Y with minimum cost(Y), include Y as the right-most node of the root X in T,
   Mark(Y), let X be Y and go to 2).
  If X is not a root, then let X be a parent of X in T, go to 2).

A term whose all variables are marked or ground is said to be marked. For a node X, cost(X) gives a cost for finding an input clause whose head is unifiable with the atom X and is defined in 6.1. The cost measure is a number of applications of access functions. It is clear that the following proposition holds according to the definition.

[Property] For every edge between nodes X and Y in TG, X and Y are in a root-to-leaf path in the navigational tree for TG.

Each edge indicates that the parent is a BK-node of the child. Fig.7 shows an example of a navigational tree for Fig.6 and Fig.8 shows its SLD deduction. A node which include any target variable is a target node. For example, Emp(Y,?N) is a target node. The navigational tree denotes a similarity class.

A depth-first ordering < of nodes in T is defined as follows and gives a selection sequence of atoms in a refutation.

1) X<Y iff Y is greater than X in a depth-first order of T.
2) X<<Y iff X<Y and no node Z such that X<Z<Y.
3) X=>Y iff Y is included in a subtree whose root is X, i.e. X is an ancestor of Y.
4) X>>Y iff X=>Y and no Z such that X=>Z=>Y, i.e. X is a parent of Y and Y a child of X.

In Fig.7, Pel=>Proj, PE>>Proj, EP<Proj, and Pel<<EP. We introduce the notations for a node X
in T.

    tail(X) = a node Y such that X=>Y and no node Z such that X=>Z and Y<Z.
    Ltarg(X)= a target node Y such that Y<X and no target node Z such that Y<Z<X.
    Rtarg(X)= a target node Y such that Y>X and no target node Z such that Y>Z>X.

Here, a join node Z of nodes X and Y in T is one such that Z=>X, Z=>Y, and no node U such that
Z=>U=>X and Z=>U=>Y.

    LJoin(X)= a join node of X and Ltarg(X).
    RJoin(X)= a join node of X and Rtarg(X).
    Rnext(X)= a node Y such that RJoin(X)>>Y=>X.

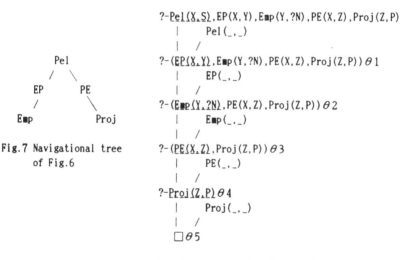

Fig.7 Navigational tree
of Fig.6

Fig.8 SLD Deduction for Fig.7.

6. Access Procedures

We discus how to synthesize access function procedures from the navigational tree T for a
similarity class SPi, which can get all answer substitutions efficiently in SPi.

6.1 Simple Access Procedures

First, we try to construct one class of access procedures, called simple access procedures (SAPs), which can find one refutation for SPi without meaningless backtracking. A SAP is
a set of cells linked by directed arcs. Each cell is an object which is composed of an ordered
set D(X) and a set of access functions on D(X). D(X) is really OE-set or OF-set in the navigational database V.

Cells communicate with others by sending messages via arcs. An arc exists from an output port 0 of a cell X (denoted by X.0) to an input port I of the other Y (denoted by Y.I). This arc is written as X.0-->Y.I. Each cell X has two input ports, X.FIRST and X.NEXT, and two output ports, X.SUCC(ess) and X.FAIL(ure). The arc reliably delivers messages from X.0 to Y.I. A SAP is constructed by the following procedure. Fig.9 shows a SAP of Fig.7.

1) For every node X in a navigational tree T, generate a cell X.
2) Generate two special cells, a start cell ST and output cell OP. They have an input port IN and an output port OUT.
3) For every nodes X and Y in T, generate the following arcs.

    X.SUCC-->Y.FIRST if X<<Y   X.FAIL-->Y.NEXT if Y>>X
    ST.OUT-->X.FIRST, X.FAIL-->ST.IN if X is a root of T
    X.SUCC-->OP.IN, OP.OUT-->X.NEXT if X is a last node in T.

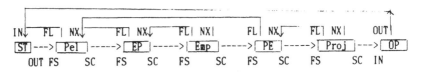

SC:SUCC FL:FAIL FS:FIRST NX:NEXT

Fig.9 Simple Access Procedure.

The action of the cell is activated on receipt of a message from the input port, and inactivated by sending a message from the output port. Messages carry substitutions.

[Behavior of SAP cells]
1) First, ST sends a message $<\varepsilon>$ from ST.OUT. On receipt of a message at ST.IN, all cells are made terminated.
2) When a cell X (except ST and OP) receives $<\theta>$ at X.FIRST (or X.NEXT). $D(X\theta)$ is sequentially accessed by using the access functions from the top (or from the lastly-accesed one). An element d in $D(X\theta)$ such that a unit clause for d and $X\theta$ are unifiable with an mgu σ is tried to be found. If found, $<\theta\sigma>$ is sent from X.SUCC. Otherwise, $<\theta>$ is sent from X.FAIL.
3) On receipt of $<\theta>$ at OP.IN, OP outputs an answer substitution from θ and sends $<\theta>$ from OP.OUT.

We show you what is the ordered set $D(X)$ and how to access $D(X)$ with cost(X).
1) [X is an E-type atom $E(K,T1,...,Tn)$ for an E-type $E=(@E,A1,...,An)$]
    If K is marked, $D(X)$ contains only e in E where $@E(e)=K$. $D(X)$ is directly accessed by dtopE/@E. Hence, cost(X)=1.
    If Ti is marked and Ai is a direct access one, $D(X)=E\%Ai[Ti]$. Since $D(X)$ is sequentially accessed by dtopE%Ai and dnextE%Ai, cost(X) is $|D(X)|$ whose estimated value is $|E|*$(selectivity[HEVN] of Ai in E), where for a set S let $|S|$ denote its cardinality.
    Otherwise $D(X)=E/@E$. All tuples in E are sequentially accessed by topE/@E and nexE/@E. So, $D(X)=|E|$.
2) [X is an F-type atom $F(K1,K2)$ where $F=(E1,E2)$]
    If K1 is marked, $D(X)=<e1,e2>$ such that $@E1(e1)=$ an instance of K1. Since $D(X)$ is accessed by one application of F, cost(X)=1.
    If K2 is marked, $D(X)=F\%T[$an instance of k2$]$ where T is some attribute of E1. Since $D(X)$ is accessed sequentially by ftopF%T and fnextF%T, cost(X) is an expected number of E-tuples in the domain which are associated with one in the range.

3) [X is a rule] cost(X) is a constant M. By increasing M, the selection of rules can be delayed.

It is clear that we can obtain one refutation for the navigational tree by the SAP.

6.2 General Access Procedures

Next, let us consider a problem how to obtain all answer substitutions for the navigational tree T. Two output ports RSUC and LFAL for every cell X and the following directed arcs are added to the SAP.

1) X.SUCC-->Rnext(X).FIRST   if Rnext(X) exists,
   X.RSUC-->OP.IN   otherwise.
2) X.LFAL-->Ltarg(X).NEXT   if Ltarg(X) exists,
   X.LFAL-->SP.IN   else if X is a root of T,
   X.LFAL-->Y.NEXT   if Y⇒X.
3) OP.OUT-->Ltarg(X).NEXT   if X is a last node in T.

An access procedure augmented with these arcs and ports is said to be general. A general access procedure (GAP) for Fig.9 is shown in Fig.10.

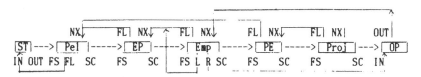

SC:SUCC FL:FAIL FS:FIRST NX:NEXT L:LTARG R:RTARG

Fig.10 General access procedure.

[Behavior of GAP cells] Messages are in a form $(<X,Y>,\theta)$ where X and Y are cells and θ an substitution.
1) First, ST sends $(<R,tail(R)>,\varepsilon)$ from ST.OUT where R is a root of T. On receipt of a message, all cells in the GAP are made terminated.
2) [On receipt of $(<Y,Z>,\theta)$ at X.FIRST or X.NEXT] If Y=Z=NULL, let Y be X and Z be tail(X). D(X) is accessed in the same as the SAP.
    If d in $D(X\theta)$ and $X\theta$ are unifiable with an mgu σ, then if X=Z, $(<NULL,NULL>,\theta\sigma)$ is sent from X.RSUC, else $(<Y,Z>),\theta\sigma)$ from X.SUCC.
    Otherwise if X≠Y, $(<Y,Z>,\theta)$ is sent from X.FAIL, else(X=Y) if $LJoin(X)\geqslant X$, $(<NULL,NULL>, \theta)$ is sent from X.LFAL, else from X.FAIL.
3) [On receipt of $(<Y,Z>,\theta)$ at OP.IN] OP outputs an answer substitution from θ and sends $(<NULL,NULL>,\theta)$ from OP.OUT.

In Fig.10, on receipt of a token θ, OP outputs an answer substitution, i.e. a refutation is found, and then sends θ to the target cell Emp. Then, Emp gets next substitution θ' and sends it to OP from Emp.RSUC. By this, redundant refutations are decreased.

7. Concluding Remarks

In this paper, we discussed problems that conventional network databases are viewed as a set of ground unit clauses in Prolog and how to augment inference mechanism with the conventional network database systems. Our refutation procedure can reduce the search space by avoiding meaningless backtracking and decreasing redundant refutations. Also, our procedure is applicable to conventional file systems with access paths, i.e. indexing, hashing, pointers, clustering. This means that logic systems can be implemented directly on the file systems without using the relational database systems. Also, our system can be used as a common Prolog interface to heterogeneous database systems in distributed database systems [TAKI80,83].

At present, LIP (logic language interface processor on the database system) based on the concept presented in this paper has been implemented on the AIM/DB which is a network database management system of Facom M-380Q. Also, LIP is implemented in a workstation.

References

[APT] Apt,R. and van Emden,M.H., "Contributions to the Theory of Logic Programming," JACM, Vol.29, No.3, 1982, pp.841-862.
[CAMP] Campbell,J.A., "Implementations of Prolog," Ellis Horowood Limited, 1984, pp.175-278.
[CHAN] Chang,C.L., "On Evaluation of Queries Containing Derived Relations in a Relational Data Base," Logic&Database, Plenum Press, 1981.
[CODA73] CODASYL DDL Committee, "CODASYL Data Description Language," Journal of Development, 1973.
[CODA78] CODASYL DDL Committee, "CODASYL Data Description Language," Journal of Development, 1978.
[CODD] Codd,E.F., "A Relational Model of Data for Large Shared Data Bank," CACM, Vol.13, No.6, 1970, pp.337-387.
[DATE] Date,C.J., "An Introduction to Database Systems," Addison-Wesley, 1981.
[DAYA] Dayal,U. et al., "Query Optimization for CODASYL Database Systems," Proc. of the ACM SIGMOD, 1982, pp.138-150.
[ENDE] Enderton,H., "Mathematical Introduction to Logic," Academic Press, 1972.
[GALL] Gallaire,H. et al., "Logic and Databases: A Deductive Approach," ACM Computing Survey, Vol.16, No.2, 1984.
[HENS] Henschen,L.J. and Naqvi,S.A., "On Compiling Queries in Recursive First-Order Databases," JACM, Vol.31, 1984, pp.47-85.
[HEVN] Hevner,A., et al., "Query Processing on a Distributed Databases," Proc. of the 3rd Berkely Workshop, 1978, pp.98-107.
[JACC] Jaccob,B.E., "On Database Logic," JACM, Vol.29, No.2, 1982, pp.310-332.
[KOBA] Kobayashi,I., "Classification and Transformations of Binary Relationship Schemata," Suuno Institute of Business Administration, 1985.
[KOWA] Kowalski,R., "Logic for Problem Solving," North-Holland, 1979.
[LI] Li,D., "A Prolog Database," Research Student Press, 1984.
[LLOY] Lloyd,D., "Foundation of Logic Programming," Springer-Verlag, 1985.
[OHSU] Ohsuga,S., "Developing a Deductive Relational Database for Uniform Handling of Complex Queries," JIP(of IPSJ), 1983, pp.123-137.
[OLLE] Olle,T., "The CODASYL Approach to Data Base Management," John Wiley and Sons, 1978.
[TAKI80] Takizawa,M., et al., "Query Translation in Distributed Databases," Proc. of the IFIP'80, 1980.
[TAKI83] Takizawa,M., "Distributed Database System - JDDBS," JARECT, Vol.7 (Computer Science and Technologies, Kitagawa,T. ed.), Ohmsha and North-Holland, 1983, pp.264-283.
[ULLM] Ullman,J.D., "Implementation of Logical Query Language for Databases," ACM TODS, Vol.10, No.3, 1985, pp.289-321.

Programming in Modal Logic :
An Extension of PROLOG based on Modal Logic

Yasubumi SAKAKIBARA

IIAS-SIS, Fujitsu Ltd.
140 Miyamoto, Numazu
Shizuoka, JAPAN 410-03

Abstract

In this paper, we will attempt to give a procedural interpretation to modal logic. Modal logic is used as a programming language and then its procedural interpretation defines a computational procedure for the language. This is done within the framework of logic programming and is one of extensions of PROLOG based on modal logic. Further, we will demonstrate some advantages of the extension such as modurality, hierarchy or structure of logic programs.

1. Introduction

Recently, various forms of logic programming are presented and developed. Logic programming is based on first-order predicate logic and uses it as a programming language. However first-order predicate logic can deal with as its domain only one world in which the truth of an expression does never change and does not depend on place and time. Thus it lacks the expressive power of structure of space, state or time. In order to overcome this shortcoming, various improvements of logic programming are studied [1,2,3,6,8]. In this direction, based on modal logic we will propose an extension of logic programming, and we call it *modal logic programming*. That is to say, we will give a procedural interpretation to modal logic. To do this, we first have to consider semantics of modal logic. Modal logic is one of nonstandard logic in the sense that it is different from first-order logic, and has two kinds of semantics, one of which is axiomatic semantics and the other is possible-world semantics based on the possible-world model developed by Kripke. In our study, we will use the possible-world semantics. Consequently, we will enjoy multi-worlds as modules or as procedures on logic programming. Furthermore, compared with other studies of extensions, we can have the exact logical argument of modal logic programming and never introduce any impure primitive, and this is not the integrated way of two different programming paradigms such as logic programming and object-oriented programming. Thus modal logic programming is a simple and natural extension of logic programming, and further we will demonstrate that this has a good advantage to analyse structure or modularity of logic programs in the logical framework and to practice program debugging based on logical semantics.

2. Modal logic ([4])

Modal logic is a logic which deals with modality such as necessity or possibility, and its model-theoretic semantics is possible-world semantics based on possible-world model. A possible-world model is a triple (V,R,W) where V is a value assignment, R is an accessibility relation from one world to another and W is a set of worlds. Given two worlds w_i and w_j, w_iRw_j means that w_j is accessible from w_i. The truth of a modal expression is decided based on this relation R. Actually, for a proposition p and a world $w \in W$, p is necessarily true in w (i.e. $V(\Box p,w)=1$) iff for all $w_i \in W$ such that wRw_i, p is true in w_i (i.e. $V(p,w_i)=1$), and p is possibly true in w (i.e. $V(\Diamond p,w)=1$) iff there exists at least one world w_i such that wRw_i and p is true in w_i. Then we can define the validity of a modal expression A : A is valid iff for all possible-world models (V,R,W), $V(A,w)=1$ for all $w \in W$. The correspondence to the proof theoretic semantics is that A is valid iff $S \vdash A$ (A is derived from S) where S is the axiom set for modal logic and the symbol $\vdash$ means a derivation in that axiom system. The differences among some of the most important axiom systems for modal logic correspond exactly to certain restrictions on the accessibility relation of the possible-world models of those systems. This result was proved by Kripke. For example, by restrictions on the accessibility relation to reflexive, symmetric or transitive or these combinations we get several modal axiom systems of type T, S4 or S5.

Now we discuss what the modal logic programming is. There are at least two ways of it. One way is to regard a written program P as axioms and derive theorems T as answers from those axioms. This is analogous to logic programming like PROLOG. On the other hand, it is possible to describe one possible-world model as a program and use modal expressions interpreted in that possible-world model. In this paper, we take the latter and in the following sections we describe it in detail.

3. Programming in modal logic

3.1. Syntax of modal logic program

Definition atom

An *atom* is $p(t_1,...,t_n)$ where p is an n-ary predicate symbol and $t_1,...,t_n$ are terms.

Definition modal atom

A *modal atom* is either $\Box p(t_1,...,t_n)$ or $\Diamond p(t_1,...,t_n)$ where p is an n-ary predicate symbol and $t_1,...,t_n$ are terms.

Definition program clause

A *program clause* is of the form : $A \leftarrow A_1,...,A_n$ where A is an atom and each A_i is an atom or a modal atom ($1 \leq i \leq n$).

Modal atoms appear only in the body of a program clause.

Definition program

A *program* is a finite set of program clauses.

Definition world

A *world* definition defines its world name and program in it. A world is of the form :

>   world <world name> of

>>   <program>

>   fo.

A program defined in a world is considered as an axiom set which represents various attributes and relations hold in that world. A world is also considered as a module. Thus a world definition provides a framework to express a structure of a program.

Definition relation

A *relation* definition defines an accessibility relation between two worlds. We use a special predicate symbol "re", a relation atom and a relation clause which constitute from them to write an accessibility relation. A *relation atom* is $re(w_1,w_2)$ where each of w_1 and w_2 is a world name or a variable. The meaning of a relation atom defined for two worlds w_i and w_j is $re(w_i,w_j)$ which means that w_j is accessible from w_i. A relation clause is $R \leftarrow R_1,...,R_n$ where $R,R_1,...,R_n$ are relation atoms. A relation is a finite set of relation clauses of the form :

>   relation of

>>   {a finite set of relation clauses}   fo.

We can flexibly define various accessibility relations or structures between worlds by using these relation clauses. This is one of advantages of our way.

Example

    relation of

        re(w1,w2);

        re(w2,w3);

        re(X,X);   (reflexive)

        re(X,Y)←re(Y,X);   (symmetric)

        re(X,Y)←re(X,Z), re(Z,Y);   (transitive)

    fo.

In this relation definition, re(w1,w2), re(w2,w3), re(w1,w1), re(w2,w2), re(w3,w3), re(w2,w1), re(w3,w2), re(w1,w3) and re(w3,w1) are true.

Definition modal logic program

A *modal logic program* consists of several world definitions and one relation definition between them, and is of the form :

      relation of

         {a finite set of relation clauses}

      fo.

      world <world name> of

         <program>

      fo.

         . . .

      world <world name> of

         <program>

      fo.

3.2. Semantics of modal logic program

In this section, we will give a procedural interpretation based on possible-world semantics for modal logic program. As we mentioned before, we use modal expressions interpreted in the possible-world model expressed by a modal logic program for an extension. First we will give a model-theoretic semantics.

3.2.1. Model-theoretic semantics

Definition Let P be a modal logic program. Let (V,R,W_p) be a possible-world model where W_p is a set of all world names in P.

(1) For w and $w' \in W_p$, a relation atom re(w,w') is *true* in R iff $(w,w') \in R$.

(2) A ground relation clause $R_0 \leftarrow R_1,...,R_n$ is *true* in R iff R_0 is true in R or at least one of $R_1,...,R_n$ is not true in R.

(3) A relation clause is *true* in R iff each of its ground instance is true in R. (A ground instance of a relation clause is obtained by replacing every occurrence of a variable in the relation clause by a world name in W_p.)

(4) A set of relation clauses is *true* in R iff each clause in it is true in R.

We say R is an *accessibility relation model for* the relation in P if the set of relation clauses defined in it is true in R and we write R(P). Clearly the intersection of all accessibility relation models for the relation in P exists and we write $\cap R(P)$. We mean the model-theoretic semantics of the relation in P by $\cap R(P)$.

Definition Let P be a modal logic program. Let $(V,\cap R(P),W_p)$ be a possible-world model where W_p is a set of all world names in P.

(1) A ground atom A is true in a world $w \in W_p$ in V iff V(A,w) = 1.

(2) A ground modal atom $\Diamond A$ is true in w in V iff there exists at least one world w' such that $(w,w') \in \cap R(P)$ and A is true in w' in V.

(3) A ground modal atom $\Box A$ is true in w in V iff for all $w' \in W_p$ such that $(w,w') \in \cap R(P)$, A is true in w' in V.

(4) A ground program clause $A_0 \leftarrow A_1,...,A_n$ is true in w in V iff A_0 is true in w in V or at least one of $A_1,...,A_n$ is not true in w in V.

(5) A program clause is true in w in V iff each of its ground instance is true in w in V.

(6) A set of program clauses is true in w in V iff each program clause in it is true in w in V.

There exists the problem of quantifications and identifiers among different possible worlds. We adopt Herbrand interpretations in which constants and functions are literally interpreted and hence each term has the same denotation in every possible world. The domain in every possible world is the Herbrand universe which is the set of all ground terms which can be formed out of the constants and functions appeared in a modal logic program P. Then a ground instance of an atom, a modal atom or a program clause is obtained by replacing every occurrence of a variable in it by a term in the Herbrand universe of P.

We say $(V, \cap R(P), W_p)$ is a *possible-world model for* P if the set of program clauses defined in each world $w \in W_p$ is true in w in V. For an atom or a modal atom A, we say A is a *logical consequence in* w of P if, for all possible-world models $(V, \cap R(P), W_p)$ for P, A is true in w in V and we write $P, w \vDash A$. Thus we mean the model-theoretic semantics of a modal logic program P by $P, w \vDash A$, and therefore $(V_\vDash, \cap R(P), W_p)$ is the possible-world model expressed by a modal logic program P where $V_\vDash$ is a value assignment such that $V_\vDash(A, W) = 1$ iff $P, W \vDash A$.

3.2.2. Procedural semantics

Now we define a proof procedure for modal logic program and simultaneously give a procedural interpretation by it.

Definition goal

A *goal* is a list of pairs of the form :

$$((\leftarrow A_1, W_1), ..., (\leftarrow A_n, W_n))$$

where each A_i is an atom or a modal atom and W_i is a world name $(1 \leq i \leq n)$.

Before giving the definition of a proof procedure, we need to enumerate all of ordered pairs (w, w') of world names in P such that (w, w') in $\cap R(P)$ (i.e. w' is accessible from w). Since the set of all world names W_p is finite, there is an algorithm to enumerate them. Therefore we suppose that the list of them is calculated by some algorithm.

Definition (proof procedure)

Let P be a modal logic program, G be a goal of the form : $((\leftarrow A_1, W_1), ..., (\leftarrow A_m, W_m))$ $(m > 0)$ and $(\leftarrow A_k, W_k)$ be a selected pair. Let L_p be the list of all of ordered pairs (w, w') in $\cap R(P)$. Then proof procedure *derives* the new goal as follows :

(a) Suppose A_k is an atom, $B_0 \leftarrow B_1, ..., B_n$ $(n \geq 0)$ is a program clause defined in the world W_k and θ is a most general unifier of A_k and B_0. Then the derived goal G' is

$$((\leftarrow A_1, W_1), ..., (\leftarrow A_{k-1}, W_{k-1}), (\leftarrow B_1, W_k), ..., (\leftarrow B_n, W_k), (\leftarrow A_{k+1}, W_{k+1}), ..., (\leftarrow A_m, W_m))\theta$$

(b) Suppose A_k is a modal atom of the form $\diamond A$ and (W_k, Wa) in L_p (i.e. Wa is an accessible world from W_k). Then the derived goal G' is

$$((\leftarrow A_1, W_1), ..., (\leftarrow A_{k-1}, W_{k-1}), (\leftarrow A, Wa), (\leftarrow A_{k+1}, W_{k+1}), ..., (\leftarrow A_m, W_m))$$

(c) Suppose A_k is a modal atom of the form $\Box A$ and $(W_k, Wa_1), ..., (W_k, Wa_h)$ are all of ordered pairs in L_p such that the first element of each ordered pair is W_k. Then the derived goal G' is

$$((\leftarrow A_1, W_1), ..., (\leftarrow A_{k-1}, W_{k-1}), (\leftarrow A, Wa_1), ..., (\leftarrow A, Wa_h), (\leftarrow A_{k+1}, W_{k+1}), ..., (\leftarrow A_m, W_m))$$

In (b) and (c), θ is the identity substitution.

Definition derivation

Let P be a modal logic program and G be a goal. A *derivation* of G is a sequence $G_0 = G$, G_1, G_2, ... of goals such that each G_{i+1} is derived from G_i by proof procedure. A derivation is *successful* if it is finite and its last goal is empty.

For an atom or a modal atom A, we say A is *proved to be true* in a world W if a derivation of (←A,W) is successful. By this, we mean the procedural semantics of P.

Example

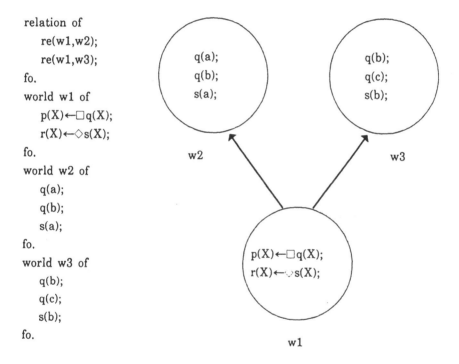

```
relation of
    re(w1,w2);
    re(w1,w3);
fo.
world w1 of
    p(X)←□q(X);
    r(X)←◇s(X);
fo.
world w2 of
    q(a);
    q(b);
    s(a);
fo.
world w3 of
    q(b);
    q(c);
    s(b);
fo.
```

In the world w1, □q(b), ◇q(a), ◇q(c), ◇s(a) and ◇s(b) are proved to be true and so are p(b), r(a) and r(b). Thus modal logic programming introduces hierarchic structures into logic programming.

Next our work is to show the soundness and completeness of the above proof procedure. More precisely, it is to show the following : Let P be a modal logic program, A be an atom or a modal atom and W be a world name.

(Soundness) If there exists a successful derivation of ($\leftarrow$A,W), then A is a logical consequence in W of P, i.e. P,W$\models$A.

(Completeness) If P,W$\models$A, then there is a successful derivation of ($\leftarrow$A,W).

It is easy to show the soundness. It may take more work to show the completeness.

3.2.3. Semantics of negation

In standard logic program, the negation as failure rule is used to infer negative information. This rule states that if all derivations of $\leftarrow$A are finitely failed, then infer not(A). We define the negation as failure rule in the same way as standard logic program.

Definition finitely failed

Let P be a modal logic program and G be a goal. A derivation of G is *finitely failed* if the derivation is finite and ends with a goal where the atom A of the selected pair ($\leftarrow$A,W) does not unify with the head of any program clause defined in the world W.

Then we can state that the negation as failure rule in a modal logic program P is the rule that, for an atom or a modal atom A and a world name W, if all derivations of ($\leftarrow$A,W) is finitely failed, then we infer that not(A) is true in W. In this procedural interpretation of "not" and the procedural interpretation of modal operators $\Box$ and $\Diamond$ defined in the previous section, $\Box$A $\equiv$ not($\Diamond$not(A)) can be established.

Now we summarize the special feature of modal logic programming. A modal logic program expresses a possible-world model and modal expressions in it is procedurally interpreted in the possible-world model. The proof procedure may correspond to the "semantic tableau method". And various relationships among worlds can be defined by relation definitions. Furthermore modal logic programming can keep its logical consistency. This is one of the advantages compared with other ways such as an integrated way of logic programming and object-oriented programming or a way of introducing impure primitives like module into logic programming. This is very useful for the program debugging.

4. World as Module or Procedure ?

From the programming language point of view, we can consider worlds as modules or procedures. Then a world limits the scope of validity of each predicate name, and a relation definition limits the scope of availability of the program in each world(i.e. it defines the accessibility relation of that program). These introduce program structures and also hierarchization into logic programming. Thus we can use multi-worlds mechanism in modal logic programming. These also realize the polysemy of a predicate name.

In the next section, we will describe a simple interpreter for modal logic program.

5. A Simple Interpreter for modal logic program

```
solve(true, W) :- !, true.
solve((A, B), W) :- !, solve(A, W), solve(B, W).
solve( A, W) :- !, rel(W, W1), solve(A, W1).
solve(□A, W) :- !, allrel(W, W1), allsolve(A, W1).
solve(A, W) :- !, clause(<A←B, W>), solve(B, W).
allsolve(A, []).
allsolve(A, [W | W1]) :- solve(A, W), allsolve(A, W1).
rel(W, W1) :- solve(re(W, W1), relation).
allrel(W, W1) :- W1 is a list of all worlds w such that re(W, w).
```

where it assumes that the modal logic program P is represented as clauses "clause(<A←B, W>)" for any program clause A←B in the world W and the relation definition is represented as clauses "clause(<A←B, relation>)" for any relation clause A←B.

For example, the above interpreter exactly corresponds to the axioms in Moore's first-order theory of knowledge [5] if we consider a □ operator as a KNOW operator and a compatible relation K as an accessible relation re.

Here we also describe a simple backtrace program debugger which is a modification of the Shapiro's contradiction backtracing algorithm [7].

```
backtrace((A,B),W,CE) :- !, backtrace(A,W,CE), backtrace(B,W,CE).
backtrace( A,W,CE) :- !, rel(W,W1), backtrace(A,W1,CE).
backtrace(□A,W,CE) :- !, allrel(W,W1), allbacktrace(A,W1,CE).
backtrace(A,W,CE) :-
    clause(<A←B,W>), backtrace(B,W,CE), resolve((A←B),W,CE).
allbacktrace(A,[],CE).
allbacktrace(A,[W | W1],CE) :- backtrace(A,W,CE), allbacktrace(A,W1,CE).
resolve((A←B),W,CE) :- var(CE), !,
    ask(A,W,V), (V=false, CE=(W,A←B); V=true).
```

```
resolve((A←B),W,CE).

ask(A,W,V) :- recordedfact(A,W,V), !.

ask(A,W,V) :- repeat, write(A), write(in), write(W), put(63), nl,
              read(V), (V=true; V=false), assert(recordedfact(A,W,V)).
```

6. Comparison with other studies

The MOLOG [3] is an extension of PROLOG using modal logic and so very similar to our direction. However its system axiomatically interprets modal operators and so different from our way based on possible-world semantics. They give a proof theory for the universal modal operator know(a) in the system S5. Prolog/KR [6] and metaProlog [1] are very related to and have inspired our study. Prolog/KR has the concept of "worlds" and is also based on modal logic semantics. The metaProlog is also an extension to consider metatheory and has "theories" like our worlds.

7. Concluding Remarks

One of further issues which we are now working on is to extend modal logic programming so as to deal with several modalities simultaneously. Specifically, by adding to modal operators an extra argument for representing a name of a modal logic system (i.e. name of a relation), we will extend modal logic programming so that we may describe several relations each of which corresponds to each modal logic system. Following illustrates some images of the extension :

```
        relation m1 of

            . . .

        fo.
        relation m2 of

            . . .

        fo.

            . . .

        world w1 of
            p←m1 pos q(X);
            p←m2 nec s(X), m4 pos t(b);

                . . .

        fo.
```

where nec and pos are infix operators which respectively represent necessity and possibility and have two arguments. For example, "m1 nec" means the necessity operator in m1 modal system.

Acknowledgements

The author would like to thank Dr. T.Kitagawa, the president of IIAS-SIS, Dr. H.Enomoto, the director of IIAS-SIS, for giving us the opportunity to pursue this work and helping us with it. He is deeply grateful to Dr. T.Yokomori, IIAS-SIS, for reading the draft of this paper and giving us many valuable comments. He is also indebted to Mr. Y.Takada, IIAS-SIS, for many fruitful discussions and comments.

This work is part of the major R&D of the FGCP, conducted under program set up by MITI.

References

[1] Bowen, K.A. : Meta-Level Programming and Knowledge Representation, *New Generation Computing*, 3(1985), 359-383.

[2] Chikayama, T. : ESP Reference Manual, *ICOT Technical Report TR-044*, 1984.

[3] Fariñas del Cerro, L : MOLOG : A System That Extends PROLOG with Modal Logic, *New Generation Computing*, 4(1986), 35-50.

[4] Hughes, G. E., & Cresswell, M. J. : An Introduction to Modal Logic, London : Methuen.

[5] Moore, R. C. : A Formal Theory of Knowledge and Action, in *Formal Theories of the Commonsense World* (J.R.Hobbs, & R.C.Moore, Eds.), Ablex, New Jersey, 319-358.

[6] Nakashima, H. : Prolog/KR - language features, *Proc. of the 1st Intern. Logic Programming Conference*, Marseille, 1982, 65-70.

[7] Shapiro, E. Y. : Inductive Inference of Theories from Facts, *Research Report 192*, Dept. of Computer Science, Yale University, 1981.

[8] Warren, D. S. : Database Updates in Pure PROLOG, *Proc. of the Intern. Conf. on FGCS' 84*, Tokyo, 1984, 244-253.

On Parallel Programming Methodology in GHC

— Experience in Programming A Proof Procedure of Temporal Logic —

Kazuko TAKAHASHI and Tadashi KANAMORI

Central Research Laboratory, Mitsubishi Electric Corporation

ABSTRACT

Parallel programming methodology in GHC is discussed based on our experience in programming a proof procedure of temporal logic. It is said that GHC can express basic constructs of parallel processing such as communication and synchronization very simply, but we have not yet had enough experiences with parallel programming in GHC. By programming a proof procedure of temporal logic in Prolog and GHC, we compare the thinking style in sequential programming and that in parallel programming. Parallel programming methodology is discussed based on the experience.

1. INTRODUCTION

"Guarded Horn Clauses (GHC)" is a language designed for execution on highly parallel architecture [Ueda 85] and is regarded as the core of Kernel Language One (KL1) of the Fifth Generation Computer System (FGCS) project in Japan. GHC is a descendant of other Prolog-like parallel programming languages such as Concurrent Prolog [Shapiro 84] and PARLOG [Clark and Gregory 84]. It is said that GHC not only provides us with basic functions for parallel processing, such as communication and synchronization, but also imposes less burden of implementation than Concurrent Prolog such as multiple environments. But we have not yet had enough experience with parallel programming in GHC. Particularly, we do not yet know whether GHC in practice gives us enough expressive power or what transition of programming style is necessary for GHC.

In this paper, we show our experience in programming a proof procedure of temporal logic in GHC. The proof procedure, called ω-graphs refutation, was known to us before programming it in GHC [Fusaoka and Takahashi 85]. We had its sequential implementation in Prolog. Fortunately or unfortunately, the sequential version contains subprocedures which embody three typical styles of programs. The first one is the general recursive style, the second one is the repetitive (tail-recursive) style and the third one is the backtracking style. We show what difficulties we have encountered in programming these procedures in GHC and discuss the parallel programming methodology based on the experience.

2. PRELIMINARIES

A GHC program is a finite set of Horn clauses of the following form ($m \geq 0, n \geq 0$):

$$H \text{:- } G_1, ..., G_m \mid B_1, ..., B_n.$$

where G_i's and B_i's are atomic formulas as usually defined. The part of the clause before '|' is called a *passive part* or a *guard*, and the part after '|' is called an *active part*.

Informally, execution of a clause is done in the following manner: When a goal is called, the clauses whose heads are unifiable are invoked. Execution of the goals in the passive part of these candidate clauses are tried in parallel, and if goals in the passive part of some clause succeed, then the clause is *committed* and the active part of the clause is executed. Any piece of unification invoked in the passive part of a clause cannot instantiate a variable appearing in the caller.

Temporal Logic [Manna and Pnueli 81] is an extension of first order logic to include a notion of time and deal with logical description and reasoning on time. It is a branch of *modal logic* [Hughes and Cresswell 68], in which the relation between worlds is considered a temporal one. The temporal logic we consider in this paper is a propositional one called Propositional Temporal Logic (PTL). Three temporal operators used in PTL have the following intuitive meanings:

□ F (always F) : F is true in all future instants

◇ F (eventually F) : F is true in some future instant

○ F (next F) : F is true in the next instant

For example, a formula □◇P indicates that P will be true infinitely often.

Let F be a formula of PTL. A *complete assignment* for F is a function which assigns truth value (t or f) to every propositional variable in F. A *model M* for F is an infinite sequence $K_0, K_1, K_2, ...$ of complete assignments for F. F is said to be *true(false)* in M if F is assigned t(f) by K_0. F is *satisfiable* if there exists a model in which F is *true*. F is *valid* if it is true in every model.

A model of PTL can be represented by a path of a graph with its edges labeled with complete assignments. For example, consider the following graph. Intuitively, the edges in the graph correspond to complete assignments. The edge from the node N_0 to the node N_1 corresponds to a complete assignment that assigns t to P, the edge from N_1 to N_2 corresponds to one that assigns f to P and the edge from N_2 to N_1 corresponds to one that assigns t to P. Then, the infinite path of $N_0 \rightarrow N_1 \rightarrow N_2 \rightarrow N_1 \rightarrow N_2 \rightarrow N_1 \rightarrow N_2 \rightarrow ....$ corresponds to a model for □◇P where the assignment for P is the sequence in which t and f appear alternately (t,f,t,f,t,f,...).

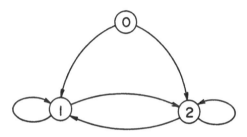

Figure 1   Graph Representation for □◇P

3. ω-GRAPHS REFUTATION PROCEDURE

An ω-*graph* is a graph in which each node is labeled with an expression called a *node formula*. When a formula of PTL is given, the ω-graphs refutation procedure shows as follows whether the formula is valid or not:

(1) Negate the given formula.

(2) Compute the initial node formula of the negation of the given formula

(3) Construct an ω-graph by starting from the initial ω-graph consisting of only one node corresponding to the initial node formula and successively expanding nodes in the ω-graph.

(4) Check ω-loop freeness of the constructed ω-graph. If it is ω-loop free, the given formula is valid.

First, we explain each procedure, *compute_initial_node_formula*, *expand_node_formulas*, *construct_omega_graphs*, and *check_omega_loop_freeness* and discuss parallel programming for each procedure. Then, we show the top level implementation.

3.1. Computation of Initial Node Formula

The negation of a given formula is once converted to its negation normal form in order to compute the initial node formula before constructing the ω-graph.

Let G be a formula obtained from a formula F by applying the rules below as far as possible. Then G is called the *negation normal form* of the formula F.

[Rule NNF1] remove implication and equivalence

$$A \supset B \implies \neg A \vee B$$
$$A \equiv B \implies (A \wedge B) \vee (\neg A \wedge \neg B)$$

[Rule NNF2] move negation inwards

$$\neg(A \wedge B) \implies \neg A \vee \neg B$$
$$\neg(A \vee B) \implies \neg A \wedge \neg B$$
$$\neg \Box A \implies \Diamond \neg A$$
$$\neg \Diamond A \implies \Box \neg A$$
$$\neg O A \implies O \neg A$$
$$\neg \neg A \implies A$$

For example, $\neg \Diamond \Box \neg P$ is converted into $\Box \Diamond P$ by applying NNF2. Negation normal forms are unique. Note that the negation normal form of a formula is valid if and only if the original formula is valid.

Later, we need to check whether we have constructed an ω-graph corresponding to a set of models of PTL in which the eventualities in a negation normal form are satisfied. We compute the eventuality set of the formula F_0 in a negation normal form in order to use it at that time. The set of all subformulas G, such that $\Diamond G$, is a subformula of F_0 is called *the eventuality set of F_0*. For example, the eventuality set of the formula $\Box \Diamond P$ is $\{P\}$.

Let F be a formula. *An initial node formula $[F_0]_{\{\ \}}$* of F is a formula suffixed by $\{\ \}$, where F_0 is in a negation normal form of F. The top level of the procedure *compute_initial_node_formula* in GHC is implemented as follows:

compute_initial_node_ formula(F,NNF,EveSet) :- true |
      negation_normal_form(F,NNF),
      compute_eventuality_set(NNF,EveSet).
negation_normal_form(F,G) :- true |
      remove_implication_and_equivalence(F,F0),
      move_not_inwards(F0,G).

Three subprocedures *remove_implication_and_equivalence*, *move_not_inwards*, and *compute _eventuality_set* were written in a general recursive style in Prolog. They are easily transformed into GHC programs with a few syntactical modifications.

3.2. Expansion of Node Formulas

An ω-graph is a graph whose nodes are labeled with expressions called *node formulas*.

Let ES_0 be the given fixed eventuality set. A node formula $[F]_H$ is a formula F suffixed by a subset H of ES_0, where F is in a negation normal form and may contain $\Diamond^*$ instead of $\Diamond$, and the suffix H is called a *history set*. For example, $[\Box \Diamond P]_{\{\}}$, $[\Box \Diamond P]_{\{P\}}$ and $[\Diamond^* P \wedge \Box \Diamond P]_{\{\}}$ are node formulas. $\Diamond^* G$ is semantically identical to $\Diamond G$. $\Diamond^* G$ is called a *marked formula*. A node formula $[F]_H$ is logically equivalent to the formula F. An initial node formula is a special node formula. The intuitive meanings of the mark and the history sets will be explained later.

In our proof procedure, we construct the ω-graph of F_0 by starting from an initial ω-graph and successively expanding nodes in the graph. This is based on the tableau method [Wolper 81]. Suppose we are trying to expand a node labeled with $[F]_H$. New node formulas are obtained by converting F to its next prefix form F_{NPF}, then converting F_{NPF} to its disjunctive normal form F_{DNF} and expanding F_{DNF}. Validity of the formulas is kept throughout these transformations.

Let F be a formula in a negation normal form and G be a formula obtained from F by applying the rules below as far as possible to subformulas not inside the next operator $\leq$, then G is called *the next prefix form of F*.

[Rule NPF1] postpone $\Box$

$$\Box A \implies A \wedge O \Box A$$

[Rule NPF2] postpone $\Diamond$ and $\Diamond^*$

$$\Diamond A \implies A \vee O \Diamond^* A$$
$$\Diamond^* A \implies A \vee O \Diamond^* A$$

For example, a formula $\Box \Diamond P$ is converted into $(P \vee O \Diamond^* P) \wedge O \Box \Diamond P$ by first applying NPF1, then NPF2.

Let F be a formula in a next prefix form and G be a formula in the form

$$(E_1 \wedge O F_1) \vee (E_2 \wedge O F_2) \vee .... \vee (E_m \wedge O F_m)$$

where $E_1, E_2, ..., E_m$ and $F_1, F_2, ..., F_m$ are formulas other than *false*. $E_1, E_2, ..., E_m$ do not contain temporal operators, and F_i and F_j are not literally identical if $i \neq j$. If G is obtained from F by applying the following rules to subformulas of F as far as possible, then G is said to be *the disjunctive normal form of F*. (Note that each F_i is in a negation normal form.)

[Rule DNF1] distribute $\wedge$ over $\vee$

$$A \wedge (B \vee C) \implies (A \wedge B) \vee (A \wedge C)$$
$$(A \vee B) \wedge C \implies (A \wedge C) \vee (B \wedge C)$$

[Rule DNF2] eliminate simple contradictions and duplication

$$P \wedge \neg P \implies false \quad \text{where } P \text{ is an atomic formula}$$
$$\neg P \wedge P \implies false \quad \text{where } P \text{ is an atomic formula}$$
$$false \wedge A \implies false$$
$$A \wedge false \implies false$$
$$false \vee A \implies A$$
$$A \vee false \implies A$$
$$A \wedge A \implies A$$

[Rule DNF3] supplement next part

Current formula A is in the form $C_1 \vee C_2 \vee ... \vee C_n$ where each C_i is a conjunction of literals or the formula whose outermost operator is $\bigcirc$.

$$C_i \implies C_i \wedge \bigcirc \square true \quad \text{where } C_i \text{ is a conjunction of literals (i.e.includes no } \bigcirc\text{-formulas)}$$

[Rule DNF4] ordering in each conjunction

$$\bigcirc B \wedge A \implies A \wedge \bigcirc B \quad \text{where } A \text{ is not in the form of } \bigcirc A'$$

[Rule DNF5] merge $\bigcirc$ in each conjunction

$$\bigcirc A \wedge \bigcirc B \implies \bigcirc(A \wedge B)$$

[Rule DNF6] combination by next part

$$(A \wedge \bigcirc C) \vee (B \wedge \bigcirc C) \implies (A \vee B) \wedge \bigcirc C$$

For example, $(P \vee \bigcirc^{\bullet} P) \wedge \bigcirc \square \diamond P$ is converted into $(P \wedge \bigcirc \square \diamond P) \vee (\diamond^{\bullet} P \wedge \square \diamond P)$ by first applying DNF1, then DNF5.

Expansion of node formulas is the basic operation in constructing ω-graphs, and is defined by using next prefix forms and disjunctive normal forms as follows:

Let ES_0 be the given fixed eventuality set, $[F]_H$ be a node formula and

$$(E_1 \wedge \bigcirc F_1) \vee (E_2 \wedge \bigcirc F_2) \vee ... \vee (E_m \wedge \bigcirc F_m),$$

be a disjunctive normal form of the next prefix form of F. Then $[F_i]_{H_i}$ is an expansion of $[F]_H$ if and only if

$$H_i = \begin{cases} ES_0 - ES_i & \text{if } H = ES_0 \\ (ES_0 - ES_i) \cup H & \text{otherwise} \end{cases}$$

$$\text{where } ES_i = \{G \mid \diamond^{\bullet} G \text{ is a subformula of } F_i\}.$$

$\diamond^{\bullet} G$ denotes that the realization of G is postponed in that expansion. Each H_i is called a *history set(h-set*, in short*)* of F_i. It is introduced to ensure that the eventuality will actually be realized in expanding nodes successively in the construction of an ω-graph. Each element of h-set indicates the history of the realization in a sequence of expansions.

The expansions of the node formula $[\square \diamond P]_{\{\}}$ where the eventuality set is $\{P\}$ are $[\square \diamond P]_{\{P\}}$ and $[\diamond^{\bullet} P \wedge \square \diamond P]_{\{\}}$.

As the parallel programming of the procedure *expand_node_formulas* is rather complicated, we divide it into the following three subprocesses which run in parallel: (1) conversion from NNF to NPF (2) conversion by using DNF1 (3) conversion by using DNF2 ~ DNF6 and compute h-sets. The top level of expansion of node formulas is implemented as follows.

```
expand_node_formulas(F,H,Xn,ES0,NodeFormulas) :- true |
        next_prefix_form(F,NPF),
        distribute_and_over_or(NPF,DNF1),
        simplify_formulas(ES0,H,Xn,DNF1,NodeFormulas).
```

3.3. Construction of ω-Graphs

Let F_0 be a formula obtained by converting the negation of a given formula to its negation normal form and ES_0 the eventuality set of F_0. An ω-graph of F_0 is the minimum graph satisfying the following conditions.

(1) Each node is labeled with different node formulas.

(2) There is a special node N_0, called an *initial node*, that is labeled with $[F_0]_{\{\}}$.

(3) When there exists a node N labeled with $[F]_H$ and $[F_1]_{H_1}, [F_2]_{H_2}, \ldots, [F_m]_{H_m}$ are all expansions of $[F]_H$, there exist m nodes $N_1, N_2, \ldots, N_m$ labeled with $[F_1]_{H_1}, [F_2]_{H_2}, \ldots, [F_m]_{H_m}$ and m directed edges from N to $N_1, N_2, \ldots, N_m$.

In parallel programming of construction of the ω-graph of a formula, each node is considered as a process and we try to execute expansion of each node formula in parallel. Since new node formulas are generated as an output stream of each node process simultaneously, it is impossible for each node process to decide whether the node formula is an existing one or not. It is necessary in the system to introduce some graph manager which manages all node formulas. It creates a *node_process* if a new node formula is generated and aborts it if the expansion of the node formula is over. It also stores a current list of node formulas and checks whether a newly generated node formula is an existing one or not. If all node formulas are expanded, then the *graph_manager* terminates.

A graph is represented as a list of quadruples $(NodeNmbr, OutStrm, InStrms, NodeType)$ where $NodeNmbr$ is the associated node number, $OutStrm$ is the associated stream variable, and $NodeType$ is either *omega* or *not_omega*. $InStrms$ is a list of the stream variables associated with the node which has an edge flowing into the node $NodeNmbr$. Thus, at the end of the *construct_omega_graphs* procedure, the *graph_manager* generates an output in this form.

For example, the ω-graph of a formula $\Box \Diamond P$ is represented as:
$$[\ (0,\ X0,\ [\ ], \qquad \text{not-omega}),$$
$$(1,\ X1,\ [X0,X1,X2],\ \text{omega}),$$
$$(2,\ X2,\ [X0,X1,X2],\ \text{not-omega})\ ]$$
and this output is shown in Figure 1.

Parallel Construction of An ω-Graph of F_0

Let F_0 be a given formula in NNF.

(1) Create the processes of graph manager GM, multiplexor MUX, and node process NP_0 corresponding to the node formula $[F_0]_{\{\}}$. Initialize $Exist$ to $\{\ \}$ and $Graph$ to $\{\ \}$. For each process, do step (2).

(2) NP : For each node process NP, let NF be the corresponding node formula. Do the following.

Expand NF. Assume that $NF_1, \ldots, NF_k$ are the node formulas generated from NF.

For each i, send MUX a pair of (NF_i, X) where X is the stream variable corresponding to NF_i.

MUX : Merge the input streams into $MrgdStrm$ and send it to GM. If every stream gets to the end_of_stream, it terminates.

GM : Repeat the following procedure until $MrgdStrm$ is $\{\ \}$.

Take a node formula NF_i from $MrgdStrm$.

If NF_i is a member of $Exist$, then send a message to the corresponding NP_i (as a result, X is added to the tail of $InStrms$ of NF_i).

If NF_i is not a member of $Exist$, then register NF_i to $Exist$ as a new node formula, and create the corresponding node process NP_i. (the head of the $InStrms$ of NP_i is X). Add the node to $Graph$.

This procedure terminates in finite steps, since there exist only a finite number of node formulas generated from F_0.

The top level of parallel construction of ω-graphs is implemented as follows, while it is in a repetitive style in sequential version.

```
construct_omega_graphs(JudgeStop,ES0,F,Graph) :- true |
       Exist=[[No0,X0,I0,F]|NewExist],
       Graph=[[No0,X0,I0,not-omega]|NewGraph],
       node_process(JudgeStop,ES0,0,Exist,StrmList),
       multiplexor(JudgeStop,StrmList,MrgdStrm),
       graph_manager(JudgeStop,ES0,0,MrgdStrm,Graph,Exist).
```

3.4. Check of ω -Loop Freeness

Let F_0 be a formula in a negation normal form and ES_0 its eventuality set. A node N, labeled with $[F]_H$ in the ω-graph of F_0, is called an ω-node when $H = ES_0$. The loop which starts from an ω-node W and returns to the same ω-node W is called an ω-loop of W. (A loop may pass through several nodes). If there is no ω-loop, then the graph is said to be ω-loop free. For example, in Figure 1, N_1 is an ω-node, $N_1 \rightarrow N_1$ and $N_1 \rightarrow N_2 \rightarrow N_1$ are ω-loops of N_1.

As we gave an intuitive explanation in the example in Section 2, some infinite paths in the ω-graph of F_0 correspond to models of F_0. Moreover, we can show that the ω-graph of F_0 is not ω-loop free if there is a model of F_0. Hence, ω-loop freeness of the ω-graph indicates that F_0 is not satisfiable.

In Prolog programming, every path outgoing from each ω-node is checked one by one via a backtracking mechanism. Because GHC has no backtracking mechanism, we have to change the algorithm for the GHC program. We use a programming technique similar to one in [Shapiro 83]. Each node is considered as a process sending messages to each other. Moreover, an extra argument, 'Judgestop,' is added as a termination flag. It can stop other processes as soon as an ω-loop is found.

Parallel Check of ω-Loop Freeness of ω-Graphs

(1) For each node, instantiate the head of X_N by its node number N and add $InStrms$ to the tail of X_N. (As a result, $InStrms$ becomes the list of paths flowing into that node. The length of a path may be infinite.)

(2) For an ω-node whose node number is N, initialize $CGraph$ to the set of all nodes in the ω-graph and $RecMes$ as [ ], and repeat step (3).

(3) If $CGraph = \{ \}$, then stop with failure.
   If $JudgeStop = stop$,
   then stop with the answer "There exists an ω-loop".
   Otherwise, assume that $InStrms$ is in the form of $[[A|X]|Paths]$, then do (3)-1 and (3)-2 in parallel.
   (3)-1 If $N = A$, then set $JudgeStop$ to 'stop'.
       If $N \neq A$, then append $[A]$ to $RecMes$, extract a node from $CGraph$.
   (3)-2 Let $InStrms$ be $Paths$ and repeat (3).
If all the processes for the nodes stop with failure, then answer "The graph is ω-loop free."

The top level of the parallel check of ω-loop freeness is implemented as follows. In the program, the third argument B of $check\_omega\_loop\_freeness/3$ plays the role of the flag as well as $JudgeStop$. A slot is cut for each node process from B and if a process finishes checking without finding an ω-loop, then 'end' is put in the slot. If all the slots are filled with 'end,' then the whole process terminates.

```
check_omega_loop_freeness(JudgeStop,Graph,B) :- true |
       check_omega_loop_freeness(JudgeStop,Graph,Graph,B).

check_omega_loop_freeness(stop,_,_,_).
check_omega_loop_freeness(JudgeStop,CGraph, [[N,Xn,INs,omega]|Gs],B) :- true |
       B=[H|B1], Xn=[N|Xn1], Xn1=INs,
       find_omega_loop(JudgeStop,CGraph,[ ],N,Xn1,H),
       check_omega_loop_freeness(JudgeStop,CGraph,Gs,B1).
check_omega_loop_freeness(JudgeStop,CGraph, [[N,Xn,INs,not-omega]|Gs],B) :- true |
       Xn=[N|Xn1], Xn1=INs,
       check_omega_loop_freeness(JudgeStop,CGraph,Gs,B).
check_omega_loop_freeness(_,_,[ ],B) :- true | B=[ ].
```

3.5. ω-Graphs Refutation Procedure

Lastly in this section, we show the top level of the parallel ω-graphs refutation procedure for checking the validity of the given formula.

```
prove(F) :- true |
        refute(not(F),A,B),
        write_answer(A,B,F).

refute(F,JudgeStop,B) :- true |
        compute_initial_ node_formula(F,F0,ES0),
        construct_omega_graphs(JudgeStop,ES0,(F0,[ ]),Graph),
        check_omega_loop_freeness(JudgeStop,Graph,B).

write_answer(stop,_,F) :- true | pretty_print(F), pretty_print('is valid').
write_answer(JudgeStop,[end|B],F) :- true | write_answer(JudgeStop,B,F).
write_answer(JudgeStop,[ ],F) :- true | pretty_print(F), pretty_print('is not valid').
```

Refute consists of three parallel processes each of which again consists of many parallel processes. Note that *construct_omega_graphs* and *check_omega_loop_freeness* have a common variable *JudgeStop*. It is set to 'stop' in order to terminate the graph construction if an ω-loop is found in the *check_omega_loop_freeness* process. Our program consists of about 500 lines in total.

4. PARALLEL PROGRAMMING METHODOLOGY IN GHC

In this section, we discuss the parallel programming methodology in GHC.

4.1. General Principles for Enhancing Concurrency

First, we discuss general principles for enhancing concurrency.

4.1.1. Early Publication

Information should be made public to other processes as soon as it is fixed in one process.

```
negation_normal_form(F,G) :- true |
        remove_implication_and_equivalence(F,F0),
        move_not_inwards(F0,G).

remove_implication_and_ equivalence(imply(F,G), F0) :- true |
        remove_implication_and_equivalence(F,F1),
        remove_implication_and_equivalence(G,G1)
        F0=or(not(F1),G1).
```

In this program, three processes can run in parallel so that the intermediate result 'F0' is propagated without waiting for the success of both processes of *remove_implication_and_equivalence(F, F1)* and *remove_implication_and_equivalence(G, G1)*. Then the head unification of *move_not_inwards* succeeds before 'F0' is instantiated to a non-variable term.

4.1.2. Early Commitment

Each process should run independently as far as possible without being suspended by the delay of another process, even if they share common variables.

```
union([X|S1],S2,L1,L2,S) :- member(X,L2,yes) | union(S1,S2,L1,L2,S).
union([X|S1],S2,L1,L2,S) :- member(X,L2,no) | S=[X|NewS], union(S1,S2,[X|L1],L2,NewS).
union(S1,[X|S2],L1,L2,S) :- member(X,L1,yes) | union(S1,S2,L1,L2,S).
union(S1,[X|S2],L1,L2,S) :- member(X,L1,no) | S=[X|NewS], union(S1,S2,L1,[X|L2],NewS).
union([ ],S2,L1,L2,S) :- true | S=S2.
union(S1,[ ],L1,L2,S) :- true | S=S1.
```

member(X,[Y|S],Answer) :- X==Y | Answer=yes.
member(X,[Y|S],Answer) :- X\=Y | member(X,S,Answer).
member(X,[ ],Answer) :- true | Answer=no.

In this program, the third and the fourth arguments of *union*, which accumulate the set elements already output so far, are always completely instantiated to lists. Hence, the unification of *member* in the passive part is never suspended. In general, in order to realize early commitment, predicates in the passive part should be written so that the clause is committed even if the shared variables are partially instantiated.

4.1.3. Decision Distribution

Decisions should be made in the distributed manner as far as possible if it does not increase the overall communication cost excessively.

bounded_buffer_communication :- true | produce(0,100,H), buffer(N,H,T), consume(H,T).
produce(N,Max,[M|L]) :- N < Max | M=N, N1:=N+1, produce(N1,Max,L).
produce(N,Max,[M|_]) :- N >= Max | M='EOS'.

buffer(N,H,T) :- N>0 | H=[_|H1], N1:=N−1, buffer(N1,H1,T).
buffer(N,H,B) :- N=:=0 | B=H.

consume([H|Hs],B) :- H\= 'EOS' | B=[_|Ts], write(H), consume(Hs,Ts).
consume([H|Hs],B) :- H=='EOS' | B=[ ].

This is the bounded buffer problem discussed by Ueda [Ueda 85]. *Produce* creates a stream of integers and puts the integer to the slot if there is a slot in the buffer. The process *produce* itself never creates a slot. If the head of the buffer is instantiated, *consume* reads it and makes a new slot at the tail. The head and tail of the stream are initially related by the goal *buffer*. These three processes run in parallel. As *buffer* only manages the relations of slots, and the values put to each slot are decided independently, *consume* does not have to wait until *produce* generates the values for slots. This is a typical example which shows the effectiveness of decision distribution using difference lists.

4.1.4. Efficient Communication Network

Communication network connected by shared variables should be as simple as possible if the cost of devising simple networks pays.

GHC uses streams for process communication similar to other concurrent programming languages. We show below a fair merge of streams in the communication between several sender processes and one receiver process. The necessity of *internal merge* in 'communication from multiple processes to one process' was also a problem in Concurrent Prolog [Shapiro 83]. Kusalik gave a solution to this problem [Kusalik 84].

In the *construct_omega_graph* procedure, we used a multiplexor based on Kusalik's algorithm to merge the messages from multiple node processes, the number of which changes dynamically. The multiplexor manages a stream of stream variables, each of which corresponds to output from each sender process. It behaves as described below.

If the head of a stream variable from a sender process is instantiated to a non-variable term, then it is eventually received by the receiver process. If some sender process generates some output, a *merge process* receives it, decreases the priority of this sender process, and check whether the other processes have generated output. If a new sender process is generated, the multiplexor creates a new channel to communicate that process. If the merge process receives [ ] as a sign of end_of_stream from some sender process, it aborts that process.

4.1.5. Equal Opportunity

Each process should have the independence and equal opportunity to decide whether it commits the selected clauses without being affected by the results of other OR-parallel processes. Consider the following two programs:

Program (A)
union([X|S1],S2,S) :- member(X,S2) | union(S1,S2,S).
union([X|S1],S2,S) :- otherwise | S=[X|NewS], union(S1,S2,NewS).
union([ ],S2,S) :- true | S=S2.

member(X,[Y|_]) :- X==Y | true.
member(X,[Y|S]) :- X\=Y | member(X,S).

Program (B)
union([X|S1],S2,S) :- member(X,S2,yes) | union(S1,S2,S).
union([X|S1],S2,S) :- member(X,S2,no) | S=[X|NewS], union(S1,S2,NewS).
union(S1,[X|S2],S) :- member(X,S1,yes) | union(S1,S2,S).
union(S1,[X|S2],S) :- member(X,S1,no) | S=[X|NewS], union(S1,S2,NewS).
union([ ],S2,S) :- true | S=S2.
union(S1,[ ],S) :- true | S=S1.

member(X,[Y|S],Answer) :- X==Y | Answer=yes.
member(X,[Y|S],Answer) :- X\=Y | member(X,S,Answer).
member(X,[ ],Answer) :- true | Answer=no.

Program (A) is a direct translation from the Prolog version. The predicate *otherwise* succeeds when the passive part of all other OR-parallel processes have failed. It is harmful since the execution depends on the passive part of other clauses. On the other hand, program (B) realizes fair OR-parallel execution in the passive part. Therefore, we try to use the predicate *otherwise* as little as possible. To avoid use, we should write passive parts symmetrically.

4.2. Programming Paradigms in GHC

Next, we discuss programming paradigms, i.e., the patterns of representing parallel algorithms in GHC.

4.2.1. Synchronization in Passive Parts

Any piece of unification invoked in the passive part of a clause cannot instantiate a variable appearing in the caller. We should not violate this synchronization mechanism when we apply program transformation such as partial evaluation to GHC programs. We reconsider an example of *remove_implication_and_equivalence*.

remove_implication_and_ equivalence(imply(F,G), A) :- true |
        remove_implication_and_equivalence(not(F),F1),
        remove_implication_and_equivalence(G,G1)
        A=or(F1,G1).

This program is written according to the fact that $F \supset G$ is logically equivalent to $\neg F \vee G$. *remove_implication_and_equivalence(F,F1)* in this clause allows the commitment of another *remove_implication_and_equivalence* process without instantiating $F, F1$. Therefore, we can apply partial evaluation. The program shown in 4.1.1 is the result in which evaluation proceeds one step ahead of that in this program.

4.2.2. Communication through Shared Variables

In logic programming, communication through shared variables provides interesting programming paradigms as was investigated by Shapiro. Here, we show a problem encountered in our programming, the *termination-flag*.

Termination-flag *JudgeStop* is a shared variable among several processes. If it is instantiated to 'stop' by some process, the message is propagated to other processes to stop them. It makes some kinds of parallel programs efficient because it releases the system from executing superfluous computations as soon as an answer is found. In the ω-graphs refutation procedure, it makes the system very efficient in the way that *construct_omega_graph* and *check_omega_loop_freeness* run in parallel with a common variable

JudgeStop. When the process *check_omega_loop_freeness* finds an ω-loop early in the computation, it sets *JudgeStop* to 'stop' to terminate the subprocesses in *construct_omega_graph*. Therefore, it does not need to treat a large graph or superfluous expansion of nodes.

4.2.3. Use of Partially Specified Data Structures

Partially specified data structures are especially useful for utilizing potential concurrency. They are an important concept to write better programs together with that of communication through shared variables.

As was described above, we can sometimes find an ω-loop before the ω-graph is completely constructed. Therefore, we can check ω-loop freeness on the current partial graph while constructing the ω-graph. Two processes, *construct_omega_graph* and *check_omega_loop_freeness*, have a shared variable *Graph* which is partially specified during computation.

4.2.4. Use of Decision Distributible Data Structures

Difference list is a typical data structure which is suited for decision distribution. It enables processes to be distributed into each step and decide the output data independently. Its use provides us with the possibility to increase efficiency of GHC programs, though it might be costly in some cases.

4.2.5. Paradigms in Sequential Programming Revisited

Are the paradigms in sequential programming, such as *divide and conquer,dynamic programming* and *generate and test*, completely of no use in parallel programming ? Or are they useful with some modification ?

Divide and conquer is a paradigm to divide the problem into partial subproblems, solve each subproblem independently, and synthesize the results to the solution of the whole problem. This paradigm naturally takes the form of general recursive style. Since sequential programs in general recursive style are almost directly translated to corresponding GHC programs with AND-parallel processes, this paradigm is suited for GHC programming. We use this paradigm in *compute_initial_formula* procedure.

Dynamic programming is a technique used to convert non-repetitive programs with redundant computation into repetitive(tail-recursive) ones with tables to store the results when they have been computed once. No matter how many resources we can assume in parallel computation, we should still avoid limitless redundant computation. In order to utilize the results computed in one process before, we must pass the results either through shared variables directly to other processes or through the common table accessible from other processes. If we use shared variables, we need to span the communication network by the shared variables. The paradigm of dynamic programming helps us to figure out the network. If the network is too complicated and we use common tables, *the multiplexor* discussed before is a useful programming concept.

Generate and test is a paradigm to find a solution by enumerating candidates in sequence and testing each candidate to see whether it is the desired one. When the generated candidate is not the desired solution, the program must backtrack and generate another candidate. Because backtracking is not supported in GHC, the principle "if fail, then redo," should be changed to "test all candidates at the same time and if one succeeds, then stop the other processes." Besides, we can sometimes find a more suitable algorithm for parallel execution. For example, in *check_omega_loop_freeness*, each node is considered as a process sending messages to each other, which is more suitable and efficient than the algorithm obtained by modifying the sequential one.

4.3. Programming Style in GHC

Lastly, we discuss programming style, i.e., the patterns of the activities in constructing GHC programs.

We usually start GHC programming by conceiving a rough and still vague parallel algorithm at an appropriate level of modules and develop it in two directions, downwards (refine parallelism within each module) and upwards (adjust and modify inter-module parallelism). In the process to reach the final GHC program, we need several tools and an environment devised for parallel programming.

If we borrow the viewpoint of Kowalski, GHC programs also consist of a *logic part* and a *control part*. Different from Prolog, we cannot consider both parts simultaneously in GHC since the control part in GHC programs contains more subtle problems and needs more concentration from programmers. We usually would like to confirm the logic part as early as possible before considering these subtle control problems in parallel programs. In refining the parallelism within each module, we sometimes modify parallel GHC programs into sequential ones and test them first. The reason for this is two fold: complicated tracing and scheduler's overhead (especially under the breadth-first search scheduling on the sequential machine).

In general, it is difficult to trace the computation of parallel programs compared with that of sequential programs, because it is difficult to know when variables are instantiated or clauses are suspended. Even if each process, executed independently, behaves as we expected, the whole program might behave quite differently from our expectations. The more the number of processes which run in parallel increases, the more serious this problem becomes. As one solution of this problem, we propose programming by incremental parallelization. First, we divide the whole problem into modules of a proper size, and make parallel programming in each module, paying attention to the interface between the modules. Next, we try to accomplish parallelism at the upper level. We used this programming style in the upper level parallelism for programming the ω-graphs refutation and its three modules *compute_initial_node_formula*, *construct_omega_graph*, and *check_omega_loop_freeness*.

More powerful debugging aids would make our programming in GHC more comfortable. Currently, GHC has two types of debuggers: a tracing type and an algorithmic debugging type. The former is the conventional debugger which traces the execution of computation. The algorithmic debugger of GHC programs [Takeuchi 86] employs the 'divide and query' algorithm and detects the bug location by getting the requisite information from the programmer. It can find the bug in the case of deadlock as well as that of termination with an incorrect answer. Though it imposes less burden on a programmer, it is still difficult to grasp the behavior of the whole program. We should use them properly according to the requirement.

In constructing GHC programs, we needed to check whether the GHC program at hand was efficient enough for parallel execution. There are several measurements of performance e.g.,CPU time, memory space, and 'parallelism.' We used the compiler developed on DEC10-Prolog by Miyazaki [Miyazaki 85], which translates the GHC(not flat) source program to Prolog code and compiles it by DEC10-Prolog Compiler. Because the compiler employs breadth-first scheduling, the system reports the number of cycles in the execution. We can take the number of cycles as a rough base for evaluation of parallelism. For example, the ω-graphs refutation of the formula $\Diamond \Box \neg P$ needs 10064ms CPU time, 42 cycles, and 12457 global stack size. Among these measurements to better judge of the GHC program, we gave higher priority to time efficiency than space-efficiency because development of a parallel execution machine for GHC will solve the space problem to some degree. And we gave higher priority to parallelism than time-efficiency because the execution time reported by the current system does not necessarily reflect the theoretical one.

5. CONCLUDING REMARKS

We have reported our experience in programming a proof procedure of temporal logic in GHC and discussed the parallel programming methodology in GHC. Through the experience, we have found many interesting facts and encountered some difficulties due to differences in the thinking style between GHC and sequential programming. Further research on parallel programming methodology and the accumulation of experience need to be done simultaneously with the development of the GHC system itself and parallel machines for execution of GHC.

ACKNOWLEDGMENTS

This research was done as one of the subprojects of the Fifth Generation Computer Systems (FGCS) project. We would like to thank Dr.K.Fuchi, Director of ICOT, for the opportunity of doing this research and Dr.K.Furukawa, Chief of the 1st Laboratory of ICOT, for his advice and encouragement.

REFERENCES

[Clark and Gregory 84] Clark,K.L. and S.Gregory, "PARLOG: Parallel Programming in Logic," Research Report DOC 81/16,Imperial College of Science and Technology,1984.

[Fusaoka and Takahashi 85] Fusaoka,A. and K.Takahashi, "On QFTL and the Refutation Procedure on ω-graphs," pp.43-54,TGAL85-31,IECE,Japan,1985.

[Hughes and Cresswell 68] Hughes,G.E. and Cresswell,M.J., " An Introduction to Modal Logic," Methuen and Co. Ltd, 1968.

[Kusalik 84] Kusalik,A.J., "Bounded-Wait Merge in Shapiro's Concurrent Prolog," New Generation Computing, pp.157-169,Vol.2,No.2,1984.

[Kripke 69] Kripke,S.A., "A Completeness Theorem in Modal Logic," The Journal of Symbolic Logic,Vol.24, No.1,March 1969.

[Manna and Pnueli 81] Manna,Z. and A.Pnueli, "Verification of Concurrent Programs, Part1: The Temporal Framework," Stanford TR 81-836,1981.

[Miyazaki 85] Miyazaki,T., "Guarded Horn Clause Compiler User's Guide," unpublished, 1985.

[Shapiro 83] Shapiro,E.Y., "A Subset of Concurrent Prolog and Its Interpreter," ICOT TR-003,1983.

[Shapiro 84] Shapiro,E.Y., "Systems Programming in Concurrent Prolog," Proc.11th Annual ACM Symposium on Principles of Programming Languages, pp.93-105,1984.

[Takahashi and Kanamori 86] Takahashi,K. and T.Kanamori, "On Parallel Programming Methodology in GHC," ICOT TR-184,1986.

[Takeuchi 86] "Algorithmic Debugging of GHC Programs and Its Implementation in GHC," ICOT TR-185,1986.

[Ueda 85] Ueda,K., "Guarded Horn Clauses," ICOT TR-103,1985.

[Wolper 81] Wolper,P.L., "Temporal Logic Can Be More Expressive," Proc.22nd IEEE Symposium on Foundation of Computer Science, pp.340-348,1981.

An Optimizing Prolog Compiler

Hideaki Komatsu, Naoyuki Tamura, Yasuo Asakawa and Toshiaki Kurokawa

IBM Tokyo Research Laboratory,
5-19 Sanban-cho, Chiyoda-ku, Tokyo 102, JAPAN

Abstract

In this paper we report on our experiment on Prolog compiler technology. Targeted properties of the compiler are efficiency and portability. The generated code attained so far is efficient enough to gain more than 1 MEGA LIPS on IBM 3090. One of the specialities of the compiler is in the intermediate Virtual Prolog Machine Code, which enhanced efficiency and portability. Another advantage of the compiler is to generate PL.8 code which can be used on multiple machines including the IBM 370 and IBM RT-PC. We also introduce some declarative extensions , which are compatible with Prolog and powerful enough to produce efficient code.

1 Our Goals and Approaches

The goals of our optimizing Prolog compiler technology development were the following:

1. Development of the technology to produce one of the world's fastest Prolog compilers.
2. To achieve both efficiency and portability achieved in the same framework
3. To conduct the feasibility study of the compiler technology in a reasonably short period.
4. Evaluation of various machine architectures from the standpoint of the Prolog compilation.

To achieve these goals we have employed the following techniques:

1. Extension of the Prolog language for the generation of efficient code while maintaining compatibility.
2. Adoption of the Virtual Prolog Machine scheme as the intermediate stage of the compilation process for effective optimization.
3. Use of the machine independent and efficient system programming language, PL.8 (See Auslander and Hopkins 1982) as the object code.

In this paper, we present the newly introduced declarations, an overview of the compilation and an evaluation of the compiler. We have omitted arguments about Prolog such as in Kurokawa (1982), and assumed the readers have some familiarity with Prolog language and programming (Clocksin and Mellish 1981).

2 Prolog Language Extensions

There are two newly introduced extensions to Prolog language: *notrail* and *type*. Both are declarations which can be attached to any predicate. So far, *mode* declaration in DEC-10 Prolog (Bowen 1981) is the only declaration used for optimizing compilation.

- *Notrail* declaration indicates that the annotated predicate actually behaves rather as a function so that there is neither backtracking nor ambiguous head selection. This declaration usually follows the *usage* declaration explained below.

- *Type* is declared actually in part of the *usage* declaration where input/output *mode* is also declared for the predicate. With it, we can declare the data type of each argument, not of each variable. So far, we limit type categories among the built-in data types such as *atom, nil, list, integer, structure, variable*, and their combinations.

For example, we can define the list concatenation program, *append*, that is deterministic and accepts two input lists (possibly *nil*) and produces one output list. It is actually the same as the well-known *append* predicate but is declared as in Fig 1.[1]

```
<- usage append(in:(list+nil),
                in:(list+nil),
                out:(list+nil)).
<- notrail append(*,*,*).

append({},X,X).
append({A|X},Y,{A|Z}) <- append(X,Y,Z).
```

Figure 1: APPEND with declarations

The introduction of *type* annotations is natural, in the sense that most contemporary high-level programming languages, even Lisp, have type declarations. However, the *notrail* declaration is special to the Prolog language, and may need some explanation. This declaration is introduced mainly for the following two reasons:

1. For the compiler writer, it helps the decision to eliminate the trailing of variables. Without it, all variables have to be trailed, or at least checked for whether they must be trailed or not, even if the execution is deterministic.

2. For the Prolog programmer, this declaration eliminates the use of the *cut* operation. It is commonly observed that a novice programmer either puts in too many cuts or forgets to puts in cuts at all. Most of the Prolog predicates tend to be deterministic, especially when Prolog is used for system programming.

The benefit of the deterministic declaration varies with machine architectures. For the ordinary commercially available machines such as IBM S/370 or IBM RT-PC (IBM 1986), the gain is significant because the trailing operation requires more instructions compared with special Prolog machines such as Tick and Warren's Pipelined Prolog Machine (Tick

---

[1]Note that we use VM/Prolog (IBM 1985) syntax. In DEC-10 Prolog, square brackets ([]) would be used to indicate list data instead of curly braces ({, }).

and Warren 1984). We have also introduced two auxiliary declarations: *key* and *entry*. *Key* declaration can be used to specify the argument which will be indexed. *Entry* declaration is used to declare the entry point and an entry declaration is necessary for a compilation unit. More complicated examples of these declarations are shown in appendix A, which is really used for benchmark tests. That original version is defined in Prolog contest (Okuno 1984).

3 Outline of The Compilation Process

As noted in our goals, our emphasis lies in *optimization* and *portability*. We adopt a *virtual machine* as an intermediate stage of our compilation so that we can enhance both of these. The virtual machine, which we have adopted, is based on Tick and Warren's machine. However, considering from the viewpoint of optimizing Prolog compiler, the level of its instructions is too high. For example, its instruction "*get_list A1*" implies the following:

```
test the tag of register A1
if reference then
     do dereference
     and retry
if unbound variable then
     create a list cell
     bind it to the variable
     check whether trailing is necessary or not
     if necessary then do trailing
     set the address of the list cell to register S
     set write mode
if list then
     set the address of the list cell to register S
     set read mode
otherwise
     fail
```

In so far as "*get_list A1*" is a primitive instruction and it can not be decomposed into lower level instructions, there is no opportunity for optimization even if it is known that A1 is always a list. Therefore, in our virtual machine many low level instructions , which basically correspond to each statement in the above example are introduced. The optimizer in our compiler eliminates redundant type-checking and mode-checking at this level.

Another special point of our approach is the adoption of PL.8 as an object code. PL.8 compiler provides a low-level optimization. For example, we need not care about the register allocation. It also provides the portability between the S/370 and RT-PC. The compilation process is summarized in Fig 2.

3.1 Lower level instructions

Our approach is through the adoption of the lower level instruction set as the intermediate language so that the optimizer can estimate redundant test operation of data tags and read/write modes. The *case* instruction is used to test a data type (including bound or unbound) or read/write mode. The *case* instruction is used in *get* and/or *unify* instructions, and also used as the alternative of *switch_on_term* instruction. The conditions are exclusive like a guarded command. For example, the *get_list(a(1))* instruction (this is the same wit *get_list A1* of WAM) is decomposed as follows:

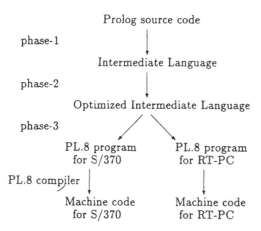

Figure 2: The outline of our compilation process

```
L1: case type(a(1)){
      ref(\undef) -> {     /* a(1) is a bound variable. */
        deref(a(1));
        goto(L1)
      };
      ref(undef) -> {      /* a(1) is an unbound variable. */
        get_list_w(a(1));
        trail(a(1));
        setmode(write)
      };
      list -> {            /* a(1) is a list. */
        get_list_r(a(1));
        setmode(read)
      };
      nil+atom+int+struct ->    /* otherwise */
        failure
    }
```

The *get_list_w* and *get_list_r* instructions correspond to *write mode* and *read mode* respectively. The *setmode* instruction will set the mode bit to write or read. And the *unify_variable(x(1),0)* instruction (the second argument 0 specifies an offset position of the element to be unified) will be decomposed as follows:

```
case mode {
  write -> unify_variable_w(x(1),0);
  read  -> unify_variable_r(x(1),0);
}
```

Now, most of the instructions are straightforward and don't include the implicit test operations.

3.2   Phase-1

In this phase, Prolog program is translated to an intermediate language. This is considered a mapping process of Prolog language into the virtual machine. From this point of view, some optimization is done. For example,

- Tail recursion optimization (Warren 1980)
- Decision of unification order using *mode* information
- Detection of *unsafe variable* using *type* and *mode* information
- Selection of the best code for built-in predicates using *type* information
- Variable classification

Type and mode information is also generated so that optimization can be done effectively in the following phase. In Fig 3, a part of output of phase-1, which is generate from *append*, is shown. It corresponds to the indexing part and unification of the first argument of the second clause in Fig 1. This will be expanded to low-level code before the optimization process. Expansion is very simple and straightforward. An example of expanded code is shown in Fig 4.

```
asa3:
   assertion(type(a(1)) = list + {}
                          + ref( \= undef));
   select type(a(1)) of {
     ref( \= undef) -> {
        deref(a(1));
        goto(asa3) };
     {} -> goto(asa1);
     list -> goto(asa2);
     otherwise -> failure};
   ............................
asa2:
   get_list(a(1))
         where trail = no &
               type(a(1)) = list + {}
                            + ref( \= undef) &
               deref = no;
   unify_variable(x(1),0);
   unify_variable(x(2),1);
   ............................
```

Figure 3: A part of output of phase-1 for *append*

3.3   Phase-2

In this phase, the intermediate code is translated into a graph for optimization. The optimizer is designed to cover the following optimizations:

1. Elimination of never selected cases: If there are never selected entries in a case statement, those entries can be omitted. For example, when the compiler knows some

```
asa3 :                                          write ->
    case type(a(1)) of {                            goto(tn58);
      ref( \= undef) ->                         read ->
          goto(tn82);                               goto(tn57)
      {} ->                                     };
          goto(asa1);                       tn58 :
      list ->                                   unify_variable_w(x(1),0);
          goto(asa2);                       tn53 :
      atom + int + struct + ref(undef) ->       case mode of {
          goto(tn81)                              write ->
    };                                                goto(tn55);
tn82 :                                            read ->
    deref(a(1));                                      goto(tn54)
    goto(asa3);                                   };
. . . . . . . . . . . . . . . . . . . . .     tn55 :
asa2 :                                            unify_variable_w(x(2),1);
    case type(a(1)) of {                      tn52 :
      ref ->                                  . . . . . . . . . . . . . . . . . . . . .
          goto(tn64);                         tn54 :
      list ->                                     unify_variable_r(x(2),1);
          goto(tn62);                             goto(tn52);
      {} + atom + int + struct ->           tn57 :
          goto(tn60)                            unify_variable_r(x(1),0);
    };                                          goto(tn53);
tn64 :                                      tn62 :
    get_list_w(a(1));                           get_list_r(a(1));
    setmode(write);                             setmode(read);
tn56 :                                          goto(tn56);
    case mode of {                          . . . . . . . . . . . . . . . . . . . . .
```

Figure 4: Example of expanded code

variable is already dereferenced, the entry for a bound variable can be deleted. Also, read mode *unify* instructions preceded by a *put* instruction can be eliminated.

2. Elimination of redundant testing: If there is only one selectable entry in a case statement, the case statement can be skipped. This redirection can be performed for each control flow which goes to that case statement. For example, suppose there is a chain of type tests for a same variable (such as *switch_on_term* followed by *get_list*), the second type test can be skipped. And also, same mode *unify* instructions can be chained in a sequence by this optimization.

3. Elimination of unreachable instructions: Unreachable instructions can be deleted.

The optimizer uses a graph representation of the intermediate language. The graph consists of nodes and directed edges, and represents the control flow of the intermediate code. The following two steps are applied repeatedly for the graph:

1. Tracing the graph to infer the behavior of the intermediate code by *semantic definition of the intermediate language*

2. Modifying the graph by *graph reduction rules*

Table 1: Our effect measured with optimization and no optimization of our compiler. The unit is number of node.

	No declaration		Mode,Type declaration	
	No optimize	Optimize	No optimize	Optimize
List Append	103	95	99	51
nreverse	162	143	156	86
Quick Sort	260	235	254	169
N Queen	327	287	317	177

This optimization process is repeated several times and after that the optimized graph is translated back to the intermediate code. Detailed discussions about this optimization techniques will be found in our accompanying paper (Tamura 1986), especially from the *knowledge-based* viewpoint. Figure 5 shows the result of optimization of the code shown in Fig 4. Table 1 shows the improvement of the optimization for a list append program , nre-

```
asa3 :
    case type(a(1)) of {
        ref( \= undef) ->
            goto(tn82);
        {} ->
            goto(tn77);
        list ->
            goto(tn62)
    };
tn82 :
    deref(a(1));
    goto(asa3);
.........................
tn62 :
    get_list_r(a(1));
    setmode(read);
    unify_variable_r(x(1),0);
    unify_variable_r(x(2),1);
.........................
```

Figure 5: Output of Phase-2

verse, quick sort and nqueen. In the case of list append with no declaration, the performance is improved by a factor of 1.79, and when mode and type declaration are added, the factor becomes 1.99. This measurement of optimization is only in Phase-2.

3.4 Phase-3

The code obtained in Phase-2 is machine independent. In Phase-3, the code is translated into PL.8 program. During this translation information which depends on the target machine is used to optimize the following:

- Design of tag

- Primitive operations

- The order of case entries

The case statement of our intermediate language is guarded command. We compute the cost of each checking instruction of case labels by using the target machine information. We reorder the checking instructions in order of small cost. The function of cost evaluation is following: *Total cost = # of memory access cycles + # of instructions* Figure 6 is an example of PL.8 code generated for S/370 from the code shown in Fig 5.

```
asa3:
select;
when(  shiftr(a1,28)=4 )
goto tn62;
when( a1= ('30000000'xb^('0FFFFFFF'xb &0)) )
goto tn77;
otherwise
goto tn82;
end;
tn82:

/*** DEREF(a1)***/
a1 =
ptr(
a1
,memory)->w;
goto asa3;
........................
tn62:

/*** G_LIST_R(a1)***/
s = ('00000000'xb^('0FFFFFFF'xb &a1));
mode = rmode;

/*** U_VAR_R(x1,0)***/x1=s->strfrm.w0;

/*** U_VAR_R(x2,1)***/x2=s->strfrm.w1;

........................
```

Figure 6: Output of Phase-3(for S/370)

3.5 PL.8 compiler

As described in Auslander and Hopkins (1982), the PL.8 compiler performs many kinds of optimization, including register allocation, dead code elimination, code motion, value numbering, dead store elimination, straightening, and so on. Of course, those are also effective in our method. These are done from a global viewpoint. The PL.8 compiler can also do the optimization considered in Warren's "Abstract Prolog Instruction Set"(Warren 1983) level.

The value numbering and register allocation algorithm used in PL.8 compiler can do same optimization as shown in Fig 7[2].

```
get_list A1
unify_variable X4
unify_variable X5    -->  unify_variable A1
get_variable X6,A2   -->  (deleted)
get_list A3
unify_value X4
unify_variable X7    -->  unify_variable A3
put_value X5         -->  (deleted)
put_value X6         -->  (deleted)
put_value X7         -->  (deleted)
execute append/3
```

Figure 7: Example of Warren's Abstract Prolog Instructions level optimization

4 Evaluation

The compiler itself is written entirely in high-level programming languages, VM/Prolog and PL.8. Due to the quality of the debugging environment for VM/Prolog (Numao 1985). and for PL.8, the prototype compiler has been developed in a short term. The compiler itself runs on VM/CMS on the IBM S/370, producing code both for the IBM S/370 and the IBM RT-PC. Although the full facilities of Prolog are not yet implemented, enough have been realized to handle list processing and the arithmetics. With these functions, we can measure LIPS[3] values presented in Table 2. We also measured the performance by more complicated programs such as the classical "eight-queen problem", which is shown in appendix A. The measured execution times are shown in Table 3.

As our current prototype compiler has several points to be tuned up, we can reasonably expect that the final LIPS values will be better than those presented in Table 2. Note that the speed on the IBM 3090 has exceeded one MEGA-LIPS, which is a good intermediate step towards achieving the goals raised in the Fifth Generation Computer Project (Moto-oka 1982). Also note that in the figures for the IBM RT-PC, all system overheads are included. In other words, we measured real time performance in the IBM RT-PC. Table 4 shows the effectiveness of the optimizations which are done in Phase-2 and in PL.8 compiler. From this table it is found that the optimizer in PL.8 compiler does the optimization considered in Warren's Instruction level, shown in Fig 7. But it is also found that optimization in low-level virtual machine instructions is also effective and a combination of these two level optimization is very effective.

Table 5 shows the effectiveness of newly introduced declarations. According to this table, *mode* declaration by itself is of little useful for optimization. A combination of *mode* and *type* declaration, we call it *usage* declaration, is very effective. *Notrail* declaration is also effective, especially for the RT-PC, which is the so-called workstation and whose memory is much slower than that of host-class machines.

---

[2]This example is found in Tick and Warren (1984) and Warren (1983).

[3]LIPS (Logical Inferences Per Second) is usually measured by a simple list manipulation program, *i.e.* a simple *append* or a naive *reverse*.

Table 2: LIPS value measured on the IBM S/370 and the IBM RT PC. The unit is KLIPS. The benchmark program is *simple append* with 1000 elements. Hints mean *mode, type,* and *notrail* declarations.

	RT-PC	3081K	3090
Without hints	56	611	1000
With hints	87	827	1420

Table 3: Execution time of 8-queen problem. The unit is millisecond. Hints mean *mode, type,* and *key* declarations.

	3081K		RT-PC	
	Without hints	With hints	Without hints	With hints
First	14	5	178	65
All	232	92	2860	1066

5   Concluding Remarks

It is not an easy task to conclude in this kind of evolutionary activities. However, it should be noted that our main emphasis lies in the technology development, not in the product development. In other words, when one tries to make a product-level Prolog compiler based on our technology, there may necessarily be a trade off of efficiency for functionality.

Our prototyping is, to use an analogy from physics, an experiment conducted only to prove the correctness or feasibility of our approaches. We conducted an extensive review of similar works, and as far as we know, our compiler has achieved the highest performance yet for Prolog compilation.

Table 4: Effect of optimization: relative values of LIPS in case of append. Hints mean *mode, type,* and *key* declarations.

	3081K		RT-PC	
	Without hints	With hints	Without hints	With hints
No optimization	1	1.06	1	1.09
Prolog only	1.68	1.92	1.62	1.86
PL.8 only	1.64	1.85	1.68	1.74
Prolog+PL.8	3.30	4.47	2.80	4.35

Table 5: Effect of declaration: relative values of LIPS in case of append. Optimization is done both in phase-2 and PL.8 compiler.

	3081K		RT-PC	
	Without notrail	With notrail	Without notrail	With notrail
None	1	1.08	1	1.15
Mode only	1.03	1.26	1.04	1.30
Type only	1.07	1.16	1.23	1.36
Mode+Type	1.24	1.40	1.47	1.97

Acknowledgement

Dr. Peter Y. Woon and Dr. Tetsunosuke Fujisaki have provided us one of the best environment for this work. Ahmed Chibib at IBM Austin, helped us to fix the usage of PL.8 language.

References

Auslander M. and Hopkins M.(1982) "An Overview of the PL.8 Compiler", *Proceedings of the SIGPLAN '82 Symposium on Compiler Construction*, Volume 17, Number 6.

Bowen D.L.(1981) "DEC system-10 PROLOG USER'S MANUAL", Dept. of Artificial Intelligence, Univ. of Edinburgh.

Clocksin W. F. and Mellish C. S.(1981), " Programming in Prolog", Springer-Verlag.

International Business Machines Corporation(1986), "VM / Programming in Logic, Program Description / Operations Manual", No.SH20-6541-0.

International Business Machines Corporation(1985), "RT Personal Computer Technology", No.SA23-1057.

Kurokawa T.(1982), "LOGIC PROGRAMMING – What does it bring to the software engineering", *Proceedings of First International Conference on Logic Programming*, pp.134-138, Marseille.

Moto-Oka T.(1982), (ed.) "Fifth Generation Computer Systems", North-Holland.

Tamura N.(1986), "Knowledge based optimization in Prolog compiler", to appear in Proc. of the 1986 ACM/IEEE Computer Society Fall Joint Computer Conference.

Numao M. and Fujisaki T.(1985), "Visual Debugger for Prolog", *Proc. of The Second Conference on Artificial Intelligence Applications*, pp.422-427, IEEE Computer Society.

Okuno H.(1984), "The benchmarks for The Third Lisp Contest and The First Prolog Contest", Information Processing Society of Japan, WGSYM No.20-4.

Tick E. and Warren D.H.D.(1984), "Towards a Pipelined Prolog Processor", *Proc. of 1984 International Symposium on Logic Programming*, IEEE Computer Society.

Warren D.H.D.(1980), "An Improved Prolog Implementation which Optimises Tail Recursion",*Proc. of Logic Programming Workshop*, pp.1-11.

Warren D.H.D.(1983), "An Abstract Prolog Instruction Set", SRI International Technical Note 309.

Appendix

A A program to find all solution of 8-queen problem

```
<- entry queen8.

<- usage try(in:int,in:(list+nil),
              in:(list+nil),out:(list+nil),
              in:(list+nil),in:(list+nil)).
<- usage generate(in:int,out:(list+nil)).
<- usage selectx(in:(list+nil),
                 out:int,out:list).
<- usage notmem(in:int,in:(list+nil)).

<- key(try(*,*,*,*,*,*),2).
<- key(notmem(*,*),2).


queen8 <- start_timer & queen(8,L) & fail.
queen8 <- display_timer.

queen(N,L) <-
    generate(N,L1) & try(N,L1,{},L,{},{}).

generate(0,{}).
generate(N,N.L) <-
    gt(N,0) & diff(N,1,N1) & generate(N1,L).

try(*,{},L,L,*,*).
try(M,S,L1,L,C,D) <-
    selectx(S,A,S1) &
    sum(M,A,C1)  & notmem(C1,C) &
    diff(M,A,D1) & notmem(D1,D) &
    diff(M,1,M1) &
    try(M1,S1,{A|L1},L,{C1|C},{D1|D}).

selectx({A|L},A,L).
selectx({A|L},X,{A|L1}) <- selectx(L,X,L1).

notmem(*,{}).
notmem(A,{B|L}) <- ine(A,B) & notmem(A,L).
```

A Prolog Based Object Oriented Language SPOOL and its Compiler

Shinji Yokoi

Tokyo Research Laboratory, IBM Japan Ltd.
5-19 Sanbancho, Chiyoda-ku, Tokyo 102, Japan

ABSTRACT

A Prolog based object oriented language, SPOOL, is introduced and its language processor, which compiles SPOOL codes into Prolog codes, is described. This paper considers optimizing compilation techniques for generating efficient codes which reduce not only number of accesses to the Prolog database, but also the dynamic method search. Internal representations of methods and states of objects are also presented so that the above techniques can be realized. Finally, this language processor is evaluated and compared with an earlier interpreter which we developed.

1. INTRODUCTION

We are developing a knowledge representation language SPOOL (Fukunaga et al. 1985, 1986) which is a combination of a logic programming language and an object oriented language. In designing a knowledge representation language, it is the ability to express knowledge and then to manipulate this knowledge that is important.

In an object oriented language, knowledge is described as a collection of objects. Interactions between objects are allowed only through a uniform communication mechanism called message passing, and tasks to be performed by the object receiving a message are described in the method of its class. This mechanism increases the modularity of each object. An inheritance mechanism among objects is another important concept. Using this mechanism, new objects can be defined by specializing the existing ones. This feature contributes to the hierarchical representation of knowledge. For these reasons, we are much interested in adopting an object oriented language as a framework for knowledge representation. However, representation of knowledge in a method is in many cases limited to procedural rather than to declarative.

In a logic programming language, on the other hand, one can describe declarative knowledge and the application independent inference mechanism solves the problem. Therefore, program developing amounts to constructing a knowledge base for the problem domain. These features of a logic programming language are promising for the design of a knowledge representation language. We have therefore decided to combine an object oriented language and a logic programming language.

In SPOOL, methods are represented as clauses of a logic programming language and message passing to an object corresponds to the invocation of a Prolog goal. Advantages of this combination idea are:
1) It can create objects with inference facility
2) It supports declarative description of methods
3) It can do a message transmission with specific conditions to an object

We have developed several applications on SPOOL. PROMPTER (Fukunaga 1985) is a program which automatically generates annotations to the source codes written in an assembly language. Objects in PROMPTER are instructions or data that essentially organize a hierarchical structure. In this application, a multiple inheritance mechanism, a feature from an object oriented language, is a must. INK (Yokoi 1986) is a toolkit which easily creates a graphic user interface to an interactive system with multiple window facilities. INK was used for creating a user interface of PROEDIT2 (Morishita et al. 1986) which is an advanced version of a visual Prolog debugger PROEDIT (Numao et al. 1985) and was quite useful. In this application, however, we were dissatisfied with its low execution speed of SPOOL. When programs written in SPOOL are used for further applications, as in the case of INK, high execution speed is required for application designers, though our design aimed for expressive power and understandability rather than execution speed.

There was an attempt (Suzuki 1984) to improve the performance of the object oriented language by restricting the language features. But we wanted to enjoy the usefulness of the combination of an object oriented language and a logic programming language. So, without restricting the language features, we developed a compiler which compiles SPOOL codes to Prolog codes.

Section 2 shows an overview of SPOOL. The special features of the compiler, described in Section 3, are that it avoids costly dynamic methods search and reduces the number of accesses to the Prolog database. Internal representation methods of objects to incorporate these features are also presented. In Section 4, we evaluate the performance of this compiler by comparing it with the interpreter which we developed earlier. Our conclusions are presented in Section 5.

2. OVERVIEW OF SPOOL

SPOOL is an object oriented language implemented on top of Prolog and has concepts of a class and an instance like Smalltalk-80 (Goldberg 1983). A class and an instance are each an object. Behavior of an object is defined by the class it belongs to. A class in SPOOL has five properties: superclasses, metaclass, instance variables, class variables and methods. The meaning of these properties is similar to that of Smalltalk-80. In SPOOL, a class may have more than one superclass (i.e. multiple inheritance is allowed) and method search is done in a Flavor-like manner. Class definition has the form:

```
class <class name> has <properties>
```

A method has a form similar to a Prolog clause: it consists of a head and an optional body. A method is defined as:

```
<head> :- <body>
```

We can most clearly explain the overview of the execution of a SPOOL program by using an example. The SPOOL program in Fig. 1 defines two classes *employee* and *manager* and two instances *snoopy* and *charlie*. *Snoopy* is an instance of *employee* and a value of *his_manager* is *charlie*. *Charlie* is an instance of *manager* whose superclass is *employee* and a value of *his_manager* is *linus*.

A message passing in SPOOL has the form:

```
<receiver> << <message>
```

By the execution of the last line in Fig. 1, the message *request(domestic_trip)* is sent to *snoopy*. Since this message can be unified to a method defined in the class *employee*, *snoopy* retrieves the value of its instance variable named *his_manager* and sends the message *give_me_approval(domestic_trip,Answer)* to it. The instance *charlie* receives this message. Three *give_me_approval* methods are defined in the *charlie*'s class *manager* and all of them can be unified to the message. These methods are tried in the order of definition. In this case, the first one succeeds because *unimportant(domestic_trip)* holds for all *managers*. So, *approved* is unified to the variable *Answer* and control is returned to *snoopy*. Finally, a Prolog goal *display(domestic_trip,approved)* is executed and the result is displayed.

```
class employee has
    super_class root_class ;
    instance_var his_manager ;
    methods
        request(Subject) :-
            his_manager :: M &
            M < < give_me_approval(Subject,Answer) &
            #display(Subject,Answer);
end.

class manager has
    super_class employee ;
    methods
        give_me_approval(Subject,approved) :- unimportant(Subject);
        give_me_approval(Subject,rejected) :- unreasonable(Subject);
        give_me_approval(Subject,pending);
        unimportant(domestic_trip);
        unimportant(presentation);
        unreasonable(double_salary);
end.

instance snoopy is_a employee
    where   his_manager : charlie.

instance charlie is_a manager
    where   his_manager : linus.

snoopy < < request(domestic_trip).
```

Figure 1.   A sample SPOOL program

3. SPOOL COMPILER

We first created an interpreter of SPOOL written in Prolog and developed several applications on it. When the size of applications becomes large, however, we have not been satisfied with the performance. We believe the reasons for obstruction are:
1) language processor is an interpreter rather than a compiler
2) the means of representation of state of an object is not good
3) methods are dynamically searched at a run-time
we developed a compiler to resolve these problems. Details are explained below.

3.1 Internal Representation of a Method

Object oriented languages support instance variables and class variables as a means for maintaining a state of an object. A state has a global nature and in the implementation of it in Prolog, the only way is to represent in the Prolog database. In the SPOOL implementation, these variables are asserted as facts in the database. So, every time an object refers to or assigns a value to these variables during the execution of methods, access to the database is required. Access to the database, however, is extremely costly in execution and is an obstacle to the improvement of the performance.

We intended in the first place to reduce the number of accesses to the database. We changed the representation of an instance method as a Prolog clause, shown in Fig. 2, so that a state is kept as arguments. A state of an object which executes the method is unified to the argument *context1* before the execution of the method and the state after the execution of the method is unified to the argument *context2*. The second argument *object* is unified to the name of the object which

> class_name(method_head,object,sender,context1,context2) < - method_body.
>
> | | |
> |---|---|
> | class_name | the name of the class in which the method is defined |
> | method_head | the head of the method |
> | object | unifies to the name of the object which executes the method |
> | sender | unifies to the name of the object which sends a message to the object |
> | context1 | unifies to the state of the object before the execution of the method |
> | context2 | unifies to the state of the object after the execution of the method |
> | method_body | Prolog codes which are the result of compilation of the method |
>
> **Figure 2.   Internal representation of a method**

executes the method and the third argument *sender* is unified to the name of the object which sends a message to *object*. If a message transmission is self-addressed, that is, a sender and a receiver of a message are the same, then these two arguments are unified to the same object.

In this representation, when an object is activated by receiving a message, the state of the object is first read from the database. As changes in the state (such as an assignment to instance variables) during the execution are maintained as the arguments, there is no need to have access to the Prolog database until a message transmission to another object is executed.

This representation of method contributes not only improved performance, but also to the understanding of execution of a program. For example, a tracer of SPOOL can make use of the representation. If a tracer displays which message is sent from which object to which object, and how the state of the object is changed as a result, the behavior of a program is quite obvious. This is very effective for the debugging of programs.

For example, the method *add(V1,V2)* of *classG* is represented as the next class.

```
class classG has
   super_class classF; classD;
   instance_var inst_var7;
   methods
      method1 :-
         inst_var7 :: V1 &
         inc(V1,V2) &
         inst_var7 ::= V2;
      add(V1,V2) :-
         inst_var2 :: V3 &
         #(V2 := V3 + V1);
      method5 :-
         inst_var7 :: V1 &
         instE1 << methodE1(V1,V2) &
         inst_var7 ::= V2;
      method6 :-
         inst_var7 :: V1 &
         instE1 << methodE2(V1,V2) &
         inst_var7 ::= V2;
   end.
```

A class hierarchy structure

Figure 3.   A sample program: A sample program defines nine classes from *classA* to *classI* which organize a class hierarchy structure as on the right (root_class is provided by the system). An arrow represents a superclass. Instance variables from *inst_var1* to *inst_var9* are defined respectively in the class definition from *classA* to *classI*. A class definition of *classG* is on the left.

---

get_nth(3,*.*.I.*,I).
put_nth(3,V1.V2.*.V3,I,V1.V2.I.V3).

Figure 4.   Predicate for list processing

```
classG(add(V1,V2),V3,V4,V5,V6) <-
        get_nth(2,V5,V7) & V8=V5 & V2:=V7+V1 & V6=V8.
```

Get_nth and *put_nth* are predicates to refer to and assign a n-th item in a list. *get_nth(3,List,Item)* and *put_nth(3,List,Item,List1)* are, for example, defined as in Fig. 4 which respectively refers to and assigns the third item in a list. If a language processor of Prolog supports an indexing of the first argument, the search for the clause takes little time. Referring to and assigning n-th item in a list can be executed by making use of the variable binding mechanism of Prolog. Therefore, these predicates are also executed effectively.

If an object *obj_a* send a message *add(10,*)* to an object *instG* in *classG*, the fourth argument *context1* in Fig.4 unifies to the state of *instG* and a goal *classG(add(10,V1),instG, obj_a,{undef,20,undef,10,undef,undef},V2)* is executed. The result becomes to *classG(add(10,30),instG,obj_a,{undef,20,undef,10,undef,undef},{undef,20,undef,10,undef,undef})*.

3.2 Internal Representation of a State of an Object

In an interpreter of SPOOL, a state of an object was represented as facts of the form *object_name(class_name,variable_name,value)* where *object_name* is the name of the object, *class_name* is the name of the class in which the variable is defined, *variable_name* is the name of the instance variable and *value* is the value of the variable. The first argument *class_name* is used to distinguish those variables which have the same name and are defined in different classes. For example, the state of the object *snoopy* in Fig. 1 is as in Fig. 5.

---

snoopy(employee,his_manager,charlie).

Figure 5.   A state representation of snoopy (old version)

---

classG(var,{classD:inst_var4,classC:inst_var3,classA:inst_var1,
        classB:inst_var2,classF:inst_var6,classG;inst_var7}).

Figure 6.   An order of the representation of instance variables

---

instG(var,{undef,20,undef,10,undef,undef}).

Figure 7.   A state representation of instG (new version)

This representation method seems a natural way to represent a state of an object in Prolog. But with this method, every time a value is referred or assigned to the variable, the Prolog processor has to dynamically search for the fact from the head which represents the value of the variable among the facts which represent the state of the object, and therefore the performance is poor. Thereupon we decided to represent the value of instance variables of an object as a list of the forms that values of each variable take, and to list these in reverse of the method search order. In this representation, if specified conditions are satisfied, the location of the instance variable can be decided at compile time and dynamic method search can be avoided. For example, instance variables of an object which belongs to *classG* are always represented as the order shown in Fig. 6.

Figure 7 shows a fact which represents values of instance variables of *instG* which belongs to the class *classG*.

In this representation, common offset from the head in a list can be available in instance variables not only of objects which belong to the same class, but also of objects which belong to different classes.

3.3 Reduction of the Dynamic Search of the Method

Object oriented languages provide an inheritance mechanism among classes. When an object receives a message, it first finds a method that is unifiable to the message in the object's class. If none of the methods in the class are applicable, the methods are searched in the next class according to the method search order. This mechanism is useful for classifying knowledge with programming in object oriented languages, but performance is very poor, since the dynamic search of the method necessarily occurs in execution time. However, if conditions mentioned below are satisfied, an ordered set of methods unifiable to the message can be identified by statistically analyzing a program at a compile time. Then cost of the method search is reduced, and performance will be improved.

SPOOL terms describe the action that make up a method. They are either message transmissions or invocations of Prolog goals. Message transmissions are of two types: self-addressed and to another object. In the following, we describe self-addressed message transmissions.

Self-addressed message transmissions are also divided into two types: the invocation of user defined methods and system built-in methods. Built-in methods are provided for referring to and assigning a value to variables.

Case I: User defined method

First we describe conditions so as to be able to determine at a compile time the methods to be executed, and thus eliminate a dynamic methods search.

Condition A: a message is not represented as a variable
If a message is represented as a variable which will be unified to a concrete value at a run-time, it is impossible to optimize at a compile time.

Condition B: No method should be defined whose head is unifiable to the message in all the subclasses of the class in which the method is defined
For example, a method defined in the *classG* can be executed by several objects which may belong to the *classG*, *classH* or *classI*. If a method whose head is unifiable to the message is defined in the *classH* or *classI*, an actually to be executed method differs depending on the executing object, and it is impossible to determine at a compile time which of the methods will be executed.

Condition C: there should be no multiple inherited classes who are members of all sub-classes of the class in which the method is defined
For example, a method search order of each object which belongs to the *classG*, *classH* and *classI* are respectively shown in Fig. 8. If *classH* multiply inherits *classE* and *classG*, a method search order of objects in *classH* is H,B,A,root_class,G,F,C,D and the search order differs in the part after *classG*. Thus, the search order differs depending on the executing object and the method to be used cannot be determined.

---

classG: G,F,B,A,root_class,C,D
classH: H,G,F,B,A,root_class,C,D
classI: I,G,F,B,A,root_class,C,D

Figure 8. Search order of each class

Generation of optimized codes:
We now will consider the search order of the methods which are unifiable to the self-addressed message described in a method of the specified class. If condition C holds, this search order in the following specific class coincides with the search order of an object which belongs to this specific class, whatever the executing object of this self-addressed message might be. Therefore, a possible set of methods to be executed can be determined.

For example, the search order of methods unifiable to a message within a method of *classG* is identical in the part after *classG* as in Fig. 8 regardless of what class an executing object belongs to among the class G, H and I. Furthermore, if condition B holds, there are no methods unifiable to the message in the search order before *classG*. So, *method1* in *classG* can be compiled as follows:

```
classG(method1,V1,V2,V3,V4) <-
              get_nth(6,V3,V5) & V6=V3 &
              (classF(inc(V5,V7),V1,V2,V6,V8) |
               classA(inc(V5,V7),V1,V2,V6,V8) )
              put_nth(6,V8,V7,V4).
```

Here we suppose there are defined methods whose head is unifiable to the message *inc(V1,V2)* in *classF* and *classA*. A code is generated which first executes *classF(inc(V1,V2),...)* and, if this fails, then executes *classA(...)*. During the execution of the message *inc(V1,V2)*, this code does not require a dynamic search at all and performance is greatly improved.

Last but not least, since this message transmission is self-addressed, save and load of a state are not required. That is to say, once a message is sent from one object to another and the state of the object is loaded, there is no need to have access to the Prolog database until a message transmission to the other object is done.

Case II: Built-in method

In SPOOL, reference and assignment of a state are executed by using system built-in methods. The referring to and assigning a value of variables is described respectively as < variable > :: < value > and < variable > :: = < value >. Conditions A, B and C in this case correspond to conditions A1, B1 and C1 respectively.

Condition A: a variable is not represented as a Prolog variable

Condition B: there should be defined no variable whose name is the same as the variables defined in the all sub-classes of the class in which the variable is defined
For example, variables defined in *classG* can be referred not only from objects of *classG* but also from objects which belong to its subclasses *classH* and *classI*. If a variable of the same name is defined, for example, in *classH*, the reference to the variable in an object of *classH* is the reference to the variable defined in *classH*. Therefore the variables cannot be identified in methods defined in *classG*.

Condition C: there should be no multiple inherited classes who are members of all sub-classes of the class in which the method is defined
We represent values of instance variables of objects in a list and assert it in the Prolog database as a fact. The represented order of variables in a list is the reverse of the methods search order. For example, the represented order of variables of objects in *classG* and *classH* are as follows.
classG(var,{classD:inst_var4,classC:inst_var3,classA:inst_var1,classB:inst_var2,
classF:inst_var6,classG:inst_var7}).
classH(var,{classD:inst_var4,classC:inst_var3,classA:inst_var1,classB:inst_var2,
classF:inst_var6,classG:inst_var7,classH:inst_var8})
In this representation, the first six items in a list represent the common variables regardless of whatever classes objects belong to among all subclasses of the class including *classG*. But, if *classH* also multiply inherits *classE*, the reverse of the methods search order of objects in *classH* is classes

D, C, F, G, A, B, E and H. In this case, objects in *classG* and *classH* differ in the representational order of variables in a list. So, the location of instance variables from the head in a list cannot be determined.

Generation of optimized codes:
As described in section 3.1, since the fourth argument of a clause head representing a method is unified to a state of an object before executing the method, if the location of a variable to be referred to or assigned in a list is determined at a compile time, an operation is executed at high speed using predicates *get_nth* and *put_nth* in Fig. 4.

If condition C1 holds, the common order is assured for variables defined in classes that are after the class in which the method is defined in the method search order. Furthermore, if condition B1 holds, there are no instance variables of the same name to the right of the variable in the list (that is, before the class in the methods search order) and the location can be determined. For example, referring-to and assigning *inst_var7* in *method1* in Fig. 3 are compiled to the codes *get_nth(6,V3,V5)* and *put_nth(6,V8,V7,V4)*.

3.4 Reduction the Dynamic Search of the Method

As mentioned in section 3.1, when a method is executed, a state of the executing object at that time is passed as an argument. When a message is sent from a sender object to the receiver object, a state of the sender object has to be saved in the Prolog database. This is normally done by executing the following operations:

```
(1)  save the state of the sender
(2)  load the state of the receiver
        (at the same time, delete it from the database)
(3)  execute a message transmission
(4)  save the state of the receiver
(5)  load the state of the sender
        (at the same time, delete it from the database)
```

Operations (1) and (5) are needed since there is a chance that in the operation (3) a message transmission to the sender object will be executed and the contents of the state of the sender object might be changed. For example, the result of the compilation of the *method5* is the *classG*, as in the following:

```
classG(method5,V1,V2,V3,V4) <-
            get_nth(6,V3,V5) & V6=V3 &
            addax(V1(val,V6))(1) &
            delax(instE1(val,V7)) &
            classE(methodE1(V5,V8),instE1,V1,V7,V9) &
            addax(instE1(val,V9)) &
            delax(V1(val,V10)).
```

A state of the object which executes this method is saved in the operation *addax(V1(val,V6))*. (variable *V1* is bound to the object at a run-time. In the operation *delax(instE1(val,V7))*, a state of the object *instE1* is deleted from the database and at the same time variable *V7* is bound to the state as a side-effect.

Here a future definition is needed:

---

[1] Since a variable is not allowed as a predicate name, the exact form is $VV =.. \{V1,val,V6\}$ & *addax(VV)*.

```
def M1 a method which does not send a message to the other object
        a method in which there are no operations that send a message to
        the other object

def M2 a method which does not change a state
        a method in which there are no operations that change a state
```

If a method which is executed according to the message transmission satisfies definition M1, the method does not change the state of the other object. Therefore the state of the sender object is not changed and operations (1) and (5) can be omitted. If a method satisfies definition M2, deletion of the state in operation (2) and operation (4) can be omitted.

The following is the result of compiling *method6* of *classG*.

```
classG(method6,V1,V2,V3,V4) <-
        get_nth(6,V3,V5) & V6=V3 &
        ax(instE1(val,V7)) &
        classE(methodE2(V5,V8),instE1,V1,V7,V9) &
        put_nth(6,V6,V8,V4).
```

Here we suppose that *methodE2* is defined in *classE* and satisfies definitions M1 and M2. Therefore, save and load of the state which will be bound to a variable *V1* are omitted and save of the state of the object *instE1* is also omitted.

4. EVALUATION

Table 1 shows a comparison of the compiler and the interpreter in execution speed. Targeted programs are extracted from facilities of INK, an application of SPOOL.
Table 1. Comparison of execution speed of processors (in microsecond)

	interpreter	compiler	ratio
● display of help facility	200	60	3.3
● creation of window	182	90	2.0
● movement of window	184	76	2.4
● deletion of window	163	109	1.5
● display of class hierarchy structure	3557	1217	2.9
● deletion of displayed structure	1104	325	3.4

As seen in this table, execution speed is improved about threefold. Conditions for optimization stated in this paper seem fairly strict, but when we examined the above targeted codes, almost all codes satisfied the conditions and optimized compile codes were generated. An exception is in the case where a receiver object of a message transmission is represented as a Prolog variable whose value is unified at a run-time.

Change of representation of a state from facts for each variable to a list as a whole improves performance about 20 percents. This percentage is below our original estimate. The reason for this, we think, is because access to the Prolog database is not so slow in VM/Prolog (IBM 1985) compared with the binding speed of variables. Also, a list notation's memory needs are less.

While the technique described in section 3.4 depends on the internal representation of a state described in section 3.2 and is peculiar to SPOOL, the technique described in section 3.3 is generally applicable to object oriented languages.

5. CONCLUSION

We have described an internal representation method of objects and a compilation technique to generate optimized codes in order to improve the performance of a program of SPOOL, a knowledge representation language based on a combination of object oriented programming and logic programming. In generated Prolog codes, the dynamic search of the method and the number of access to the Prolog database are reduced, and the efficiency of execution is improved.

In considering development of a toolkit for creating a user interface such as window systems by using object oriented languages, it seems an important step will be improving processing speed. In fact, the need for a fast SPOOL compiler is demonstrated by the unsatisfactory execution speed in creating the user interface of a Prolog programming environment using an application of SPOOL.

The introduction of a type is yet another technique for improving performance, in addition to the ones mentioned in this paper: A type is information on the class an object might belong to. For example, when the receiver of a message is unknown, and if the name of the class of the receiver is determined at a compile time, a set of methods unifiable to the message can be determined. Furthermore, when a new object is generated by the *new* message, if a variable representing the generated object is traced, the type of the object is determined. Future investigation of this concept appears highly promising.

Acknowledgement

The author would like to thank Mr. Shin-ichi Hirose for his valuable suggestions about this research.

References

Fukunaga K (1985) PROMPTER: A Knowledge Based Support Tool for Code Understanding. Proc 8th International Conf on Software Engineering

Fukunaga K, Hirose S (1985) Prolog based Object-Oriented Language SPOOL and its applications. the 2nd JSSST

Fukunaga K, Hirose S (1986) An Experience with a Prolog-based Object-Oriented Language. Proc of the ACM Conf on Object Oriented Programming Systems, Languages and Applications

Goldberg A, Robson D (1983) Smalltalk-80: The Language and its Implementation. Addison-Wesley

IBM Corporation (1985) VM/Programming in Logic, Program description/Operation Manual. SH20-6541

Morishita S, Numao M (1987) Prolog Computation Model BPM and its debugger PROEDIT2. Logic Programming '86, Springer-Verlag

Numao M, Fujisaki T (1985) Visual Debugger for Prolog. Proc IEEE the 2nd Conf on Artificial Intelligence Application

Suzuki N (1984) Creating Efficient Systems for Object Oriented Languages. Proc ACM SIGACT-SIGPLAN Principles on Prog Lang

Yokoi S (1986) Interactive Systems Kit: INK. Proc of 32nd Annual Convention of IPSJ

DEVELOPMENT OF C-PROLOG COMPILER

Ken'ichi Kakizaki, Kuniaki Uehara, and Jun'ichi Toyoda

The Institute of Scientific and Industrial Research
Osaka University
8-1 Mihogaoka, Ibaraki, Osaka 567, Japan

ABSTRACT

We describe the design, implementation and performance for C-Prolog Compiler. C-Prolog Compiler is an in-core, incremental and native code compiler based on C-Prolog interpreter developed by Pereira et. al. (1984) The compiler runs on Data General's MV/8000II, and the produced code gains about 25K LIPS.

1 INTRODUCTION

Prolog is a simple but powerful general purpose programming language. Prolog has been used extensively in the field of artificial intelligence. A highly interactive environment is essential for artificial intelligence research. According as the number of users increases, requirements for high performance and easy-to-use facility are increasing. In order to cope with these requirements, we have developed a Prolog compiler, which allows users to compile Prolog programs into the machine code incrementally. That is, we can compile selected predicates rather than whole programs. Extremely fast program execution speeds have been achieved by use of such techniques as indexing and tail recursion optimization.

2 DESIGN METHODOLOGY

Main requirements for the design of the compiler implementation are as follows:

1) Interpreter based compiler
An interpreter is mainly used for debugging. This means that the performance of the interpreter is very important to develop programs efficiently. Almost all Prolog interpreters which have their own compilers have been written in Prolog, therefore, these interpreters does not gain so far high performance. In our approach, we have developed C-Prolog compiler based on the architecture of C-Prolog interpreter, considering efficient implementation. Both of our system, interpreter and compiler, thus, can achieve high performance.

2) In-core compiler
From the user's point of view, the compiler should be convenient to use. With the in-core compiler, compiling a program is just as easy for the user as reading it in to the interpreter. For example, in our compiler, we can compile a predicate in a currently running Prolog session, and after successful

compilation, the compiled predicate is available for execution, without any separate linking and loading.

3) Native code compiler
For the purpose of achieving high performance, our compiler produces the native code of MV/8000II instead of the intermediate code which is executed by an intermediate code emulator. The code can be stored into a file in the form of a relocatable object.

4) Almost all parts of compiler are written in Prolog
For maintenance and portability, it is desirable that almost all parts of the compiler should be written in Prolog itself.

3 COMPATIBILITY BETWEEN INTERPRETER AND COMPILER

C-Prolog is a Prolog interpreter written in C for 32-bit machines, which was developed at University of Edinburgh. Its design was based on DEC-10 Prolog (Warren 1980a). C-Prolog interpreter is closely compatible with DEC-10 Prolog (Pereira 1978), a de facto standard. In addition, the interpreter manipulates large address space which is approximately 2 giga ($2 ^\wedge 31$) bytes. The design of the system such as memory layout and tag architecture is well considered for maximum efficiency.

Prolog Language Machine (PLM) is proposed by Warren (1980a) for DEC-10 Prolog implementation. The instruction set of PLM is called a PLM code. PLM is a virtual target machine, although its registers and addressing modes are oriented towards the DEC-10 architecture.

Both C-Prolog and PLM use similar implementation technique. For example, they use structure sharing technique, and they have three stack areas (local, global and trail), a control frame on the local stack and same registers. Thus, PLM architecture is compatible with C-Prolog interpreter closely. We make use of PLM code on the intermediate stage of compilation.

4 IMPLEMENTATION

4.1 Compilation Phase

Compilation consists of three phases. In the first phase, Prolog programs are compiled into a PLM code. In the second phase, The PLM code is translated into an assembly language code in a macro expansion manner. In the last phase, The assembly language code is translated into a relocatable object code. The object code is finally loaded into the interpreter by linkage loader.

4.2 Registers

In PLM architecture, the current state of a computation is contained in a set of registers. Registers A, FL and C play an important role for interface between interpreted predicates and compiled predicates. Transferring control between an interpreted predicate and compiled predicate is performed according to these registers. Register A contains the address of a goal to invoke. Register FL contains the address of an alternative at which to continue if unification should fail. Register C contains the address of a next goal at which to continue if unification should success.

Consider, for example, the following program. When the 'subgoall' is being invoked by the 'goal', the register A points the goal to invoke (1), the register C points the next goal to continue (2), and the register FL points the alternative to resume (3), respectively.

```
               (1)        (2)
       goal :- subgoall, subgoal2.

       (3)
       goal :- subgoal3.
```

Fig. 1.

4.3 Memory Allocation

For the purpose of storing a compiled predicate, we add the code heap area (Fig. 2) to the original memory allocation. The top address of the code heap area is named code0. Code0 is used to distinguish the compiled predicate from the others.

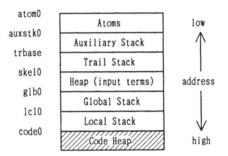

Fig. 2. Memory Layout

4.4 Compiled Code Linkage

In C-Prolog implementation, all kinds of the data related to a functor are stored into the atom area (Fig. 2). The data includes the pointer that points to a predicate definition, similar to the function definition of Lisp which is stored as one of a symbol data. We call the pointer a predicate definition pointer. If a predicate is executed by the interpreter, the predicate definition pointer points to the code heap area (Fig. 2), and the definition is emulated by the interpreter.

A compiled predicate is linked into the interpreter by a resident loader written in Prolog. When a Prolog program is compiled, the linkage is performed automatically. The loader has two tasks. First, the loader stores the compiled predicate into the code heap area. Hereupon, relocatable addresses are fixed by the loader. Second, the loader makes the predicate definition pointer point to the entry address of the compiled predicate.

In our compiler, the method of compiling predicate is divided into two methods. One is compiling each predicate individually, and the other is compiling a program (a set of predicates) all together.

In the first method, for the individually compiled predicate, in order to invoke the interpreted predicate which is called by the clause body of the compiled predicate, the control should be returned from the compiled predicate to the interpreter. This transfer control is executed through the dispatcher, taking advantage of the predicate definition pointer. The function of the dispatcher is described in section 4.5. This method has the great advantage that it is not necessary for the goal to be loaded at the loading time. However, if the predicate is a compiled one, an invocation overhead exists, because the invocation of the predicate is performed through the dispatcher instead of directly.

In the second method, if the predicate is called within a module, compiled predicates in the module are connected tightly each other. Therefore, the goal is directly invoked, and the code runs without any dispatching overhead.

These two linkage methods offer both highly interactive environment and obtain high performance. In the first method, we can compile a predicate one by one, and can also reconsult the predicate which has been already compiled. Therefore, we can compile the predicate, even if the predicate is reconsulted frequently. In the second method, we can gain the maximum performance of a program. A large program which is putted to practical use can be performed efficiently.

4.5 Dispatchers

This section discusses the interface between interpreted predicates and compiled predicates. In order for interpreted predicates to coexist with compiled predicates, transferring control between these predicates must be executed exactly. The transferring control manager (Fig. 3) is thus introduced into the original C-Prolog interpreter.

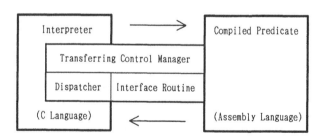

Fig. 3. Transferring Control Manager

We shall now introduce dispatchers into C-Prolog interpreter. Dispatchers manage the transferring control. For example, Figure 4 shows the outline of calling dispatcher. Dispatchers have two functions. One function is to transfer control from interpreted predicates to compiled predicates (Fig. 4 (2)). The other function is the determination of the next action, such as calling process, continuation process, and backtracking process. The process is performed by the interpreter (Fig. 4 (3), (4), (5)), when control is returned from compiled predicates.

In our implementation, it is the most important fact that spots where the transferring control occur are limited to only three spots, and the transferring is controlled by dispatchers exactly. Therefore, the interpreter and compiled predicates can be performed without any consideration of the transferring control, except for these three spots.

```
int (*compcode)() ;

/* the value of d is a definition pointer */
if (d >= code0) {     /* is it a compiled code ? */
    compcode = d ;                          /* (1) */
    switch ((*compcode)()) {                /* (2) */
        case CONTINUE:
            goto continuation ;             /* (3) */
        case FAIL:
            goto fail ;                     /* (4) */
        default:
            goto icall ;                    /* (5) */
    }
}
```

Fig. 4. The Dispatcher

The transfer control between the interpreter and compiled predicates is categorized into three cases. They are called calling process, continuation process and backtracking process. In our C-Prolog compiler, we add dispatchers where transfer control occurs. Each dispatcher is named calling dispatcher (Fig. 5 (1)), continuation dispatcher (Fig. 5 (2)) and backtracking dispatcher (Fig. 5 (3)), respectively.

Another management mechanism between these dispatchers and compiled predicates are named interface routines written in assembly language. In our implementation, a compiled predicate is invoked as a function of C language. C language has the stack which contains the management information to execute a program. However, the compiled predicate is executed without any consideration of the content of the stack. Therefore, the stack environment must be preserved before the compiled predicate is executed. Interface routines perform this preservation. We add interface routines which are named calling interface routine (Fig. 5 (4)), continuation interface routine (Fig. 5 (5)), and backtracking interface routine (Fig. 5 (6)).

4.5.1 Calling Compiled Predicates from Interpreted Predicates

Invocation of a compiled predicate from an interpreted predicate is performed by the calling dispatcher. The value of the predicate definition pointer is used as the entry address of the compiled predicate (Fig. 4 (1), 5 (8)). Invocation of the compiled predicate is performed in a function calling manner of C language (Fig. 4 (2)).

4.5.2 Calling Interpreted Predicates from Compiled Predicates

Invocation of an interpreted predicate from a compiled predicate is performed by the calling interface routine and its corresponding dispatcher. In order to invoke the interpreted predicate, the compiled predicate should also invoke the calling interface routine (Fig. 5 (4)). The routine stores the pointer which indicates the goal to be invoked into register A, and the control is returned to the

interpreter. In the interpreter, internal calling process procedure is
called by the dispatcher (Fig. 4 (5), 5 (7)), and the interpreted
predicate is invoked.

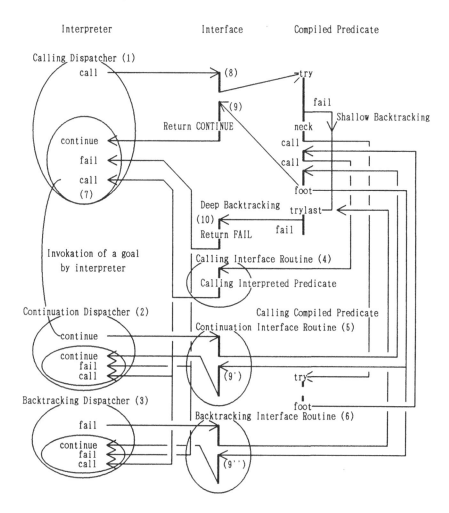

Fig. 5. Flow of the Transferring Control

4.5.3 Continuation Process

A successful exit from a goal requires the continuation process. The
process performs to resume at a continuation point which is pointed by
register C. If the value of C is greater than or equal to code0, the
parent goal is determined to be a compiled predicate. If not, the
parent goal is determined to be an interpreted predicate. If both the
current goal and parent goal are compiled predicates or both of them
are interpreted predicates, the system does not require to transfer
control between them. If not, the interpreter transfers the control to
the compiled predicate, or vis a vis. There are two cases in which the
transfer control should be required. One is from a compiled predicate
to an interpreted predicate, and the other is from an interpreted
predicate to a compiled predicate.

The first case, the continuation interface routine (Fig. 5 (5)) is invoked through the continuation dispatcher, and the routine invokes the compiled predicate which is pointed by register C to performs continuation process.

The second case, a interface routine which is pointed by register C is invoked (Fig. 5 (9), (9'), (9'')), and the routine performs the transfer control. The interface routine returns the value of CONTINUE which indicates currently executing continuation process, and according to the returned value, the interpreter invokes internal continuation procedure by a dispatcher (Fig. 4 (3)).

4.5.4 Backtracking Process

The method of backtracking process is divided into two cases, one is shallow backtracking, and another is deep backtracking. In shallow backtracking, there are other alternatives for the current goal. All that has to be done in this case is to resume execution at the instruction indicated by FL.

However, in deep backtracking, the execution of an alternative which is indicated by register FL is resumed. If the value of FL is greater than or equal to code0, the alternative is determined to be a compiled predicate. If not, the alternative is determined to be an interpreted predicate. If both the current goal and resumed goal are compiled predicates or both of them are interpreted predicates, the system does not require to transfer control between them. If not, the interpreter transfers the control to the compiled predicate, or vis a vis. There are two cases in which the transfer control should be required. One is from a compiled predicate to an interpreted predicate, and the other is from an interpreted predicate to a compiled predicate.

The first case, in order to perform deep backtracking process, backtracking interface routine (Fig. 5 (6)) is invoked through the backtracking dispatcher. Finally, execution is resumed at the compiled predicate indicated by FL.

The second case, the subroutine (Fig.5 (10)) which executes backtracking process is invoked by a compiled predicate, and the routine performs the transfer control. The subroutine returns the value of FAIL to the interpreter. The value indicates currently executing deep backtracking process, and according to the returned value, the interpreter invokes internal deep backtracking procedure by a dispatcher (Fig. 4 (4)).

5 OPTIMIZING COMPILER

5.1 Intermediate Stage Code

For the purpose of producing an optimized code, PLM code is slightly modified. The formalism of the extended code has much in common with the abstract machine design of Warren (1983). The extension of the code are categorized into three groups. The first is used for indexing, such as 'switch_list'. The second is used for tail recursion optimization, such as 'tro_enter', 'execute' and 'proceed'. The third is used to execute an unification, such as 'unify_variable', 'get_list', 'unify_value' and 'get_value'. The extended PLM code realize efficient clause indexing and tail recursion optimization. For example, the optimized code for 'concatenate' is shown in Fig. 6.

```
:- mode concatenate(+, +, -).

concatenate([X|L1], L2, [X|L3]) :- concatenate(L1, L2, L3).
concatenate([], L, L).


concatenate, 3,
    tro_enter([+, +, -]),
    switch_list( [
            unify_variable(+, car, 3),
            unify_variable(+, cdr, 0),
        get_list(-, 2),
            unify_value(-, car, 3),
            unify_variable(-, cdr, 2),
        execute(concatenate, 3)
    ], [
        get_value(1, 2),
        proceed
    ] )
```

Fig. 6. Optimized Code

5.2 Indexing

Efficient clause indexing (Warren 1980a) can be very important for the performance of predicates with a large number of clauses. Indexing also improves the systems ability to detect determinacy, which is important to conserve the working memory space. In our compiler, the clause is indexed by the predicate name and principal functor of the first argument in the head.

Clause indexing consists of two steps. The first step, clauses are indexed according to the instance type of a first argument in the head, such as atoms, a list structure and other structures. The second step, clauses in each type are also indexed according to the name of the atom or the functor of the structure, respectively.

The latter step of clause indexing uses hash method instead of search method. When atoms (functors) are read into the interpreter, hash keys are calculated from their symbol names. These keys are stored into the atom area associated with their atoms (functors). When a compiled predicate is being executed, clause indexing is performed according to these hash keys. Therefore, clause indexing is performed without any overhead which is necessary to calculate the hash key.

In a Prolog program, the 'list' structure is used widely, and most of the 'list' structure manipulation programs have a possibility that these program are applied to tail recursion optimization. Accordingly, for the purpose of achieving high performance, we introduce an instruction named 'swith_list' (Fig. 6), which performs clause indexing of a 'list' structure efficiently.

5.3 Tail Recursion Optimization

In tail recursion optimization (TRO) (Warren 1980b), the tail recursion structure of a deterministic predicate is translated into a loop structure. This technique improves the space and time efficiency. When unification is being performed by a tail recursion optimized predicate (TRO predicate), the contents of argument cells are overwritten and their values are lost completely. Therefore, argument cells within the goal molecule should not be used directly. We now introduce argument registers. These registers are used for the unification which is performed by the TRO predicate.

In C-Prolog and PLM architecture, arguments are passed by a pair of skeleton and environment. We call this combination a goal molecule, and the goal molecule contains argument cells. When the goal is invoked, register A indicates the skeleton, and registers X and X1 indicate the environment. The X and X1 point local stack and global stack, respectively.

A method of argument passing is divided into three cases. First, a TRO predicate is invoked from a TRO predicate (itself or another), arguments are passed through argument registers. Second, a TRO predicate is invoked from a non-TRO predicate or an interpreted predicate, arguments are passed through the goal molecule, and arguments are copied from the molecule into the registers by 'tro_entry' instruction. This situation is shown in Figure 7 (1). Third, a non-TRO predicate or an interpreted predicate is invoked from a TRO predicate, the goal molecule is constructed by 'tro_call' and 'execute' instructions using information contained in the argument registers. This situation is shown in Figure 7 (2).

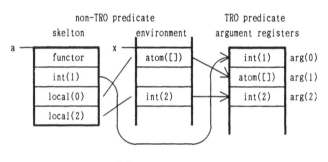

(1) Argument Copy

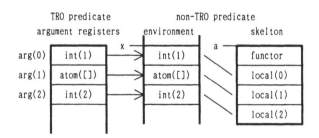

(2) Goal Molecule Construction

Fig. 7. Argument Passing

6 System

6.1 Software Components

C-Prolog Compiler system comprises six packages of programs, each of which is written in Prolog itself. A function and overview of each package is shown below:

1) comp package 150 lines
   This package integrates all of the packages depicted below, and offers user interface.
2) plm package 300 lines
   This package parses a source program, and generates a PLM code.
3) gen package 450 lines
   This package translates the PLM code into an assembly code.
4) apis package 250 lines
   This package translates an optimized PLM code into an assembly code.
5) subr package 700 lines
   This package is a collection of subroutine programs which are used by the compiled code.
6) asm package 550 lines
   This package produces a relocatable code from the assembly code.
7) load package 200 lines
   This package loads the relocatable code into a memory.

6.2 Modifications of C-Prolog Interpreter

Modifications of C-Prolog interpreter were about 150 lines, an outline of each modification is shown below.

1) Memory Management
   A code heap area is added to the original memory allocation. The area is used to store compiled predicates.
2) Built-in Predicate
   Seven built-in predicates are introduced into the original C-Prolog interpreter. These predicates are used to load compiled predicates.
3) Dispatcher
   Three dispatchers are introduced into the original C-Prolog interpreter. They are used to transfer control between interpreted predicates and compiled predicates.

7 PERFORMANCE

The benchmark results contained herein were gathered by running C-Prolog compiler on an MV/8000II with 4M bytes of physical memory. The benchmark programs are 'nreverse' and 'qsort' (Okuno 1985). Each program performs 496 LI and 609 LI, respectively. The result of the benchmark is shown in Table 1. The execution time is measured by CPU time, and LIPS means a Logical Inference Per Second.

The compiled predicates which are optimized run approximately 16 times as fast as the interpreted predicates, and are also approximately 3 times as fast as the compiled predicates which are not optimized.

	TIME (ms)	LIPS	RATE
Interpreted Predicate	280.0	1.77K	1
Compiled Predicate (non-TRO)	53.3	9.31K	5.3
Compiled Predicate (TRO)	20.0	24.80K	14.0

(1) nreverse

	TIME (ms)	LIPS	RATE
Interpreted Predicate	430.0	1.42K	1
Compiled Predicate (non-TRO)	68.3	8.91K	6.3
Compiled Predicate (TRO)	26.5	23.00K	16.2

(2) qsort

Table 1. The result of the Benchmark

8 Concluding Remarks

We have shown our approach on C-Prolog compiler implementation. C-Prolog compiler provides both highly interactive environment to develop a program and high performance to execute a program. Because of these features, C-Prolog compiler becomes our work-bench for AI research.

We are currently working on the C-Prolog compiler to improve it efficiently. Most of the essentials are already complete, but much detailed work remains to be done, and we make all necessary preparations for porting C-Prolog compiler to a SUN-3 workstation.

References

Okuno HG (1985) The proposal of the benchmarks for The Third Lisp Contest and The First Prolog Contest. No.28-4, Report of WGSYM. IPSJ
Pereira F (1984) C-Prolog User's Manual. Dept. of Architecture University of Edinburgh
Pereira LM, Pereira FCN, Warren DHD (1978) User's Guide to DECsystem-10 Prolog. Dept. of Artificial Intelligence University of Edinburgh
Warren DHD (1980a) Implementing Prolog - compiling predicate logic programs. Research Reports 39 & 40. Dept. of Artificial intelligence University of Edinburgh
Warren DHD (1980b) Improved Prolog Implementation Which Optimises Tail Recursion. Research Paper No.141. Dept. of Artificial intelligence University of Edinburgh
Warren DHD (1983) An Abstract Prolog Instruction Set. Technical Note 309. SRI International

A Framework for
Interactive Problem Solving
based on Interactive Query Revision

Masaru Ohki, Akikazu Takeuchi and Koichi Furukawa

ICOT Research Center,
Institute for New Generation Computer Technology,
Mita Kokusai Bldg. 21F, 1-4-28, Mita,
Minato-ku, Tokyo, 108, Japan

Abstract

Logic programming has been widely used because of the clearness of its semantics and its extensibility. Many inference systems have been proposed using a logic programming framework. But few of these have studied logic based man-machine interaction, apart from systems based on incremental query [Emden 1985]. Incremental query allows users to enter a part of queries incrementally instead of entering the whole query at once, as in Prolog. In this paper we investigate essential concepts of interactive problem solving and generalize incremental query further. And we propose a new query model for logic programming, which we call interactive query revision. Interactive query revision allows a user to modify queries and hypotheses and to act as a part of the inference engine, in addition to entering queries incrementally. We apply interactive query revision to an interactive LSI layout system.

1. Introduction

It has been claimed that logic programming provides a powerful framework for building inference systems. The theorem-proving capability of logic programming languages is the starting point for logic-based inference systems. The methodology for realizing inference in an expert system by computation in logic programming languages was discussed in an early work on a logic-based expert system [Clark 1982].

Basically, an inference system consists of an inference engine and a rule base. An inference engine is the kernel of the system performing basic inference. A rule base is a database of inference rules. The important characteristics of inference systems are usually all realized in their inference engines. They are the explanation facility, handling of certainty factors, query facilities used when some information is missing, multiple rule bases, frames and so on.

Logic programming has provided new concepts not only for basic inference mechanisms but also for such extended features as those listed above, which

are essential in inference systems. In APES [Hammond 1983], explanation facilities are realized by meta-level operations on the proof tree. Shapiro proposes an efficient debugging method for rules [Shapiro 1983a] and a meta-interpreter to handle certainty factors [Shapiro 1983b]. Sergot [Sergot 1983] introduced an open world assumption in his logic-based expert system in order to realize query facilities naturally if inference fails without additional information. Several researchers [Nakashima 1982, Poole 1985, Bowen 1985] introduce multiple theory models to form bases for hypothetical inference. Frame-based representation of knowledge in a logic programming language was introduced in CIL [Mukai 1985], based on situation semantics. Partial evaluation of logic programs [Takeuchi 1985] made possible customization of inference engines and rule compilations. Emden introduced a new computation model called the query interaction model, facilitating a mixed languages environment [Emden 1984].

These are just some of the many proposals for inference engines. However, almost all of them are related to logic-based inference mechanisms and, as yet, apart from [Emden 1984], no studies have directly confronted the problem of logic-based models of environments including man-machine interaction. Emden introduced a new standpoint from which logic can be seen as an interaction language and his concept of the incremental query represents a new type of query for logic programs. Emden also proved that incremental query can be a strong basis when building universally accessible interfaces for logic programs such as spreadsheets [Emden 1985].

In practical applications, many problems cannot be given as a set of goals at once. To model the whole human problem solving task, it has to be considered in two modes, horizontal and vertical modes. The horizontal mode represents the top-level tasks of problem solving such as detailed specification of the problem, only roughly specified at first, and examination of the solutions under several variations of the original problem. It often happens that the problem to be solved is too weakly specified. A user has to specify the problem in more detail in order to solve the problem by computer. Since there are many possibilities in describing the details of the problem, the user has to try to specify the problem in various ways. Furthermore the problem to be solved changes over time as the user observes the solutions under several variations of the original problem and comes to better understand the properties of the problem. In fact, problems people have in mind are very vague and can only be specified weakly. This is where the horizontal mode of problem solving comes into play. At the moment this phase is performed by the users themselves.

The vertical mode of problem solving involves solving a problem that is well specified in the horizontal mode. Many concepts have been invented to model this kind of problem solving task in the computer, such as common sense reasoning, ambiguous reasoning using certainty factors, hypothetical reasoning, default reasoning, qualitative reasoning and so on.

As stated above, there are many contributions from logic programming to the vertical mode of problem solving, but only a few address the horizontal mode. When a transformed problem cannot be solved or its solution is not satisfiable, the user has to change the detail of the problem specification added during transformation. Thus, the problem specification task is still the heavier task, even if the computer assists users in the vertical mode. We believe that "logic for problem solving" has to be extended to "logic for interactive problem solving."

In this paper, we present a new query model for logic programs to assist users in the horizontal mode of problem solving and establish ideal man-machine interaction for interactive problem solving. Our new query model is called interactive query revision model. It is based on the previous work, incremental query, of Emden et al. [Emden 1984, 1985]. They suggested that incremental query could use for interactive problem solving. But they did not investigate interactive problem solving in detail because incremental query aimed at the implementation of spreadsheet. We investigate essential concepts for interactive problem solving and we propose interactive query revision model, which realizes the concepts.

In Section 2 we describe the difficulties of current problem solving systems from the viewpoint of interaction between man and machine. In Section 3, we introduce the interactive query revision model for Prolog [Bowen 1982] and outline an implementation. Section 4 shows how interactive query revision is applied to an interactive LSI layout system and how it solves the problems described in Section 2.

2. Difficulties of problem solving and new concepts to solve them

(1) Observation 1:
The user does not know exactly what he wants in the solution.

In general, users do not know what they want exactly, however, they do know what they do not want. It is difficult for users to fully specify the problem, but easy for them to say "no" when they see unacceptable 'solutions'. For example, when a user starts to lay out an LSI, he does not often know the detailed specification and he determines these details as he goes along. If he found the LSI unsatisfactory, he may design it over again or add new constraints. In order to support such users, we need the concept of "open constraints" allowing users to add new constraints incrementally. The incremental query model is the first to realize open constraints. In the incremental query model, when the solution obtained based on the constraints entered up to a given point is unsatisfactory, the user can add constraints that exclude the solution proposed at that point as new increments.

(2) Observation 2:
The user wants to know the relation between solutions and constraints/hypotheses.

There are two ways in which a problem is said to be weakly specified. The first is that the goal to be solved is vague. The second is that the rules and facts are incomplete and contain hypotheses. If the problem initially given is weakly specified, the solutions of the problem conceptually form a set, each element of which is a solution of the strictly specified version of the original problem. There is no way to obtain the whole set of solutions for a weakly specified problem, since computers can only solve strictly specified problems. For example, in the case of LSI layout a user may want to design the best LSI among those satisfying the weak specification. Instead of directly solving the weakly specified problem, we propose the concept of "variation of solution" to allow the user to see the variations in solutions resulting from slightly modifying parts of constraints or hypotheses and select the most desirable from among them. Now, even if the user has only a vague problem in mind, he can examine solution variations with respect to several constraints or several hypotheses and find the most acceptable candidate in the set of solutions.

(3) Observation 3:
The user does not perform a function as part of the inference engine.

The inference engine is usually incomplete. In fact, it is impossible to build the perfect inference engine based on current technology. For example, a system for laying out LSIs may not include information on their sale conditions. But this is often important to designers. Instead of making a perfect inference engine, we propose a concept of the "combination of computer and man." It provides a mechanism to allow users to act as a part of inference engine. Even when the system fails to solve a part of problem, appropriate action by the user can keep the system going until it succeeds in solving the problem. This mechanism is convenient when the problem to be solved partially exceeds the range of the rule base. Of course, even if the user has the opportunity to act as a part of the inference engine, he may not solve the relevant part of the problem. Nevertheless, it is clear that a mechanism to add the power of the human brain will significantly enrich the system.

3. Interactive Query Revision

3.1 Interactive Query Revision Model

A query of Prolog is a set of goals such as the following:
$?\text{-}\ p,..,q.$
When this is entered, the Prolog system solves it and replies yes with answer substitution if the goals succeed, or no if they do not. A user cannot interact with the Prolog system in the course of computation except at input/output, an extralogical feature of the Prolog system.

The incremental query model expands the Prolog query model so that queries can be incrementally added. The idea of incremental query is that instead of entering the whole goals, a user is allowed to enter parts of the goals incrementally as he sees the intermediate solution(substitution) of some of the queries entered so far. The incremental queries are of the following form: ('???--' is the prompt for the incremental queries.)
$\quad$???-- p.
$\qquad$<answer substitution for "p">
$\quad$???-- q.
$\qquad$<answer substitution for "p and q">
$\quad$???-- r.
$\qquad$<answer substitution for "p and q and r">
where "p","q" and "r" are queries entered by the user and <answer substitution>'s are responses from the system. These queries are equivalent the Prolog goals "p,q,r". <answer substitution for "p and q and r"> is equivalent to the answer substitution of Prolog for the goals "p,q,r". In incremental query, when a new query, Q_i, is given, the current (last) answer substitution S_{i-1} is applied to Q_i. The resultant query, $(Q_i)S_{i-1}$, is then solved and the updated answer substitution, S_i, is returned. If the query Q_i cannot be solved with the current substitution,S_{i-1}, backtracking occurs. The system tries to find alternative substitution S'_{i-1} by re-solved Q_{i-1} with S_{i-2}, so that $(Q_i)S'_{i-1}$ can be successfully solved. A variant of incremental query allowing the user to cancel parts of the queries already entered is given in [Emden 1985], and its implementation in Prolog is also described.

The interactive query revision model carries the idea of incremental query a step further. It allows a user to enter a query incrementally, insert a new query between previous queries, remove parts of queries or partially replace them. It also allows the user to add hypotheses to the program, and remove them or replace them in the program incrementally. These functions realize two of the concepts stated in Section 2, "open constraint" and "variation of solution." Whatever queries or hypotheses parts are modified, the logical validity of the solution is preserved in the interactive query revision model. Suppose the following queries
$\quad$???- p. ???- q. ???- r.
$\qquad$(Queries are written in the same line.)
have been given. If a user replaces the query "q" with "q1", the above queries change as follows:
$\quad$???- p. ???- q1. ???- r.
They are solved as if equivalent to Prolog goals "p,q1,r". If a hypothesis is added to the program after the queries "p" and "q" are solved:
$\quad$???- p. ???- q. ???- <added hypothesis>.
the solution of these queries is equal to the solution of the Prolog goals "p,q" in the program to which the hypothesis is added.

We introduce the special command, "user_interaction," to realize the third concept, "combination of computer and man." It allows users to help the system by giving a solution for a part of the problem in the form of queries, and allows them to act as part of the inference engine. Assigning a solution to an unbound variable, which cannot be determined by the system, is an example of an interaction with a user. Once the mechanism recognizing the user as a part of inference engine is introduced, it is obviously necessary that interactions with a user are treated in the same manner as other logical constructs. This means that on backtracking the system needs to be able to query the user for alternatives of the previous interaction. This kind of interaction with the users is logical and entirely different from conventional input/output, which is extralogical. When the "user_interaction" command is entered, a user is asked for the queries he has in mind at that moment. Suppose the following sequence of queries:
$\quad$???-- p. ???-- user_interaction. ???-- r.
where "q1" and "q2" are entered at "user_interaction." It is handled as if equal to the following sequence of queries:
$\quad$???- p. ???-- (q1;q2). ???-- r.
These goals,"q1" and "q2", are connected with disjunction, so the user can give alternative choices or instructions to the system. These alternatives are selected one by one when backtracking occurs. If all alternatives are exhausted, the user is asked to enter other alternatives. If the user replies with another alternative, say "q3", the query sequence is then as follows:
$\quad$?- p. ?- (q1;q2;q3). ?- r.

If the user wants to backtrack beyond "user_interaction," it is possible to pass to enter an alternative.

Interactive query revision is independent of inference systems since it assists users in the horizontal mode of problem solving. Therefore, we can use various inference systems operating in the vertical mode with the interactive query revision model.

3.2 Implementation

We have implemented the interactive query revision model based on the incremental query model. First we briefly describe an implementation of incremental query [Emden 1985].

The key point of the implementation of incremental query is the stack of elements consisting of an incrementally-entered query and its environment. The environment is a set of pairs of variable and value before the query is executed. The stack is used to simulate the backtracking mechanism so that incremental query can be processed just as in Prolog. An example of a stack is given in Figure 1. When a new query is added and fails under the current environment, the system starts to simulate backtracking. It moves back along the stack one by one, gets goals, and makes new goals by combining the previous goals and the current query. The new goals are solved as the Prolog goals. If the goals fail, the system resumes backtracking.

Incremental queries	Stack token forms	environments
X = 1	('X' = 1)	('X',__)
Y = 2	('Y' = 2)	('X',1),('Y',__)
Z = 3	('Z' = 3)	('X',1),('Y',2),('Z',__)

Figure 1 An example of incremental queries the content of the stack

We have enhanced incremental query to implement interactive query revision. We added the following mechanisms to modify queries: (1) editing a stack to insert, remove and replace queries, (2) recalculating modified queries, (3) reforming a new stack. Modification of hypotheses is currently implemented by modifying the program in the global database of Prolog. When hypotheses are modified, for example, when a hypothesis is added to a program, all queries must be recalculated because it is difficult to know which queries can use the hypothesis.

The "user_interaction" command takes in solutions inferred by the user in query form. When backtracking occurs, the user interaction is also redone. If all solutions inferred by the user have

been tried,' the user is asked to enter other alternatives. The user can enter one of the following:
(1) a new alternative
   Add a new alternative to current alternatives.
(2) pass
   Leave the set of alternatives as it is at that moment and propagate backtracking beyond the "user_interaction" command.
(3) temporarily close
   Leave the set of alternatives as it is during execution of the current query and propagate backtracking beyond the command.
(4) close
   Leave the set of alternatives as it is and propagate backtracking beyond the command.

4. Application of interactive query revision to an LSI layout system

An LSI chip layout is a typical example of problem solving using computers. The system considered here lays out three kinds of component blocks, CPU, ROM and RAM, on LSI, as shown in Figure 2. It is written in CIL [Mukai 1985] and has two types of knowledge. One is the knowledge to lay out an LSI and the other is the knowledge about the component blocks. CIL is a logic programming language. Compared with Prolog, it is augmented with the "freeze" primitive [Colmerauer 1982] and an association list. An association list is denoted by "{A1/V1,..,An/Vn}", where Ai is an attribute name and Vi is its associated value. Unification of two association lists only succeeds if the values of their common attributes can be unified, in which case their attributes are merged. Otherwise, unification fails. Access to an attribute A of an association list X is denoted by the primitive function "X!A". The "freeze" primitive suspends goals with respect to a variable until the variable(called the frozen variable) becomes instantiated. A question mark, "? ", is attached to a frozen variable.

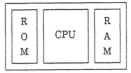

Figure 2 An example of LSI chip layout

The rules for LSI layout are described as constraints using the "freeze" primitive of CIL. One of the rules for laying three component blocks on an LSI is shown in Figure 3. An LSI chip is described as an association list containing LSI type, right, center and left component, width(w) and length(l) of the LSI, and its cost. The width and length of a component block are determined by constraints in "arrangement31_constraint." It expresses conditions such as, if the length of the left component is not given it is set equal to the length of the LSI. If

```
arrangement(LSI,[A,B,C]) :-
   !, arrangement3(LSI,[A,B,C]).
arrangement3(LSI,[A,B,C]) :-      arrange3([A,B,C],[Right,Center,Left]),
   LSI = {type/lsi3l,right/Right,center/Center,left/Left,w/W,l/H,cost/Cost},
   cost(Cost,W,H,[Right,Center,Left]),
   arrangement31_constraint(Right,Center,Left,W,H).
arrangement31_constraint(Right,Center,Left,W,H) :-
   constraint_ge(H,Left!l),
   constraint_ge(H,Center!l),
   constraint_ge(H,Right!l),
   constraint_add(W,Center!w,Right!w,Left!w).
```

Figure 3 Part of the knowledge for LSI chip layout

```
ram(RAM) :-
   Type = ram4, Access = 200, PerSpace = 6, PerCost = 2,
   template_ram(RAM,Type,Access,PerSpace,PerCost).
template_ram(RAM,Type,Access,PerSpace,PerCost) :-
   RAM = {type/Type,w/W1,l/H1,capacity/Capacity,
   r_capacity/R_Capacity, access_time/Access,cost/Cost},
   (W1?) :> 0, (H1?) :> 0,
   or_freeze([([H1,W1],ram1(Capacity,H1,W1,R_Capacity,PerSpace)),
             ([Capacity,H1],ram2(W1,H1,Capacity,R_Capacity,PerSpace)),
             ([Capacity,W1],ram2(H1,W1,Capacity,R_Capacity,PerSpace))]),
   Cost :== (R_Capacity?) * PerCost.
```

Figure 4 Part of the knowledge on RAM

it is specified, its value is checked to make sure it is less than or equal to the length of the LSI. The widths of components and the LSI are determined by the constraint that the width of the LSI is greater than or equal to sum of the widths of components. Figure 4 shows one of the rules for a component RAM. A RAM is also described as an association list containing RAM type, width and length, requested capacity and actual capacity, access time and cost. The reason why a RAM association list contains actual capacity as an attribute is that actual capacity is not always equal to requested capacity, because its shape is restricted to a rectangle. If any two of the values for width, length and requested capacity are specified, the rest is determined from them. The cost of the RAM can be determined if actual capacity is given.

Let us start to lay out an LSI chip, even though we do not completely know all the constraints. The constraints for LSI layout we have at first are as follows:

(1) The size of the LSI chip is roughly 30mm wide and 20mm long.

(2) The LSI has at least CPU and ROM.

(3) The most efficient layout should be produced.
The scenario in which we lay out an LSI chip is as follows:

(1) First, CPU and ROM are arranged on the LSI with 30mm wide and 20mm long.

(2) RAM is then placed in the remaining space.

(3) The LSI layout system does not possess knowledge on the reasonable cost/performance ratio, which is one of sale conditions of the LSI, so we pose it to the system by "user interaction."

(4) If a proposed layout fails, we try to hypothesize a new type of ROM.

(5) Using the new type of ROM we continue to lay out by trial and error to improve the design.

Now let us lay out the LSI chip. Some configurations of LSI are shown in Figure 5. Statements begun by "%" explain the course of design, and statements parenthesized by "(" and ")" are other comments.

```
| ?- iq.
      % First we try to set the width and the length of LSI to 30mm
      %and 20mm respectively.
??- LSI!w=30,LSI!l=20.
LSI = {w/30,l/20}          ("{ }" is an association list.)
             (Figure 5 (1) shows the chip at this point.)
      % Arrange two components, CPU and ROM, on the LSI.
???-- arrangement(LSI,[CPU,ROM]).
             :        (A display of values of variables is omitted.)
      % Assign substantial CPU and ROM to variables CPU and ROM
      %respectively.
???-- cpu(CPU),rom(ROM).
             :
             (Figure 5 (2) shows the chip at this point.)
      % Attempt to set ROM capacity to 300 bytes.
```

```
???--   ROM!capacity=300.
LSI = {w/30,1/20,cost/3200,type/lsi2,right/{cpu1},left/{rom1}}
CPU = {cost/2000,w/1,1/20,type/cpu1,perform/100}
ROM = {cost/600,capacity/300,access_time/100,w/15,1/20,type/rom1,r_capacity/300}
            % The first version of layout was obtained.
            %What is the space-utilization efficiency of the LSI?
???--   space(LSI,Space).
            :
Space = 53
                    (Figure 5 (3) shows the chip at this point)
            % Space-utilization efficiency is 53 %, it is very low.
            %It is necessary to redo the layout. First, let us take a look at
            %ail queries so far using the list_queries command.
???--   list_queries.
----------------------
[0]  space(LSI,Space)
----------------------
[1]  ROM!capacity=300
----------------------
[2]  cpu(CPU),rom(ROM)
----------------------
[3]  arrangement(LSI,[CPU,ROM])
----------------------
[4]  LSI!w=30,LSI!1=20
            % Attempt to change the capacity of ROM.  This attempt is an example
            %of "variation of solutions."  It is performed by the "replace_query"
            %command.  We replace an old query ROM!capacity=300 by a new query
            %ROM!capacity=500.  The argument of the command  indicates
            %the number of the query in the queries list above.
            %When the query is replaced, all queries after that query are
            %re-solved. That is, [1] and [0] in the above list are solved again.
???--   replace_query(1).
 >> Enter a query :   ROM!capacity=500.
            :
Space = 86
            % There is still space left. Now let us try to place RAM on the LSI.
            %We replace "arrangement(LSI,[CPU,ROM])" by
            %"arrangement(LSI,[CPU,ROM,RAM])".
???--   replace_query(3).
 >> Enter a query :   arrangement(LSI,[CPU,ROM,RAM]).
            :
            % Assign substantial RAM to a variable RAM.
???--   ram(RAM).
            :
            % Add a constraint specifying reasonable cost/performance ratio
            %from the point of view of expert designers
            %before we specify the RAM capacity.  Definition of the reasonable
            %ratio differs with designers and over time, and this system
            %does not have such knowledge. Enter constraints using
            %"user interaction" so that we can add alternative constraints
            %on backtracking.
???--   user_interaction.
 >> Enter comment for user interaction :
 'reasonable cost/performance ratio'
 >> Enter user_interaction query(or close/pass/temp_close) :
CPU!perform=100,ge(RAM!capacity,100),le(LSI!cost,4500).
                    ("ge" is "greater than or equal to,"
                     and "le" is "less than or equal to.")
 >> Enter user_interaction query(or close/pass/temp_close) :
CPU!perform=150,ge(RAM!capacity,50),le(LSI!cost,7000).
 >> Enter user_interaction query(or close/pass/temp_close) :
 pass.
            :
            % Now make the RAM capacity 100 bytes.
???--   RAM!capacity=100,
            :
Space = 96
                    (Figure 5 (4) shows the chip at this point.)
            % A layout is completed. But there is still space left.  Since we
            %should use the LSI space efficiently, we try to increase
            %the RAM capacity.
```

```
???--  replace_query(0).
 >> Enter query :  RAM!capacity=200.
        % Backtracking is invoked because the replaced queries fail.
        %At "user_interaction," we are asked whether we have other
        %alternative constraints.  We enter an alternative constraint as it
        %occurs to us just now looking at indeterminate solutions.
 ** Comment of user_interaction = reasonable cost/performance ratio
 >> Enter user_interaction query(or close/pass/temp_close) :
 CPU!perform=100,ge(RAM!capacity,200),le(LSI!cost,5000).
        %Backtracking occurs again and we are
        %asked still more for alternative constraints, but we temporarily
        %close interaction because we do not have any alternatives.
        %Backtracking propagates to queries before the "user_interaction."
 ** Comment of user_interaction = reasonable cost/performance ratio
 >> Enter user_interaction query(or close/pass/temp_close) :
 temp_close.
LSI = {w/30,l/20,cost/4080,type/lsi31,center/{rom1},right/{ram2},center/{rom1}}
CPU = {cost/2000,l/20,w/1,type/cpu1,perform/100}
ROM = {cost/1000,capacity/500,access_time/100,l/20,w/25,
                                        type/rom1,r_capacity/500}
RAM = {cost/480,capacity/200,access_time/100,l/20,w/3,type/ram2,r_capacity/240}
Space = 96
        % The LSI layout system selected another type of RAM.  There is
        %space left yet.  Attempt to increase the RAM capacity further.
???--  replace_query(0).
 >> Enter query :  RAM!capacity=400.
        % Backtracking occurs, but we do not have any alternative
        %conditions.  Close interaction.
 ** Comment of user_interaction = reasonable cost/performance ratio
 >> Enter user_interaction query(or close/pass/temp_close) :
 close.
LSI = {w/30,l/20,cost/4560,type/lsi31,center/{rom1},right/{cpu1},left/{ram4}}
CPU = {cost/2000,l/20,w/1,type/cpu1,perform/100}
ROM = {cost/1000,capacity/500,access_time/100,l/20,w/25,
                                        type/rom1,r_capacity/500}
RAM = {cost/960,capacity/400,access_time/200,l/20,w/4,type/ram4,r_capacity/480}
Space = 100
                    (Figure 5 (5) shows the chip at this point.)
        % We try to improve the layout.
                 :
                    (Several queries are omitted.)
        % First, we attempted to reduce the size of the LSI to 22mm wide
        %and 20mm long.  The system laid out LSI using other
        %components.  So space was generated.  We tried to increase the RAM
        %capacity to 500 bytes.  There was still space left.
        %We also tried to increase the ROM to 600 bytes.  But the access time
        %of RAM became 200ns.  The access time must be less than
        %or equal to 100ns.  So we added a new constraint for the access time.
        %We did not know the detailed specification relating to the
        %access time at first, but it was clear that the solution was
        %unsatisfactory.  We removed the unsatisfactory solution by
        %adding a new constraint. Now ROM access time became 200ns also.
                 :
        %We add a new constraint that the access time of ROM must be less than
        %or equal to 100ns.
???--  le(ROM!access_time,100).
I cannot solve the following queries.
-----------------------
[0]  le(ROM!access_time,100)
-----------------------
[1]  le(RAM!access_time,100)
-----------------------
[2]  RAM!capacity=500
-----------------------
[3]  user( CPU!perform=100,ge(RAM!capacity,100),le(LSI!cost,4500);
     CPU!perform=150,ge(RAM!capacity,50),le(LSI!cost,7000);
     CPU!perform=100,ge(RAM!capacity,200),le(LSI!cost,5000))
-----------------------
```

```
[4]   ram(RAM)
-----------------------
[5]   space(LSI,Space)
-----------------------
[6]   ROM!capacity=600
-----------------------
[7]   cpu(CPU),rom(ROM)
-----------------------
[8]   arrangement(LSI,[CPU,ROM,RAM])
-----------------------
[9]   LSI!w=22,LSI!l=20
         % The layout failed.  But, we want to know how the layout changes
         %if we provide a new type of ROM.  We add the new type of ROM
         %as a hypothesis using the "add_hypo" command.
???--   add_hypo.
 >> Enter hypothetical clause (or end) :
 rom(ROM) :- template_rom(ROM,rom0,100,3,1).
         % We use a template clause for ROM to define a new ROM,
         %whose type, access time, capacity per space and capacity
         %per cost are rom0, 100ns, 3 and 1 respectively.
 >> Enter hypothetical clause (or end) :
 end.

LSI   = {w/22,l/20,center/{rom0},cost/4160,type/lsi31,right/{cpu1},left/{ram2}}
CPU   = {cost/2000,l/20,w/1,type/cpu1,perform/100}
ROM   = {cost/600,capacity/600,access_time/100,l/20,w/10,type/rom0,r_capacity/600}
RAM   = {cost/1120,capacity/500,access_time/100,l/20,w/7,type/ram2,r_capacity/560}
Space = 81
                   (Figure 5 (6) shows the chip at this point.)
         % Attempt to reduce the cost of the LSI.
???--   le(LSI!cost,4000).
                   :
Space = 90
                   (Figure 5 (7) shows the chip at this point.)
         % Attempt to reduce its cost further.
???--   le(LSI!cost,2800).
I cannot solve the following queries.
                   :
         % The layout failed.  How would it be if we reduced the size of
         %the LSI.
???--   replace_query(11).
  >> Enter query :  LSI!w=22,LSI!l=18.
LSI   = {w/22,l/18,center/{rom0},cost/2752,type/lsi31,right/{cpu2},left/{ram2}}.
CPU   = {cost/700,l/18,w/3,type/cpu2,perform/100}
ROM   = {cost/648,capacity/600,access_time/100,l/18,w/12,type/rom0,r_capacity/648}
RAM   = {cost/1008,capacity/500,access_time/100,l/18,w/7,type/ram2,r_capacity/504}
Space = 100
                   (Figure 5 (8) shows the chip at this point.)
         % We may try to get a far better LSI while changing conditions.
                   :
                   (Several queries are omitted.)
                   :
         %We tried to reduce the cost and the size.  But we cannot get
         %a better LSI than the previous one.
         %We ought to be content with the previous layout.
```

We have completed a LSI layout, though we did not know the full detailed specification for the LSI at first. CPU and ROM were laid out first on the LSI chip, but we found that there was space left. So we placed a RAM on the LSI. Next, we modified the constraints while looking at the intermediate solutions to get a better LSI. Modification was easy using interactive query revision. We also wanted to take account of the cost/performance ratio, but the system does not have such knowledge because it differs with designers and over time. We input it to the system using "user interaction" keeping an eye on intermediate solutions. It might be difficult for even an expert designer to find it without considering the intermediate solutions. When a layout failed, we added one hypothesis to know how solutions varied using a new type of ROM. Finally, we got a satisfactory LSI. If we had not used interactive query revision, we would have had to enter many sets of goals to the LSI chip layout system and we might not have been able to include knowledge the system did not have, such as the reasonable cost/performance ratio.

It may not be easy to see the output of variables in this example. But it can be easily enhanced by connecting a special output subsystem, like the incremental query system connected to the spreadsheet interface described in [Emden 1985].

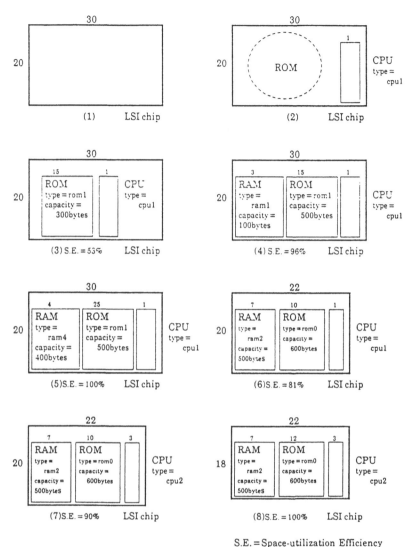

S.E. = Space-utilization Efficiency

Figure 5 LSI Configuration

5. Concluding remarks

In this paper we discussed the contribution of logic programming to inference systems and pointed out that one phase of problem solving has been ignored, which is quite indispensable from the viewpoint of interactive problem solving. The limitations of current problem solving systems are obtained from the following observations: (1) The user does not exactly know what he wants in the solution. (2) The user wants to know the relation between solutions and constraints/hypotheses. (3) The user does not perform a function as part of the inference engine. An alternative query model called the interactive query revision model was introduced to resolve these issues. Using an LSI chip layout system, it was shown how our query model has achieved man-machine interaction in a satisfactory manner, and how it can solve a problem interactively under cooperation between the user and the computer.

We developed our query model on a Prolog system. Since this query model is general, we plan to combine it with a powerful inference system that can perform various inference functions such as common sense reasoning, ambiguous reasoning using certainty factors, hypothetical reasoning, default reasoning, qualitative reasoning and so on.

Acknowledgment

We wish express our thanks to Prof. M.H. van Emden for introducing us to this research field. And we wish express our thanks to Kazuhiro Fuchi, Director of ICOT Research Center, who provided us with the opportunity of doing this research in the Fifth Generation Computer Systems Project at ICOT. We would also like to thank Kuniaki Mukai, who patiently taught us CIL, and the ICOT research staff.

References

[Bowen 1982] D.L.Bowen, L.M.Pereira, F.C.N.Pereira and D.H.D.Warren: User's guide to DECsystem-10 Prolog. Dept of Artificial Intelligence, University of Edinburgh (1982).

[Bowen 1985] K.Bowen, T.Weinberg: A Meta-Level Extension of Prolog, Technical Report CIS-85-1, Syracuse University (1985).

[Colmerauer 1982] A.Colmerauer: Prolog II: Reference Manual and Theoretical Model,Internal Report, Groupe Intelligence Artificielle, Universite d'Aix-Marseille II, (1982).

[Emden 1984] M.H.Emden: Logic as an Interaction Language, Proc. of 5th Conf. Canadian Soc. for Computational Studies in Intelligence (1984).

[Emden 1985] M.H.Emden, M.Ohki, A.Takeuchi: Spreadsheet with Incremental Queries as a User Interface for Logic Programming, ICOT Technical Report (1985).

[Mukai 1985] K.Mukai, H.Yasukawa: Complex Indeterminates in Prolog and its Application to Discourse Models, New Generation Computing, 3, pp441-466 (1985).

[Nakashima 1982] H.Nakashima: Prolog/KR - languages features, Proc. of the First International Logic Programming Conference, (1982).

[Poole] D.Pools, R.Aleliunas, R.Goebel: Theorist: a logical reasoning system for defaults and diagnosis, Waterloo University (1985).

[Sergot 1983] Marek Sergot: A Query-The-User for Logic Programming, Proc. of the European Conference on Integrated Computing Systems, P. Degano and E. Sandewall (eds.), North Holland, 1983.

[Shapiro 1983a] E.Shapiro: Algorithmic Program Debugging, The MIT Press, 1983

[Shapiro 1983b] E.Shapiro: Logic Programs with Uncertainties: A Tool for Implementing Rule-based Systems, Proc. of IJCAI'83, 1983

[Takeuchi 1985] A.Takeuchi, K.Furukawa: Partial Evaluation of Prolog Programs and its Application to Meta Programming, Proc. of Logic Programming Conference'85 (Tokyo), (1985). .

Prolog Computation Model BPM and its debugger PROEDIT2

Shinichi Morishita   Masayuki Numao

IBM Tokyo Research Laboratory
5-19 Sanban-cho, Chiyoda-ku, Tokyo 102 JAPAN

Abstract

This paper presents a debugger for Prolog 'PROEDIT2'. In order to express the complex execution mechanism of Prolog, a new execution model for Prolog 'BPM' is also proposed. PROEDIT2 shows the execution of Prolog in BPM notation.

1 INTRODUCTION

Since Prolog has a complex execution mechanism, a useful Prolog debugger must provide clear views of the execution process of Prolog. In this paper, in order to grasp the complex execution mechanism of Prolog, we propose a visual computation model BPM (Box and Plane Model) that clarifies the semantics of backtracking and cut operator in a visual way. Based on BPM, we have developed a visual debugger for Prolog PROEDIT2, which shows the execution of Prolog programs in BPM notation. PROEDIT2 first executes a goal and then displays the wider image of the execution in 2-dimensional way. This allows the user to get the global image of the execution of his program and find a shortcut to the bug.

In the following sections, we explain the details of BPM and PROEDIT2. In section 2, we discuss the complex features of Prolog execution upon which we have to concentrate, and then give an outline of a solution for these problems through BPM. Next, the definition of BPM is given, and its expressive power is shown using examples. Section 3 discusses the problems of other debuggers, introduces a Prolog debugger PROEDIT2, and shows how these problems are solved in PROEDIT2. The usage of PROEDIT2 is also presented.

2 BPM (BOX AND PLANE MODEL)

In this section, the important features of the execution model BPM are discussed, the symbols of BPM are presented, a real meaning is given for each symbol, and the expressive power of BPM is explained using some examples.

2.1 The features of BPM

The most popular execution model on which the usual debuggers are based is the box model (See Clocksin and Mellish 1981). Our model BPM is made through modifying and enhancing this box model. Therefore, before introducing BPM, we want to describe the merits and defects of the box model.

The box model gives a good representation of control flows through a given subgoal. In the box model, each goal or subgoal is represented by a box. The flow of control in and out of the boxes is represented by arrows which are named call, exit, redo and fail.

But this box model has problems. Since the box model restricts attention to one goal and represents it by a box, it cannot express the backtracking mechanism clearly. In other words, since each call of a predicate results in a change of variable binding, having only one box per predicate does not adequately represent the execution of the program. It is necessary to represent the relationship between each goal, so that the effect of changes over time should be clarified. Another problem of the box model is that it also cannot represent the scope and effect of the cut operator clearly. To be able to represent a cut operator's behavior, the box model needs to be modified and enhanced.

In order to represent these procedural aspects, such as backtracking mechanism and cut operator's behavior, the new computation model BPM is created out of the box model through modifying and enhancing it. BPM uses the same kind of symbols, boxes and arrows as the box model. But let's look at how it solves each of the problems. On the backtracking mechanism problem, the weak point of the box model is that its only interest is control flows of one subgoal. In our model BPM, the unit of interest is clauses which define the same predicate. Then this model shows the flow of control between subgoals in a clause by using 2-dimensional representation. It connects boxes corresponding to subgoals in clauses by arrows and represents control flows between boxes. These boxes are contained in a 'plane' that was introduced to express the internal control flow of an upper level box. With this 'plane', we can clearly catch the scope of the cut operator and its return place clearly in BPM.

2.2 Symbols

box There are two kinds of boxes. One is the head-box, and the other is the goal-box. A head-box is a rectangle of dotted lines. A goal-box is a rectangle of thin lines.

plane The plane contains boxes. It is a rectangle drawn by bold lines.

arrows There four different arrows, each of which has two names.

These symbols are shown in Fig. 1.

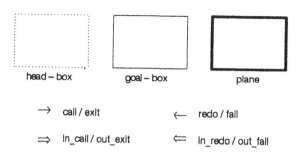

Fig. 1 Symbols of BPM

2.3 Representation of Prolog computation

Throughout this paper, we will use the following notations:

predicate name	g, g1, g2, ..., p, q, r, ...	**variable**	X, Y, Z, ...
term	T, T1, T2, S, ...	**goal**	g(T), ...
clause	g(T) ← g1(T1) & g2(T2) & ...	**execution of a goal**	← g(T).
substitution, unifier	θ, θ_1, θ_2	**substituting T to X**	T / X
composition of unifiers	$\theta_1 \circ \theta_2$		

Representation of goal execution

Let g(T) be a goal. To represent a control flow of goal g(T), a goal-box corresponding to g(T) is created, and then arrows, that is call, exit, redo and fail, are located around the goal-box. The meaning of each arrow is listed below. (See also Fig. 2)

call The initial invocation of goal g(T), with control passing into the box.

exit The goal was satisfied and that control moves out of the goal-box. In other words, the goal-box returns a result of the goal g(T), g(T) θ. We can think of it as returning a unifier θ.

redo Backtracking occurs in an attempt to find alternatives, so there is another invocation of the goal g(T).

fail The goal g(T) was not satisfied. Backtracking occurs.

The name of the goal-box corresponding to g(T) is called 'g'. We say that these arrows around the goal-box belong to it.

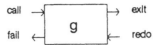

Fig. 2 Control flow of goal – box

Representation of the internal portion of goal-box

To represent the internal execution process of a goal-box, boxes and arrows are arranged in a 2-dimensional way. A plane contains these boxes and arrows. There is a unique plane which corresponds to a goal-box. In a plane, there is one head-box which represents clause selection processes. Execution of goals in a body are shown by goal-boxes and arrows where arrows connect goal-boxes.

Single arrows which belong to a goal-box are rewritten to be double arrows in the corresponding plane. That is, call($\rightarrow$), exit($\rightarrow$), redo($\leftarrow$), fail($\leftarrow$), which belong to a goal-box are represented by in_call($\Rightarrow$), out_exit($\Rightarrow$), in_redo($\Leftarrow$), out_fail($\Leftarrow$) respectively in the plane. The expressions in_call($\Rightarrow$) and in_redo($\Leftarrow$) stand for entrances into a plane. out_exit($\Rightarrow$) and out_fail($\Leftarrow$) stand for exits from a plane. (See also Fig. 3)

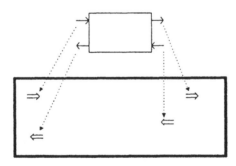

Fig. 3 Relationship between goal – box's
arrows and plane's arrows

Let g(T) be a goal. The clause selection process picks up a clause whose head can be unifiable with g(T). This process is represented by putting single arrows around a head-box. These single arrows are call($\rightarrow$), exit($\rightarrow$), redo($\leftarrow$) and exit($\leftarrow$) which have the same shape as those in a goal-box. These symbols however belong to a head-box and have different meanings. These are listed below. (See also Fig. 4)

call The Initial request for a clause whose head is unifiable with goal g(T).

exit The unifiable clause g(T0) $\leftarrow$ g1(T1) & ... was found. The unifier θ of T and T0 is returned.

redo Backtracking occurs in attempt to find an alternative clause, so there is another request for an unifiable clause.

fail No unifiable clause was found. So backtracking occurs.

The name of the head-box corresponding to g(T) is called 'g'. And we say that these arrows around the head-box belong to it.

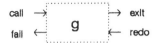

Fig. 4   Control flow of head – box

Next, we would like to explain the representation of the goal-box and plane with the following sample program.

```
descendant(X,Y) ← offspring(X,Y).
descendant(X,Z) ← offspring(X,Y) & descendant(Y,Z).
offspring(abraham,ishmael).
offspring(abraham,issac).
offspring(issac,esau).
offspring(issac,jacob).
```

Figure 5a shows the execution process of goal ← descendant(abraham,V) & fail in BPM. First, $\rightarrow_a$ invokes the goal-box descendant. Then the first result descendant(abraham,V)θ_b is returned to $\rightarrow_b$ where $\theta_b = $ ishmael/V. Successively, there are three invocations of the goal, that is $\leftarrow_c$, $\leftarrow_e$, $\leftarrow_g$, then results are returned to $\rightarrow_d$, $\rightarrow_f$, $\rightarrow_h$ respectively. These results are shown below.

$\rightarrow_d$ descendant(abraham,V)θ_d $\theta_d = $ issac/V
$\rightarrow_f$ descendant(abraham,V)θ_f $\theta_f = $ esau/V
$\rightarrow_h$ descendant(abraham,V)θ_f $\theta_f = $ jacob/V

Consequently, for the last invocation $\leftarrow_i$, the goal failed and $\leftarrow_j$ shows its failure.

Figure 5b shows the plane of the goal-box descendant from Fig. 5a. The single arrows $\rightarrow_a \sim \leftarrow_j$ of the goal-box descendant are expressed by the double arrows $\Rightarrow_a \sim \Leftarrow_j$ in the plane respectively. The clause selection process is shown by head-box descendant and the arrows belonging to it. The execution of goals of bodies in the selected clauses are shown by goal-boxes which follow the head-box.

152

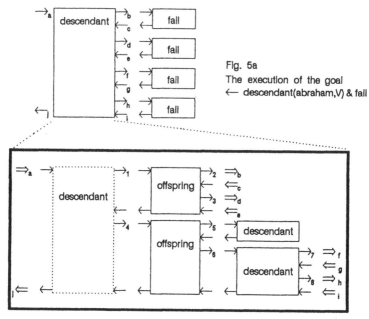

Fig. 5a
The execution of the goal
← descendant(abraham,V) & fail

Fig. 5b The Internal portion of the goal–box descendant

Fig. 5 Example of representation of control flow In BPM

Now let's check the details of the execution process and unification step by step. We want to restrict our attention to the arrows with a subscript in the plane.

$\rightarrow_1$ The first clause descendant(X,Y) ← offspring(X,Y) is chosen. A unifier $\theta_1 = \{$ abraham/X, Y/V $\}$ for descendant(abraham,V) and descendant(X,Y) is returned. Then θ_1 is applied to the selected clause. The goal of its body becomes offspring(abraham,Y). Next the goal-box of offspring(abraham,Y) is generated and put next to the head-box.

$\rightarrow_2$ The first result of the goal offspring(abraham, Y) is returned. The result is offspring(abraham, Y)θ_2 where $\theta_2 = \{$ ishmael/Y $\}$. Then no goal is left to be executed, so the flow of control exits from the plane, and $\Rightarrow_b$, is located next to $\rightarrow_2$.

$\Rightarrow_b$ This arrow corresponds to $\rightarrow_b$. Its result is descendant(abraham, V)θ_b where $\theta_b = \{$ishmael/V$\}$ as explained before. θ_b is obtained by restricting the variables of $\theta_1 \circ \theta_2 = \{$abraham/X, ishmael/Y, ishmael/V$\}$ to V.

$\rightarrow_3$ Next an answer is requested by $\Leftarrow_c$ and the goal offspring(abraham,Y) is invoked again. Then the alternative answer offspring(abraham,Y)θ_3 is returned where $\theta_3 = \{$issac/Y$\}$.

$\Rightarrow_d$ The exit $\Rightarrow_d$ is put next to $\rightarrow_3$ and it returns the result descendant(abraham,V)θ_d where $\theta_d = \{$issac/V$\}$. θ_d is obtained by restricting variables of $\theta_1 \circ \theta_3 = \{$abraham/X, issac/Y, issac/V$\}$ to V.

$\rightarrow_4$ Next backtracking occurs and the flow of control goes back to the head-box. Then the head-box selects another clause descendant(X,Z) $\leftarrow$ offspring(X,Y) & descendant(Y,Z) . And the unifier $\theta_4 = \{abraham/X,Z/V\}$ for the head of the clause chosen and descendant(abraham,V) is returned to $\rightarrow_4$. After applying θ_4 to the selected clause, the body of it becomes offspring(abraham,Y) & descendant(Y,Z). So the first goal offspring(abraham,Y) is chosen to be executed and its goal-box is generated and located next to $\rightarrow_4$.

$\rightarrow_5$ The first result offspring(abraham,Y)θ_5 of the goal offspring(abraham,Y) is returned to $\rightarrow_5$, where $\theta_5 = \{ishmael/Y\}$. Then θ_5 is applied to descendant(Y,Z), with the result that descendant(Y,Z)$\theta_5 = $ descendant(ishmael,Z). Then, the goal descendant(ishmael,Z) which is the second goal of offspring(abraham,ishmael) & descendant(ishmael,Z) is executed, but it fails. So backtracking occurs and the flow of control is returned to the goal-box offspring.

$\rightarrow_6$, $\rightarrow_7$, $\Rightarrow_f$ Successively, $\theta_6 = \{issac/Y\}$ is returned to $\rightarrow_6$ and $\theta_7 = \{esau/Z\}$ is returned to $\rightarrow_7$. Then the flow of control goes to $\Rightarrow_f$. This arrow returns the result descendant(abraham,V)θ_f where $\theta_f = \{esau/V\}$. θ_f can be obtained by restricting variables of $\theta_4 \circ \theta_6 \circ \theta_7 = \{abraham/X, esau/V, issac/Y, esau/Z\}$ to V.

$\rightarrow_8$, $\Rightarrow_h$ θ_8 is returned to $\rightarrow_8$. θ_h can be obtained by restricting variables of $\theta_4 \circ \theta_6 \circ \theta_8 = \{abraham/X, jacob/V, issac/Y, jacob/Z\}$ to V.

Representation of cut

Here we incorporate the cut operator into our framework. For cut, we prepare a special goal-box called the cut-box. If cut is invoked, the cut-box is created and it returns exit($\rightarrow$). If backtracking later returns to the cut and the cut-box is invoked by redo($\leftarrow$), it returns fail($\leftarrow$). Then out_fail($\Leftarrow$) is located next to fail($\leftarrow$). It means that the computation flow exits from the plane including the cut-box and goes to the upper plane (See Fig. 6).

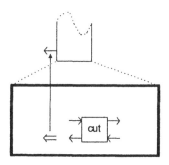

Fig. 6 meaning of cut operator

In this way, in BPM we can easily understand the scope of the cut. Furthermore if the computation flow backtracks to the cut and exits from the plane, we can catch the return place clearly. With BPM, we can see that cut offers a method for getting out of its plane at an intermediate place.

So let's turn to an example. The example program is 'not' and it is defined by using meta-call and cut as follows.

```
not(P) ← P & cut & fail.
not(P).
```

To clarify the difference between a case where cut is activated and one where cut does nothing, we will provide two figures. Figure 7a shows the execution of goal ← not(fail) . Figure 7b shows the execution of goal ← not(true) .

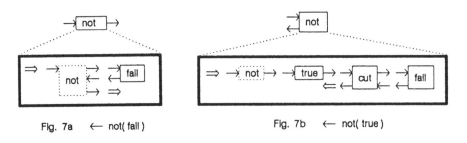

Fig. 7a ← not(fail)   Fig. 7b ← not(true)

Fig. 7 Example of execution of cut operator

Whole image of computation

In tree representations, the whole image of computation is a tree which consists of goals, and it is these units in which we are interested. In BPM, on the other hand, the goals are on planes and our interest focuses on these planes. So in BPM, the whole image is a tree which consists of planes (See Fig. 8). Each goal-box has its plane that is drawn under it. But no head-box is without a plane under it. So a leaf from this kind of tree is a plane which consists of only head-boxes.

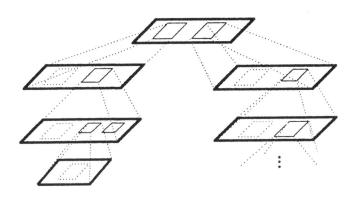

Fig. 8 Whole image of a computation

3 PROLOG DEBUGGER : PROEDIT2

In this section, we introduce PROEDIT2 which shows execution of Prolog programs in BPM notation. But before introducing PROEDIT2, we want to discuss some current approaches to debugging Prolog programs.

These seem to take two different approaches. One is to offer methods to follow the execution of the program faithfully, another is to use diagnostic programs.

An example of the former approach is the DEC-10 Prolog debugger, which uses the box model as the execution model. This kind of debugger outputs information too primitive to allow the user to grasp the global images of execution. It is especially difficult to follow backtracking. Furthermore, it usually takes many steps to reach the bug, because it follows the execution of the program faithfully. From these considerations, a useful debugger is needed to satisfy the following criteria:

- Represent global images of execution

- Offer methods not only to follow an execution faithfully, but also to reach the bug quickly

Diagnostic programs search through the computation tree of the program, and ask the user to verify each predicate. From this information, the source of the problem can be determined. Important works in this area include Algorithmic Program Debugging by Shapiro (1983), and Relational Debugging by Pereira (1984). But diagnostic approaches have some problems. The principal ones are that diagnostic approaches are not suitable for use on large programs since the debugging process is controlled by the system, and the system has the initiative of the debugging process. For a large program, it generates a large number of queries, which quickly frustrate the programmer. And these approaches meet with difficulty when the user tries to debug a program that includes side-effect predicates, such as those modifying rulebase, input and output predicates, etc. From these considerations, a useful debugger must also offer the following:

- Allow the user to take the initiative in debugging work

- Handle side-effect predicates

Our system PROEDIT2 was designed to satisfy these requirements. When the user executes a goal, the goal is executed once and PROEDIT2 creates the virtual image of its computation as Fig. 9a. The user starts debugging from the top of the planes. From these planes, the user selects planes that are necessary to be checked(See Fig. 9b). Each plane selected is displayed on the screen as a window. These selections are up to the user, the initiative of debugging rests with him rather than with the system. The content of a window is the execution flow of the program in BPM representation. Thus the user can get a global image of computation and need not follow the execution of Prolog faithfully, but can find short cuts to the bug.

In a window, the user can move the viewpoint to any arrow. This viewpoint is shown as the bold arrow in Fig. 9b. At the viewpoint, the user can check the binding of the goal specified and the state of rulebase at the point. In the Fig. 9b, Window 1 shows the names of the upper level goals of the viewpoint. The binding of the goal specified is shown in Window 2 . Window 3 shows the state of rulebase of the viewpoint. Thus, the user can get the various information from the viewpoint. If the user moves the viewpoint to the previous state, the system restores the state at the viewpoint. So programs including side-effect predicates can be handled in the system.

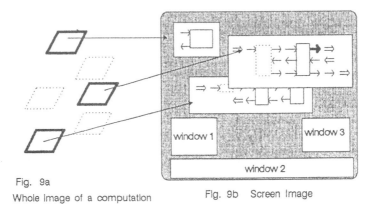

Fig. 9a
Whole Image of a computation

Fig. 9b   Screen Image

Fig. 9   Multi–window Interface

Here we show the usefulness of PROEDIT2 by using one example listed below. (In order to show the power of PROEDIT2, we intentionally put a bug in this program.)

```
push(Data) ← inc-index & push-on-stack(Data).
pop(Data) ← dec-index & pop-from-stack(Data).
init-index ← assert(index(0)).
inc-index ← retract(index(I)) & J := I + 1 & assert(index(J)).
dec-index ← retract(index(I)) & J := I - 1 & assert(index(J)).
push-on-stack(Data) ← index(I) & assert(stack(I,Data)).
pop-from-stack(Data) ← index(I) & retract(stack(I,Data)).
```

In this program, 'assert' and 'retract' are primitive predicates which modify the rulebase. Of these, assert(R) registers the clause R in the rulebase and retract(R) deletes the clause R' which matches with the clause R. The predicates 'push' and 'pop' realize the push and pop operations on the stack. The stack is realized as the global predicate 'stack(*,*)'. The first argument of the stack(*,*) stands for its index and the second argument is its data. The predicate 'index' contains the index which is the index of the top of stack.

Now let's execute the goal ← init-index & push(john) & push(morris) & pop(X) & pop(Y) in PROEDIT2. The screen of Fig. 10a will be created, and in this screen, the bold arrow shows the current viewpoint.

Suppose that we have moved the viewpoint to the exit arrow of the first goal-box of pop. Figure 10b shows its screen. In Window 2 of the screen, we can see the state of the exit arrow and this shows that the result of the pop(X) is pop(morris). But since we pushed john at the first and then pushed morris, john should have been popped. Furthermore Window3 shows the states of stack and index. These, however, are incorrect, because the content of 'index' does not point to the top of the stack, so something is wrong.

Now let's move the viewpoint to the entrance of the goal-box of pop. Fig. 10c shows the screen. At this point, Window 3 shows that the index points to the top of the stack. So we can see that this program operates correctly up to this point. From these observations, we can predict that something is wrong in the goal-box of pop. So let's expand the goal-box and look the inside of it. Fig. 10d shows the screen, and the new window corresponds to the plane which represents the internal control flow of the goal-box of pop. After expanding the goal-box, the viewpoint will be moved to the bold double arrow of the plane. Window 1 contains the goal 'pop' which creates the plane. In the plane, we can see that the predicate pop first tries to decrement the index and then pop the date of the top of stack. But in order to realize the pop operation, first the predicate 'pop' must pop the data and then decrement the index. This is the bug. To confirm this, let's move the viewpoint to the exit arrow of the goal-box dec-index (See Fig. 10e).

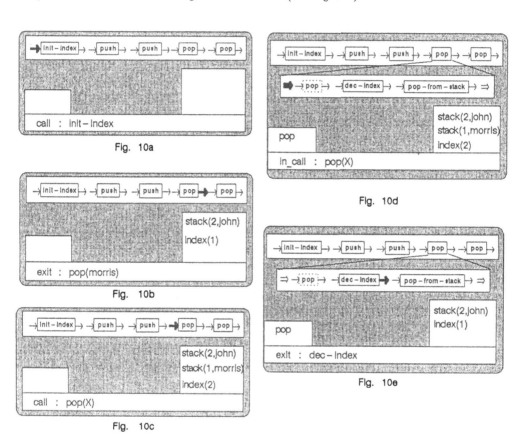

Fig. 10a

Fig. 10b

Fig. 10c

Fig. 10d

Fig. 10e

Fig. 10   Example of debugging work

4   CONCLUSION

This paper investigated the complex features of Prolog's execution mechanism and proposed the computation model BPM intended for the practical use. BPM forms the foundation of the debugger PROEDIT2.

PROEDIT2 was made by improving the previous version PROEDIT proposed by Numao and Fujisaki (1985). PROEDIT2 was developed as one of the programming environments of VM/PROLOG (VM/Programming in Logic: an IBM implementation of the Prolog programming language). It runs on color terminals, so that color coding is used to distinguish among types of flow of control. Its kernel component was implemented using VM/PROLOG and amounted to 2000 lines. Its multi-window interface component was implemented using a tool for building up interactive environments called INK (See Yokoi 1985). INK is written in the object-oriented language SPOOL proposed by Fukunaga and Hirose (1986).

We are now engaged in enhancing PROEDIT2 so that it can handle programs which go into a loop. Since this current version displays after execution, it cannot now handle these programs.

ACKNOWLEDGEMENTS

We would like to thank Tetsunosuke Fujisaki and Koichi Fukunaga for much useful discussion and encouragement. We would also like to thank Shinji Yokoi for helping us use his system INK.

REFERENCES

Clocksin W.F., Mellish C.S. (1981) Programming in Prolog, Springer-Verlag
Fukunaga K., Hirose S. (1986) An Experience with a Prolog-Based Object-Oriented Language,
    Proc. of the ACM Conf. on Object Oriented Programming Systems, Language and Applications
Numao M., Fujisaki T. (1985) Visual Debugger for Prolog,
    Proc. of the IEEE Second Conference on Artificial Intelligence Application, p422-427
Pereira L.M. (1984) Rational Debugging of Logic Programs,
    Department de Infomatica Universiade Nova de Lisboa
Shapiro E.Y. (1983) Algorithmic Program Debugging, MIT press
Yokoi S. (1986) Interactive Systems Kit: INK, Proc. of 32nd Annual Convention of IPSJ (in Japanese)

Fast Execution mechanisms of Parallel Inference Engine PIE: PIEpelined Goal Rewriting and Goal Multicasting

Hanpei KOIKE and Hidehiko TANAKA

Department of Electrical Engineering, Faculty of Engineering,
The University of Tokyo,
7-3-1, Hongo Bunkyo-ku, Tokyo 113, Japan

abstract

PIE is a highly parallel inference machine which executes logic programs based on the goal rewriting model. Goal rewriting makes goals completely independent and reduces access conflict, although it accompanies a substantial copying overhead. To cope with this overhead, two new execution mechanisms are proposed and evaluated. These methods are effective especially to raise parallelism quickly and to exploit other kind of parallelism in programs where OR-parallelism is not high.

1. Introduction

PIE [Mot84] is a highly parallel inference machine which executes logic programs based on OR-parallel processing. Two main features of PIE are the goal rewriting execution of logic programs, and the powerful activity control mechanism. In this paper, the architecture support of goal rewriting is discussed.

One of the main design points of parallel machines is whether data are to be copied to all the processors that need them, or to be shared among the processors. Copying brings overhead of data transfer between processors, while sharing is accompanied by access conflicts of shared data. Of course, the best choice is the appropriate mixture of the two extremes. However, it is clear that a highly parallel machine had better use more local copy to avoid access conflicts of shared data, and processing concentration on small number of processors. Therefore, we started our research from one of the extremes, i.e. a complete copying scheme, although some kinds of data are shared in our current model.

The point is that the copying overhead must be hidden and must not affect the execution time. This is true especially of programs where parallelism is not so high, and of the early stage of execution where parallelism has not been raised enough yet. To cope with the copying overhead, a fast execution mechanism is required based on a detailed analysis of execution time.

In the following sections, the basic concept of goal rewriting is introduced, the analysis of its execution time is discussed, and new execution mechanisms are proposed and evaluated.

2. The Parallel Inference Engine PIE and its Goal Rewriting Processing

2.1. The Parallel Inference Engine PIE

The Parallel Inference Engine PIE executes logic programs in an OR parallel processing manner based on the goal rewriting model [Got84]. Fig.1 shows the global architecture of PIE. 16 or more Inference Units (IU) share a structure memory (SM) and constructs a unit (level-1 system). Level-1 systems are connected by a network. Fig.2 shows the internal architecture of an IU. The functions of each element are as follows:

(1) Unify Processor (UP): UP rewrites goals by unification and reduction.

(2) Memory Module (MM): MM stores goals.

(3) Definition Memory (DM): DM stores definition clauses and supplies them to UP.

(4) Activity Controller (AC): AC maintains inference tree and controls the activity of goals.

2.2. Goal Rewriting Processing

The basic operation of PIE is goal rewriting. A goal frame (GF) which represents a goal is rewritten by a UP using a definition template (DT) which is an inner form of a definition clause. As a result, a new GF is generated. This processing corresponds to one cycle of inference. GF and DT consist of a literal part and a structure part. The smallest unit of them are called a cell.

The goal rewriting process is divided into two successive phases: unification and reduction [Yuh83]. In the unification phase, each argument of a literal in a GF is unified with the corresponding argument of a DT (Fig.3). In the reduction phase, the representation of the GF is compacted and copied, replacing the literal unified with the head literal of the DT in the unification phase with body literals of

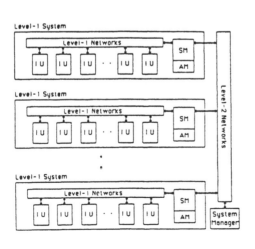

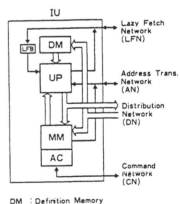

DM : Definition Memory
UP : Unify Processor
MM : Memory Module
AC : Activity Controller
LFB : Lazy Fetch Buffer

Fig.1 Global Architecture of PIE   Fig.2 Inference Unit

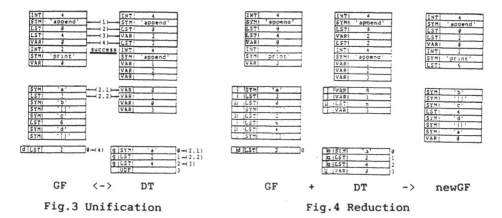

| GF | `<->` | DT | | GF | + | DT | `->` | newGF |

Fig.3 Unification   **Fig.4 Reduction**

the DT, and a new GF is generated (Fig.4). The reduction time is proportional to the size of the generated GF, which results in substantial
overhead.

3. Abnormal Behavior of the Naive-reverse Program

3.1. Experiment with the Unify Processor Pilot Machine: UNIRED

We made a unify processor pilot machine called UNIRED [Yuh84] to
study an architecture suited for the basic operations of UP: unification and reduction. From the experiment with UNIRED, we found a
remarkable result on the execution of the naive-reverse benchmark program. Fig.5 shows the relation between the length of lists and the
execution time to reverse the lists. This result shows that the execution time is cubic in the order of the length of the list rather than
square.

3.2. Analysis of the Behavior of the Naive-reverse Program

In the naive-reverse program, the predicates are called n^2 times
where n is the length of the list. In current sequential inference
machines, the time of each predicate call is constant, and is independent of the length of list. Therefore, the execution time is

Execution Time [Sec]

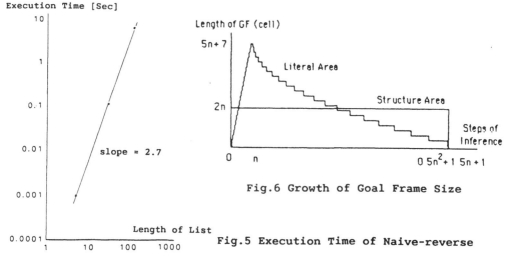

Fig.6 Growth of Goal Frame Size

Fig.5 Execution Time of Naive-reverse

proportional to square order of the list length.

On the contrary, in the unify processor pilot machine, the time of each goal rewriting is the sum of the unification time and the reduction time. This time is proportional to the size of GF. Fig.6 shows the size of the literal part and structure part of GF along the execution of the naive-reverse program. The literal part grows substantially, because the predicate nreverse calls itself recursively at the non-tail part of its body goals. The mean size of GF is proportional to the length of the list to reverse. This is why the execution time is proportional to cubic order of the list length.

4. Formulation of Execution Time

4.1. Search Time of a Solution

In PIE, the search time of a solution can be formulated as follows:

time to find a solution = a x T1 + b x T2 + T3

where

a is the search tree depth of the solution,

T1 is the mean delay time of successive goal rewriting operations for one GF,

b is the sum of $(c_i - 1)$,

where the c_i'th DT is used in rewriting on depth i,

T2 is the mean delay time of generation of alternatives,

T3 is the total time the GF is suspended and not processed.

As long as the number of GFs does not exceed the number of processors, T3 can be zero. In such a case, it is clear that T1 and T2 are the dominant factors of total execution speed.

4.2. Delay Time between Successive Rewritings of a GF

Since rewriting of a newly generated GF is assumed to start after completion of its reduction in the original goal rewriting model, delay time between successive rewritings of a GF (executions of successive AND goals) is the sum of unification time and reduction time. This makes the execution time of naive-reverse cubic order.

4.3. Delay Time between Alternative Child-GFs

Rewriting operations of a literal in one GF are assumed to be done in one UP sequentially, using several DTs of the same head predicate in the original goal rewriting model. As a result, some delay is introduced between successive child-GFs from a parent GF. The delay time is the rewriting time of the first child GF, i.e. the sum of unification time and reduction time.

5. Pipelined Goal Rewriting

5.1. Stream Processing of Goal Rewriting

Pipelined goal rewriting is a method that can reduce delay time of successive rewritings (T1) to unification time only. In pipelined goal rewriting, UPs are dynamically connected as a pipeline by a distribution network (DN). A GF is rewritten among UPs in a stream processing manner. As soon as a reduction operation starts, cells of the generated GF are transferred to the next UP through the DN, and unification proceeds in the next UP as far as possible using the incomplete GF which has arrived from the previous UP (Fig.7). Fig.8 shows a timing diagram of pipelined goal rewriting. Reduction time is hidden in the pipeline and does not affect the execution time. In other words, pipelined goal rewriting exploits another type of parallelism which can compensate the overhead of reduction. The parallelism attained by this method is formulated as follows;

$$\text{parallelism} = \frac{\text{unification time} + \text{reduction time}}{\text{unification time}}$$

As a result, the execution time of a naive-reverse program can be reduced to square order.

5.2. Transfer of GF and Synchronization Mechanism

Pipelined goal rewriting needs a synchronization mechanism to assure the 'read after write' principle. The current reduction algorithm uses a stack and traverses nested structure data in a depth-first order. In this case, the order of generation of cells has no relation to the location of the cells in the memory (Fig.9). We need to transfer both a cell and its address to locate cell properly in the next UP. We also need to add a 'presence bit' to all the memory words.

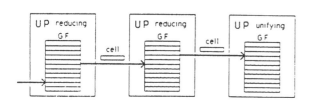

Fig.7 Pipelined Goal Rewriting

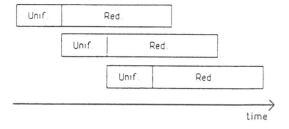

Fig.8 Timing Diagram of Fig.7

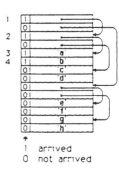

1 arrived
0 not arrived

Fig.9 Depth-first Traverse

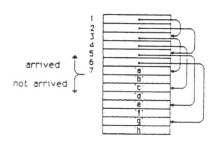

arrived
not arrived

Fig.10 Breadth-first Traverse

However, we adopted another scheme. Unification and reduction of structure data are performed in a breadth-first order in UPs. As a result, cells of a new GF are produced and transferred in the same order as their order in memory. In order to know whether a word of a GF has arrived and is accessible, a comparison of the access address with the address of last-arrived cell is enough (Fig.10).

5.3. The Effect of Breadth First Processing of Structure Data

Large and complex structure data may be copied and transferred between two UPs. Therefore, it may happen that the reduction process in the previous UP would produce data that are not needed immediately by the unification process in the next UP. In such a case, the unification process cannot proceed and must wait for necessary data to arrive. If the reduction process produces structure data in breadth-first order, however, such a situation can be avoided. The top level of structure data directly referred to by the arguments of the first literal, are supplied to the unification process first, and the next level of structure data are supplied afterwards. Since the unification process needs only a few levels of structure data (Fig.11), unification finishes just after these levels of structure data have arrived. Therefore, unification time is expected not to be prolonged.

5.4. Overhead of Distribution Network

Another problem is the overhead of network connecting time. Unless the interconnection network can connect UPs quickly, the connecting time is added to the execution time, which makes the processing slow. The throughput of a interconnection network depends heavily on the designation scheme of the destination. In our case, any free processors will do, and we don't need to designate any specific processors. Since our network has an automatic selection facility of free processors, the network itself can select appropriate processors with very little time overhead. Accordingly, the connecting time can be very short even for large interconnection networks.

5.5. Abortion of Unnecessary Reductions

Pipelined goal rewriting has another benefit. If unification fails, the whole GF becomes unnecessary and can be discarded. In such a

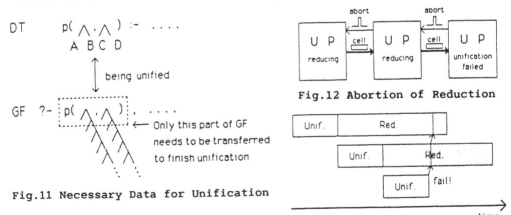

Fig.11 Necessary Data for Unification

Fig.12 Abortion of Reduction

Fig.13 Timing Diagram of Fig.12

case, the reduction process of the previous UP is wasted. In pipelined goal rewriting, the unification process is running in parallel with the reduction process that generates the GF. Unnecessary reduction processing can be detected before its completion as soon as unification fails. If unification fails and the GF has no alternative DT, UP sends an abort signal to the previous UP, and the signaled UP stops the reduction processing (Fig.12). Fig.13 shows the timing diagram of abortion. This mechanism minimizes unnecessary reduction processing with little overhead.

6. Goal Multicasting

Goal multicasting is a method to reduce delay time between alternative child-GFs (T2) to almost zero. A GF is distributed to several UPs in advance and rewritten with different DTs in different UPs in parallel (Fig.14).

There are two problems to solve in implementing goal multicasting: the way to select different candidate DTs for each UP, and the way to decide how many UPs should be multicast to. These problems are solved as follows in our implementation:

To solve the first problem with minimum overhead, two pieces of information are added on top of the header area of a GF. One is a serial number of each UP among the UPs to which the GF is multicast. This number is used as the offset from the first candidate DT, at which DTs start to be used in each UP. Though this number is transferred to each UP one by one, all the other information to be transferred is the same for all the destination UPs. The other information is the number of UPs to which the GF is multicast. This information is used as the interval at which alternative DTs are used in each UP.

The number of UPs to multicast to is decided as follows: First, the number of DTs to be used in the next rewriting is determined by clause indexing at the beginning of the reduction phase within the current UP. This number is the maximum number of UPs to multicast to. Then, the UP tries to connect to that number of UPs through the switching network. If the connecting operation takes too long because of blocking of the network, or lack of free UPs, it is timed-out, and the UP starts multicasting to fewer than the maximum number of UPs which have been connected till then.

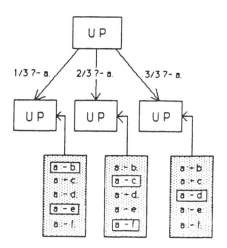

Fig.14 Goal Multicasting

Using the example in Fig.14, the offset information to the first
UP is 1, the information to the second UP is 2, and the information to
the third UP is 3. The interval information to the three UPs is 3. The
UPs choose the DTs using this information. The first UP uses the first
DT 'a:-b.' and the fourth DT 'a:-e.'. The second UP uses the second DT
'a:-c.' and the fifth DT 'a:-f.'. The third UP uses the third DT 'a:-
d.'.

7. Simulation Results

7.1. Simulation Model

We made a simulation of the methods described above. The purposes
of simulation are:

- to evaluate the maximum performance attainable by pipelined goal
  rewriting and goal multicasting, and

- to see if the reduction process produces necessary data in appropriate order in pipelined goal rewriting.

For these purposes, assumptions of the simulation are quite idealized,
i.e. the number of UPs is infinite, and the network can connect any UP
to any UP without blocking or delay. The processing time of the UPs is
determined based on the micro operations of the unify processor pilot
machine. A network without blocking is realizable as discussed in 5.4,
and delay time can be considered much smaller than unification time.
Therefore, the assumption can be considered rather realistic. The maximum number of UPs multicast to is limited to 2, because of the memory
space limitation of the simulation environment. The simulation program
is written in the language C, with a SIMULA-like event-driven simulation library.

7.2. Results

Four combinations of methods, i.e. methods with/without pipelined
goal rewriting and with/without goal multicasting, are compared. The
method with neither pipelined goal rewriting nor goal multicasting
(non.pipe.non.mult) corresponds to the original goal rewriting method
described in 2.

Benchmark programs used in the simulation are 8qa, 6q, nrev30 and
qsort50. 8qa is an eight-queens puzzle program. This program uses
nested structure data to represent a chess board and uses pattern
matching to check if queens can be put on the board without mutual
threat. This program is well suited for testing the efficient processing of complex structure data. 6q is another six-queens puzzle program.
This program uses a list of integers, and checks by arithmetic comparison. Nrev30 is a naive reverse of a list of 30 elements. Qsort50 is
a quick sort of a list of 50 elements. These two programs are typical
list processing benchmark programs, whose OR-parallelism is low.

Parallelism of 6q are shown in Fig.15. The "clock" on the horizontal axis indicates the execution time according to the processor clock,
and the "processors" on the vertical axis means the number of working
unify processors, i.e. effective parallelism.

Table.1 shows the relative execution speed where the speed of the
original method is 1. Table.2 shows the relative amount of total processing.

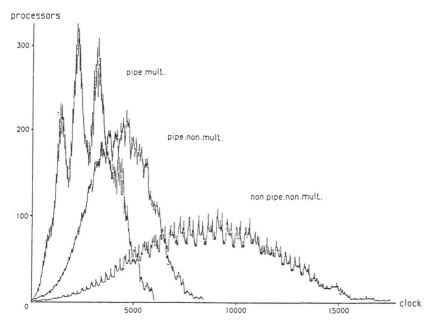

Fig.15 Parallelism of 6-queens

Table.1 Relative Execution Speed

programs		methods			
		non.pipe. non.mult.	pipe. non.mult.	non.pipe. mult.	pipe.mult.
8qa	exec. clk.	1	1.31	N.A.	2.21
	1'st ans.	1	1.82	N.A.	3.57
6q	exec. clk.	1	2.08	1.15	2.89
	1'st ans.	1	2.22	1.07	2.64
nrev30	exec. clk.	1	10.2	0.99	8.99
qsort50	exec. clk.	1	7.62	1.03	7.31

Table.2 Relative Processing Clock

programs		methods			
		non.pipe. non.mult.	pipe. non.mult.	non.pipe. mult.	pipe.mult.
8qa	total. clk.	1	0.99	N.A.	0.95
6q	total. clk.	1	1.05	1.03	1.10
nrev30	total. clk.	1	1.03	1.01	1.04
qsort50	total. clk.	1	0.74	1.00	0.72

The results of the simulation are summarized as follows:

- The execution of nrev30 is speeded up 10 times by pipelined goal rewriting.

- The execution of 8qa is 2.2 times faster by pipe.mult, and the time to get the first answer is 3.5 times faster.

- The mean reduction time decreases 20 ~ 36% by abortion of unnecessary reduction in 8qa and qsort50.

- The loss of processing caused by idle waiting in pipelined goal rewriting is 2 ~ 13% of the total processing.

- The total amount of processing is determined by a trade off of processing loss and abortion of unnecessary reduction. In 8qa and qsort50, pipe.mult is the best. In 6q and nrev30, the total amount of processing increases by pipelined goal rewriting and goal multicasting a little bit.

8. Comparison with Sequential Inference Machines

In this section, we discuss our proposed architecture through comparing with the sequential inference machines (SIM) [Tic83] in terms of the number of the operations which affect the execution time.

At first, we give the correspondence between the operations of goal rewriting and the machine instructions ('get', 'put' and 'unify') [War83] for high speed inference machines (Fig.16). Unification of a literal of GF and DT corresponds to execution of 'get' instructions. Unification of a structure of GF and DT corresponds to execution of 'unify' instructions after 'get' instruction. Reduction of body literals of DT corresponds to execution of 'put' instructions and 'unify' instructions after a 'put' instruction. Reduction includes operation not corresponded to operations of SIM, which is an overhead of goal rewriting. We assume that execution time of operations of both machines can be equal using hardware implementation technique such as pipelining.

In SIM, all the instructions above affect the time of logical inference. On the other hand, pipelined goal rewriting exploits more parallelism described below and some operations do not affect the execution time.

Copying of structure data in the head literal of a DT corresponds to execution of 'unify' instructions in write mode after 'get' instruction. In pipelined goal rewriting, this operation is delayed until unification succeeds and reduction starts. If the unification fails, unnecessary copying can be avoided. When unification succeeds, copying is hidden in the pipeline and does not affect the execution time.

Reduction of the body of a DT corresponds to the execution of 'put' instructions and succeeding 'unify' instructions. In pipelined

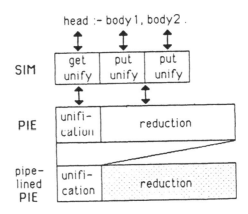

Fig.16 Correspondence of Processing

goal rewriting, this operation is hidden in the pipeline and does not affect the execution time. In other words, 'get' instructions start to be executed in the next UP as soon as 'put' instructions start to be executed. Therefore more extraction of parallelism is possible in pipelined goal rewriting.

Accordingly, the pipelined goal rewriting method can be faster than the SIM even when the program has no parallelism in it. On the contrary, disadvantages of PIE with the current pipelined goal rewriting method are:

- current implementation of UP is interpretive and removal of unnecessary operations like optimized compile code has not been studied yet,

- there is a possibility that reduction of unnecessary data would precede that of necessary data.

9. Conclusions

Two methods which exploit more parallelism and speed up the goal rewriting in PIE were presented. Pipelined goal rewriting can reduce the delay time between successive rewritings of a goal frame from the sum of unification time and reduction time to unification time only. Goal multicasting can reduce the delay time between generations of alternative child goal frames to almost zero. These methods are effective especially to raise parallelism quickly and to exploit other kind of parallelism in programs where OR-parallelism is not so high.

References

[Mot84] Moto-oka,T., Tanaka,T., Aida,H., Maruyama,T. and Hirata,K., "The Architecture of a Parallel Inference Engine - PIE -", FGCS'84, ICOT, 1984.

[Got84] Goto,A., Tanaka.H. and Moto-oka,T., "Highly Parallel Inference Engine PIE - Goal Rewriting Model and Machine Architecture -", New Generation Computing, Vol.2, OHMSHA and Springer-Verlag, 1984.

[Yuh83] Yuhara, M.Aida,H., Tanaka,H. and Moto-oka,T., "Unify Processor and its Reduction Algorithm of the Highly Parallel Inference Engine - PIE (Japanese)", Technical Research Report, EC83-30, IECE of Japan, 1983.

[Yuh84] Yuhara,M., Koike,H., Tanaka,H. and Moto-oka,T., "A Unify Processor Pilot Machine for PIE", Proc. of the Logic Programming Conference '84, Tokyo, 1984.

[Tic84] Tick,E. and Warren,D.H.D., "Towards a Pipelined Prolog Processor",International Symposium on Logic Programming, IEEE, 1984.

[War83] Warren,D.H.D., "An Abstract Prolog Instruction Set", Tech. report 309, A.I.Center, SRI International, 1983.

- FLENG Prolog -
The Language which turns
Supercomputers into Parallel Prolog Machines

Martin Nilsson and Hidehiko Tanaka
The Tanaka laboratory, Information Engineering, Department of Electrical Engineering,
The University of Tokyo, Hongo 7-3-1, Bunkyo-ku, Tokyo 113

Abstract: This paper suggests a new way of executing logic programming languages, using small-grain parallelism on vector parallel computer architectures. The main topic is the general purpose language FLENG Prolog. This is a logic programming language for arbitrary architectures, but is especially designed to run efficiently on vector architectures. The most important contribution of the paper is the described combination of the language FLENG Prolog with vector architectures.

1. Introduction

In this paper we will study

• **Why** supercomputers could be suitable for logic programming;
• **What** kind of programming language to use;
• **How** to implement it and execute it.

The main, original contribution of this paper is the combined answers to these questions.

The paper emphasizes on the FLENG Prolog language (hereafter we will just write FLENG), which is a logic programming language. It is a general purpose language for all kinds of architectures, although special consideration has been paid to vector parallel architectures. FLENG uses committed choice non-determinism, and descends mainly from GHC (Ued 86a) and (Kernel) Parlog (CG 84a), (CG 85), which in their turn are strongly related to Concurrent Prolog (Sha 83). Oc (Hir 85) is a language which was developed independently, and from a completely different standpoint, but interestingly enough still is quite similar to FLENG.

The recursive acronym "FLENG Prolog" stands for "FLENG has Logic Explicit and No Guard goals, Programming logic." i.e. it is much like GHC, but does not have any guard goals (commitment occurs immediately after head unification), and the logical semantics and control of execution is explicitly represented, not automatically "AND/ORed" like Prolog. (In fact, FLENG relates much to GHC as Kernel Parlog relates to Parlog.)

Some other differences from similar languages concern unification and system predicates. FLENG is described in more detail, with examples, in sections 3 and 4.

Although FLENG is designed to fit a variety of parallel architectures, it is particularly suitable for vector parallel (SIMD) architectures. Why? Contrastingly, current research efforts on parallel logic programming today focus on distributed (MIMD) systems, i.e. where individual processors are quite independent. Theoretically, such systems should be the most suitable for general, inhomogeneous parallel execution. However, distributed systems have serious bottlenecks in the form of communication between processors (and memories). For this reason, very few such systems exist.

On the other hand, there are already many different commercial computers with vector architecture. They don't have as serious communication problems, but their problem is that, roughly speaking, all "processors" must perform the same operation on their data. The way to execute a program in a conventional language is to use a "vectorizing" compiler. This compiler tries to detect loops in programs and convert them to special vector operations which operate on an entire matrix at a time. Vectorizing compilers are usually for Fortran, but there is also interesting ongoing work to implement a compiler for OR-parallel Prolog (Kan 85). Unfortunately, often only a small part of the processing can be done by vector operations, and the rest has to be done by a traditional scalar processor attached to the vector processor, with weak total performance as a result.

Our approach is completely different. Instead of fitting parts of a program to the architecture by a compiler, we want the programming language (FLENG) to fit the architecture from the beginning. We want this language to have very few primitive operations, which can all be executed in a fast, tight loop. Then, we can make this loop run entirely in the vector processor, with minimal scalar processor interference. One can imagine the program as in a way "floating" or "rolling" on many processing elements.

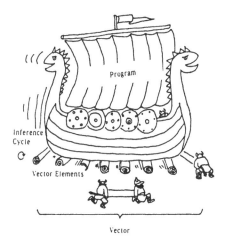

Vector

The idea why Logic Programming Languages are especially suitable for execution on vector computers is as follows: The execution cycle of logic programming languages is only a very basic inference cycle. An inference cycle is hardly anything more than clause head unification, plus execution of system primitives (evaluable predicates) for arithmetic, etc. However, the design of the unification and the system primitives are extremely important. Primitives must be as few and as simple as possible, since they will directly influence the execution cycle size and thus the execution time. They should be real time operations whenever possible. At the same time, they must be powerful enough for a general purpose programming language. Unification is the key to process synchronization and control, but can behave very unpolitely if treated carelessly.

We do not yet have a working implementation of the language on a vector computer, but we have implemented it in a pseudo-parallel way on some conventional sequential computers. For the Vax 8600 implementation, where FLENG is compiled to Franz Lisp, the speed is about 16 kLIPS. We don't believe that the vector parallel FLENG implementation we are working on will give very impressing benchmark results, since our target computer is not at all intended for this kind of application, but we believe that with small extensions, as described in section 6, vector architectures may be very suitable for parallel execution of Logic Programming Languages.

The structure of this paper is as follows: Section 2 gives the general ideas and goals behind the design of FLENG. A definition of FLENG is informally given in section 3. This definition is illustrated with examples and motivated in more detail in section 4. In section 5, translation between FLENG and other parallel languages is discussed. Section 6 discusses implementational issues of FLENG, especially for implementation on a vector architecture. Our results so far are given in section 8, and related work is cited in section 7. The research is summarized and discussed in section 9.

2. FLENG Design Principles

We want the language to be on the lowest possible level, and at the same time, easy to use, powerful (especially regarding parallelism), and machine independent.

Why do we want/what do we mean by a low-level language? A low-level language fits well to the machine architecture, and is thus easy to implement, and will execute quickly on this architecture. Of course, there is a big trade-off between the language level and its ease of use. Traditional Prolog is easy to use and machine independent, but is quite sequential in nature. Its underlying control mechanism is quite involved, and does not map easily on any machine architecture. We would like our ideal language to be as simple, easy to use, and machine independent as Prolog or GHC, while making it map more closely to the machine architecture.

As for expressional power, we want the parallel abilities of GHC, Parlog, or Concurrent Prolog. We also want programs to be first-class data structures, and we do not want any discrimination of data structures. For instance, we want to be able to detect the type of all data structures occurring in the execution, including variables. This is something which is often impossible in other logic programming languages. The reason is usually that if the language has such abilities, it will be impossible to read its statements declaratively as logical assertions.

This is a dilemma. According to our experience, primitives like metacall and type detection are really needed, especially in a low-level language, where we cannot resort to machine language subroutines. FLENG's solution is the following:

We do not require that a general FLENG clause should be readable as a statement in predicate logic. Instead, we require that a logical statement easily can be expressed in FLENG.

This means that a purely logical language, if wanted, easily can be compiled to, or implemented on top of the machine language FLENG.

The logical interpretation of a FLENG clause is given explicitly by the clause itself (this is explained in more detail in sections 3.1 and 4.1). In practice, FLENG programs will not look very different from GHC programs. The reason for that is that the AND/OR operational semantics (imposed by guards) in GHC is not necessary for, and seldom used for control of execution; the synchronization by shared variables is quite sufficient.

Note that FLENG could be interpreted logically in the same way as GHC clauses without guard goals. However, we feel that such a semantics may be a bit artificial and not to the point of the low-level language FLENG.

3. FLENG Definition Outline

3.1 Execution

A FLENG program is a set of clauses, looking just like Prolog clauses, with a head part, and a body of goals.

$$H :- G_1, G_2, \ldots G_n .$$

A program is executed by giving it a set Q of goals. Each goal is executed independently, in any order. A goal G is executed by removing it from Q and matching it with the head of all clauses in the program. For the first clause with matching head, that clause is comitted to, and the body goals of that clause are added to Q. Matching is like unification, but as in GHC, variable bindings may not be made in G (exported) during the matching. If a match of a variable in G with a non-variable is attempted, this matching is suspended, and resumes when the variable has been bound by another matching.

The execution of a goal is not associated with success, failure, or any logical truth values.

We have an additional fairness requirement: If a clause is committed to, then the execution of every one of its body goals must be guaranteed to start in the future; there may be no indefinite postponement.

3.2 Datatypes

There are four basic data types in FLENG: symbols, numbers, variables, and lists. Lists ("conses") have two fields, which may contain any FLENG data type. This is the list approach of data structure construction. Another common approach in other languages is the record approach, where structures are built of varisized arrays. This latter approach is used in Dec-10 Prolog, for instance. It is not so suitable for FLENG, since it makes execution more complicated and inhomogeneous.

3.3 System Predicates

The most important feature of FLENG primitive predicates is that it must be possible to detect their result. In other words, they must report completion in a detectable way, for instance by binding an argument variable to a non-variable, when the primitive has completed. Sometimes this is a natural effect of execution (arithmetic), and sometimes an extra argument has to be used (unification). None of the system primitives wait for their arguments to be instatiated. Such waiting can easily be implemented inside FLENG by interface predicates (cf. section 3.4). The following three predicates are considered primitive:

• unify(Result,X,Y)
Unification of term X with term Y. The variable Result is bound to true if unification is successful, and false if it is unsuccessful. Any bindings done to variables in X and Y remain in effect, even if unification fails. When Result is not needed, we can use "=" as defined by (X = Y) :- unify(Result,X,Y).

• compute(Operation,X,Y,Result)
This primitive is used for arithmetic, comparison of numbers or pointers, and bitwise numeric operations. The variable Result is bound to either a number for arithmetical and bitwise operations, or true or false for comparisons. The argument Operation should be a constant identifying the desired operation. It can be one of the following: +, -, *, / (arithmetic), and, or, xor (bitwise), =, <, sametype (comparison). = and sametype allow unbound variables as arguments.

• call(X)
This is the meta-call primitive. It does not need a result variable, since that is considered to be reported by an argument (a subterm) of the term X.

3.4 Convenience

For user convenience, we have decided to add one feature to FLENG, which is not strictly necessary. This feature is a "bind-to-non-variable" annotation (" % ") on variables in the head of a clause. If the annotation is used on a variable in the head, it is valid for that variable in the whole head. The meaning is that during head matching, an annotated variable in the head of a candidate clause must be matched with something else than a variable, or otherwise matching suspends. The same effect can be achieved by busy waiting, in a more clumsy and inefficient way.

Using this annotation, we can easily define a waiting version of the system primitive compute:

waitcompute(Op, %X, %Y,R) :- compute(Op,X,Y,R).

4 Explanations, Motivations, and Examples

4.1 Execution

In logic programming languages with guard goals, it is necessary to associate the execution with truth values, or at least success and suspension, since the result of the execution of guard goals determines whether commitment is possible. This leads to considerable overhead, difficulties in implementation of the language, and finding a proper architecture.

Another problem with guard goals is that variable binding schemes become complicated in the general case: Vaguely expressed, variables may pass bindings inside the guard, but not outside the guard. It becomes necessary to carefully remember which variable belongs to which environment.

These are the main reasons why FLENG does not have any guard goals. Still, FLENG does not lose expressional power because the synchronization mechanism by shared variables is perfectly enough for controlling the execution. In fact, practical programs in languages like GHC relatively seldom use guard goals, and when they are used, they are often only simple calls to system predicates. Furthermore, the implicit conjunctions of executed goals are used rarely. This means that typical GHC programs easily can be rewritten to FLENG. (Actually, "Flat" GHC - i.e. GHC with only system predicates as guard goals - can comparatively easily be compiled to FLENG.)

Since we don't emphasize that a FLENG clause has to be implicitly readable as a logical statement, it

might be argued that logic programming is impossible in FLENG. This is not correct. One reason is that the logic usually implicit in e.g. Prolog easily can be expressed explicitly by goal arguments in FLENG programs. Actually, compared to the implicit conjunction of goals in the body of a Prolog clause, FLENG offers greater flexibility. For instance, with the following definitions:

```
and(true,true,Result) :- Result = true.
and(false,_,  Result) :- Result = false.
and(_,false,  Result ) :- Result = false.
```

we can get the parallel AND of two goals f and g by

```
h(X,Y,Result) :-
    f(X,ResultF), g(y,ResultG),
    and(ResultF,ResultG,Result).
```

but as easily as AND, we could also define OR, exclusive OR, NOT, or any other boolean function.

Guard goals are typically used for testing arguments before commitment. This testing can as well be done before the call, as in the guard: The result of the test is passed as a parameter in the call, and is tested when matching clause heads. An example can clarify this: Consider the following GHC program:

```
prog(N) :- N < 17 | a(N).
prog(N) :- N ≥ 17 | b(N).
```

with the call prog(N). This program has a FLENG equivalent

```
prog(N) :- compute(<,N,17,Less), prog1(Less,N).
prog1(true,N) :- a(N).
prog1(false,N) :- b(N).
```

4.2 Unification

Recent logic programming languages for parallel execution seem to be converging, and have become quite similar. One of the most important differences is unification. Unification has central function for synchronization, control, and parameter passing. On the other hand, it can cause big problems by creating cyclic structures and deadlocks.

In this section, we consider mainly the unify system predicate. Head matching is similar but is somewhat easier to handle.

An important question is the grain size of unification: Should unification of two terms be split up in several unification processes to be executed in parallel? Or should unification be executed as an indivisible operation? Apparently, the latter alternative is not very good, because unification may take very long time. Parlog and GHC try to split up unification in many smaller unification processes. However, in practical programs, almost all unifications are of small size. Splitting up unification in many different processes will increase the overhead, and for average small size unifications, execution may even be slowed down.

The grain size of unification in FLENG is instead intended to be slightly larger than the average size of unification. Larger unifications have to be interruptable. The structure of unification is often such that a component in unification is often an implied test, and other components are for parameter passing. Thus we do not believe that sequential unification will impair the speed seriously. We do not prescribe sequential execution of unification in FLENG, although we believe it may be the best solution in a real implementation, especially for the purpose of detection of cyclic and other ill-behaving data structures. Note that even if execution of the unify predicate is sequential, unification of two terms f(X,Y) and f(U,V) can be parallelized by

unify(R1,X,U), unify(R2,Y,V), and(R1,R2,R)

This is one of the very important roles of the result argument. Another role is to allow variables to be full-fledged data structures. Without an extra argument, it will be impossible to non-destructively determine when a unification of a variable with another variable has been completed.

Variable bindings in the unification in FLENG remain in effect even if the unification fails, e.g. because two different constants are compared with each other. In this case, the system predicate does not suspend, but completes execution and reports failure, maintaining all variable bindings made so far. Note that in this way, unify can be used for testing both equality and inequality with correct behaviour from a logical point of view: Even if variables occuring in the arguments of unify are instantiated later, the meaning of unify does not change.

The single-assignment property of variables in a logical programming languages has a hidden, serious implication: Either we must have occur check before binding a variable, or we must be able to handle cyclic structures: After we have bound a variable in the middle of unification, we cannot change our mind, if we later find that the binding was a mistake.

As can be seen from this, unification is a delicate subject. Fortunately, there seem to be unification algorithms which can solve this problem satisfactorily (NT 86). A forthcoming paper will report more detailed results on this problem.

4.3 The Other Two System Predicates

For any low-level logic programming architecture, it is important to reduce the system predicates to a minimum. The architecture should be kept as small and simple as possible. In particular for vector architectures, it is important to minimize the size and number of system predicates: If the vector processor has to perform a (relatively) very rare operation for some process, all the other processes will probably be idle, with very low vector utilization as a result. If necessary, such operations should be performed by a front-end processor, also running FLENG, but with an extended set of system predicates for I/O and database updates.

These primitive system predicates do not necessarily check for exceptional conditions, like division with zero. Such checking can easily be done in FLENG by interface predicates.

The compute predicate operations are intended to be the basic ones of the underlying machine, like arithmetic (+, -, *, /), bitwise operations for arithmetic (and, or, xor), and pointer and numeric comparison (<, =, sametype). All these operations have a similar form, with two input arguments, a simple (real time) operation on local data, and one output. The ideal architecture has something similar to an indirect "execute" instruction, which can take the intended operation as one of its arguments. Note that the sametype and = comparisons are meaningful also for arguments which are unbound variables. For pointers, = compares addresses.

The meta-call predicate has only one argument. This not only ensures a clean semantics (cf. (Ued 86)), but is all that is needed for a meta-call facility. The completion of the call predicate itself is not interesting. The completion of the execution of the called predicate can report completion through one of its own arguments. Thus, the meaning of call is just the same as writing the called goal in the body of the clause.

We do not think the multi-argument meta-call

approach (CG 84b) is very attractive, because it is not only a meta-call, but implies an additional control construct which is very hard to implement. (For the reader familiar with Lisp terminology, it resembles not only a call to EVAL, but a call to EVAL inside ERRORSET, or UNWIND-PROTECT.) The control problem the multi-argument type of call is intended to solve, is instead swept under the carpet, and will appear when trying to implement the language. We think that FLENG solves the problem in a nicer way by letting predicates report about completion themselves.

4.4 Example Program: Generating Primes

(Ued 86a) gives the following GHC program for generating primes:

```
primes(Max,Ps) :- true | gen(2,Max,Ns),sift(Ns,Ps).

gen(N,Max,Ns) :- N<=Max | Ns=[N|Ns1], N1:=N+1,
                          gen(N1,Max,Ns1).
gen(N,Max,Ns) :- N> Max | Ns=[].

sift([P|Xs],Zs) :- true | Zs=[P|Zs1], filter(P,Xs,Ys),
                          sift(Ys,Zs1).
sift([],    Zs) :- true | Zs=[].

filter(P,[X|Xs],Ys) :-
    X mod P=:=0 | filter(P,Xs,Ys).
filter(P,[X|Xs],Ys) :-
    X mod P=\=0 | Ys=[X|Ys1], filter(P,Xs,Ys1).
filter(P,[],    Ys) :- true | Ys=[].
```

To translate this program to FLENG, we have to rewrite the non-trivial guard parts. This is quite easy as can be seen from the resulting FLENG program:

```
primes(Max,Ps) :- gen(2,Max,Ns), sift(Ns,Ps).

gen(N,Max,Ns) :-
    greater(N,Max,Greater),gen1(Greater,N,Max,Ns).
gen1(false,N,Max,Ns) :-
    Ns=[N|Ns1], add1(N,N1), gen(N1,Max,Ns1).
gen1(true,N,Max,Ns) :- Ns=[].

sift([P|Xs],Zs) :-
    Zs=[P|Zs1], filter(P,Xs,Ys), sift(Ys,Zs1).
sift([],    Zs) :- Zs=[].

filter(P,[X|Xs],Ys) :- mod(X,P,Mod), zero(Mod,Zero),
    filter1(Mod,P,[X|Xs],Ys).
filter(P,[],    Ys) :- Ys=[].
```

```
filter1(true,P,[X|Xs],Ys) :- filter(P,Xs,Ys).
filter1(false,P,[X|Xs],Ys) :- Ys=[X|Ys1],
    filter(P,Xs,Ys1).
```

with the following definitions:

```
greater(%X,%Y,Result) :- compute(<,Y,X,Result).
add1(%X,Y) :- compute(+,X,1,Y).
mod(%X,%Y,D) :-
    compute(/,X,Y,Q), times(Y,Q,P),
    difference(X,P,D).
times(%X,%Y,P) :- compute(*,X,Y,P).
difference(%X,%Y,D) :- compute(-,X,Y,D).
zero(%X,R) :- compute(==,X,0,R).
```

For a more detailed description of the execution of the primes program, we refer to (Ued 86a). Here, we would like to point out that a typical FLENG program does not become much different from a typical (Flat) GHC program. For general GHC programs, the translation of the guard is harder, but it seems that guards are usually of a simpe kind, and even where complicated user-defined guards occur, the guard often is just a test which does not try to instantiate variables in the caller. Such a guard is also easy to translate into FLENG.

5. Translation between FLENG and similar Languages

5.1 FLENG to GHC

Except for the system primitives, FLENG should be executable in GHC. The system primitive compute in FLENG can detect and identify variables, which is impossible in GHC. Also, the unification in FLENG reports completion and failed unification, which is impossible in GHC. To execute FLENG, a GHC implementation needs to satisfy the fairness requirement that the execution of goals of committed clauses must be guaranteed to be started some time.

5.2 GHC to FLENG

Flat GHC can be compiled to FLENG quite easily. We have written such a compiler in Prolog, which is about 2 pages of code long. The subset of GHC that can be easily compiled to FLENG is in fact larger than Flat GHC: What the compiler needs is knowledge about which variables in guard goals will be used for export, and which will be used for import. This information can be supplied e.g. by declarations or by thorough static analysis.

Partial evaluation may be a useful approach: (SC 86) refers to work by Codish, who has used partial evaluation for translating Concurrent Prolog to Flat Concurrent Prolog. We believe this may be a very interesting approach for translating GHC into Flat GHC, and thus into FLENG.

5.3 Other Languages: Parlog and Concurrent Prolog

We dare not say so much about the mutual expressibility of FLENG on one hand, and Concurrent Prolog and Parlog on the other hand, until we have a clear definition of the semantics of the latter languages. In particular, a critical question is the necessary system primitives: Parlog seems to require a meta-call primitive which requires quite an elaborate control mechanism "under the surface." The semantics of unification in Concurrent Prolog is also complicated, and may not be easily expressible in FLENG.

6. FLENG Architectures

6.1 Vector Parallel Architectures

The great advantages with vector parallel architectures are that they have a shared memory, and very fast communication between "processors." Processor data are actually only elements of vector registers, so processors can communicate by just shuffling data in a vector register. Global operations such as scheduling and garbage collection are very much simplified because of the shared memory. The looming dream of a vector architecture is the possibility of scaling up by just extending the vector length.

However, there are also some disadvantages with a vector architecture: The vector processor's operations cannot be specialized for a particular program, i.e. programs cannot be compiled, but an interpreting approach has to be used. It is likely that the vector processor will spend many wasted cycles executing rare system predicates.

6.2 Vector Parallel Implementation

We have spent very much time and effort trying to squeeze Prolog systems to minimal size (Nil 83), (Nil 85). Studying minimal implementations has been essential for trying to understand efficient execution of logic programming languages, and particularly so for implementation on a vector architecture: On this architecture, the program interpreter must be coded as an extremely compact loop of vector operations.

For instance, consider unification. Indeed, unification is by far the most complex operation in the inference cycle, including the other system predicates. Unification 1) has to be able to detect cyclic structures, and 2) cannot use any procedure calls, because of the restricted vector operations, but has to be opencoded as a loop. The system predicate unify is very similar to head matching. It is very important that the code of head matching and the unify predicate can be shared as much as possible.

The space for this article does not allow us to go too deeply into details of our implementation for vector parallelism, but below we will roughly sketch the main mechanisms: The kernel of the program is one loop, which basically performs N inferences simultaneously, where N is the vector size. The code in the loop is similar to a traditional interpreter. The restrictions on this code are that it may not contain jump instructions or subroutine calls. Conditionals are only allowed by using mask bits, where a machine instruction can be disabled for a particular vector element by setting the corresponding bit in a mask vector.

- First in the loop, N processes (goals) are taken from a queue of waiting processes. Then, arguments are unified with candidate clause arguments.
- Here, some processes may be suspended, or their unification may already have finished. If so, bits in a mask vector are set to disable unification for those processes.
- After so many steps of unification that most processes have finished matching, i.e. had their mask bits set, unification ends. Unifications which are not yet finished will have to wait until the next turn of the main loop.
- After unification, system primitives are checked for and executed. Processes which do not contain such calls are disabled by mask bits.
- For successful head unifications, new body goals are added to of the queue. Processes which are not yet finished, e.g. because of lengthy unifications, are also put back into the queue. Depending on where in the queue new goals are put, we get different scheduling mechanisms. If new goals are put at the back of the queue, we will get breadth-first scheduling. We can also get something similar to n-bounded depth-first scheduling (Ued 86a). n-bounded depth-first scheduling is when a goal is executed depth-first, in a way similar to Prolog, for n process reductions. Then, pending goals on the stack are added to the end of the process queue, and a new process is started from the beginning of the queue. Suppose we put new processes at the

beginning of a second queue (used as a stack), and now take processes from this queue, for n cycles. Then, we take all the processes in this second queue and add them to the end of the first queue, and repeat the procedure again.

The implementation uses a structure sharing strategy since it seems that the overhead for copying will be too large; copying is not a real-time operation, so it would have to be suspendable in the same way as unification, with a consequent increase in overhead.

6.3 Useful Improvements of Vector Computers

A practical problem today is that commercial vector processors (supercomputers) are not so much intended for non-numerical vector processing, which is indicated by the instruction set. Most modern supercomputers have instructions for so called "list vectors" (i.e. vectors containing addresses instead of data, corresponding to indirect addressing for scalar processors). They also have masking operations, which can be used for conditional operations. But what they don't have, and what would be extremely useful for the implementation of system predicates, is an "execute" instruction, such as mentioned in section 4.3. This operation can be used for taking the code of an arithmetic operation as one of its operands. It could then execute many system predicates at the same time. Such an instruction should not be too hard to implement, as it operates only on local data.

Another, even more important new instruction would be a synchronization instruction: It often happens that several processes want to store a value in the same memory location. We want to grant exactly one of them the right. One way to do this on a vector architecture is that we first write the ID numbers of the processes (i.e. the vector indices) in those locations. We wait until all values have been written, and then we read them back. A process which reads back the same value as it wrote, is granted the permission to write the location. The disadvantage with this is the long time delay for accessing the memory, although the permissions could be found by only looking at the addresses locally. In a vector register. A much more elegant way would be to have a vector instruction which sets a bit in a mask register for exactly one vector element of several elements, containing the same address.

6.4 Other parallel architectures for FLENG

A distributed architecture for FLENG has the big advantage of allowing compilation and static optimization of programs. For FLENG, no "invisible" control is necessary for relating parent and child processes, as their only links are through shared variables. On a distributed architecture, several processes can be combined to run very quickly as long as they run on the same processor. However, FLENG shares a problem with other similar languages on distributed architectures, namely how to efficiently communicate bindings of shared variables.

It is worth mentioning that the independent execution of FLENG goals suggests that a dataflow architecture for FLENG may fit well.

7. Related work

FLENG descends directly from GHC (Ued 86) and Parlog (CG 84a). The intention has been to find a low-level language, which fits current machine architectures well, but still allows programming as easily as, say, Prolog or GHC. The basic execution features are thus very close to those of GHC and Parlog. There is another recent language called Oc (Hir 85). Oc seems to be rather formally developed, with heavy emphasis on program transformation and partial evaluation. The paper describing it is very brief, so the properties of Oc are not so clear, but its basic execution mechanism seems very similar to FLENG's. However, its treatment of unification and system predicates is quite different.

The most intricate facet of FLENG, and maybe of logic programming languages in general, is unification. Recent parallel logic programming languages differ much in this respect. GHC attempts to be as general as possible and allow minimum grain parallelism, by a property called "antisubstitutability." This rougly means that unifications of large terms automatically can be split in smaller, independently executed by inserting ("antisubstituting") intermediate variables. However, there are several dangers with this approach: The completion of unification of a variable with another variable cannot be detected. This means that, for instance, the common merge program of two streams may not work properly if we want to pass general terms in the stream. It is impossible to know whether a subterm of an element in the stream is a variable, or just waits for being bound to a non-variable. Also, this approach makes proper handling of cyclic structures hard. The antisubstitutions themselves are not to blame here; the real cause of the problem is that the completion of unification cannot be detected, and this is one of the reasons why the unification primitive in FLENG has three arguments.

As for emphasizing on vector architectures for parallel logic programming languages, there are very few papers touching on this subject. (Kan 85) describes a possible implementation of how a vectorizing compiler could compile OR-parallel Prolog to fit a vector processor, by for instance moving tail recursive loops to the vector processor. This approach can only use relatively large-grain parallelism, and will rely much on a scalar processor. This contrasts to our method, where execution lies almost entirely in the vector processor. Our approach is entirely parallel in the sense that it is impossible to give a "program counter," or tell where in the program the computer is currently executing.

Another paper (BL 85) discusses the use of vector architectures for Al-languages. This article specializes on CAP, a computer with SIMD architecture. The article describes how to use the particular features of this computer for implementing the RETE matching algorithm for the OPS5 language, and how to implement an algorithm for semantical networks. However, these results are not applicable on vector parallel architectures in general, or for logic programming implementations.

8. Results

We are working on some different approaches to implementations of FLENG. So far, we have simple structure sharing and copying interpreters for FLENG written in Franz Lisp, for (sequential) Vax computers. We also have a simple compiler from FLENG to Franz Lisp. In these implementations we use n-bounded depth-first scheduling. $n = \infty$ represents depth-first search with minimal overhead, and $n = 1$ represents breadth-first search with maximal overhead, where the body goals of a reduced goal are immediately put at the end of the queue. The speed of compiled code for Vax 8600 was about 16 kLIPS for $n = \infty$, and about 4 kLIPS for $n = 1$. A normal setting of n is about 100. In this case the overhead becomes 5-10%. As a comparison, the speed of the C-Prolog interpreter on this computer is about 5 kLIPS. We estimate that the speed of FLENG can be increased by direct compilation to machine code, and some more optimizations. The structure sharing interpreter is as expected much slower than compiled code, around a factor of 20.

The different implementations of FLENG will be very different, depending on if the target architecture is a vector parallel computer, a distributed computer, or a sequential computer (pseudo-parallel implementation). There are still open questions for further research, e.g. concerning I/O and indexed data structures. Although it may be argued that these are only implementation details, we think they might influence the design so much that they had better be remembered at an early stage of the design.

9. Conclusions

We do not estimate the inherent speed of FLENG to be very much different from other similar languages on the same machine. On the other hand, the implementation will be comparatively simple, and may mean that a tailored architecture can be simplified, and speeded up, for instance by a RISC approach.

Our test implementations show that FLENG can be implemented easily and efficiently on a sequential computer. An implementation for an existing vector parallel computer will probably not be very fast since, the computer is not originally intended for this kind of application, and thus lacks some important features, most notably for process synchronization. It still seems, however, that a vector parallel design may be a very promising approach for future logic programming computers.

10. Acknowledgements

This research was possible thanks to a generous grant from the Japanese Ministry of Education. We are grateful to the members of the special interest group of inference machines, at the University of Tokyo, and to the members of the parallel programming systems working group, at the Institute for new computer technology. We would also like to thank the unknown referees of this paper for several constructive comments.

11. References

(BL 85) Brooks, R. and Lum, L.: "Yes, An SIMD Machine Can Be Used For AI." In Proc. of the Int. Joint Conf. on Artificial Intelligence. Los Angeles, 1985. p 73-79.

(CG 84a) Clark, K.L. and Gregory, S.: "PARLOG: Parallel Programming in Logic." Res. Rept. DOC 84/4. Dept. of Computing, Imperial College of Science and Technology, London. 1984.

(CG 84b) Clark, K.L. and Gregory, S.: "Notes on the Implementation of PARLOG." Res. Rept. DOC

84/16. Dept. of Computing, Imperial College of Science and Technology, London. 1984.

(CG 85) Clark, K.L. and Gregory, S.: "Notes on Systems Programming in PARLOG." In Proc. Int. Conf. on Fitfth Generation Computer Systems. Tokyo 1984.

(Hir 85) Hirata, M.: "Description of Oc and its Applications." In Proc. Second National Conf. of Japan Society of Software Science and Technology. p 153-156. (In Japanese)

(Kan 85) Kanada, Y.: "High-speed Execution of Prolog on Supercomputers." In Proc. 26th Programming Symp., Information Processing Society of Japan. 1985. p 47-55. (In Japanese)

(Nil 83) Nilsson, M.: "FOOLOG - A Small and Efficient Prolog Interpreter." Tech. Rept. no. 20. UPMAIL, Comp. Science Dept. Uppsala, Sweden. 1983.

(Nil 84) Nilsson, M.: "The worlds shortest Prolog interpreter?" In Campbell, J. (ed): "Implementations of Prolog". Ellis Horwood Ltd., Chichester, UK. 1984. p 87-92.

(NT 86) Nilsson, M. and Tanaka, H.: "Cyclic Tree Traversal." To appear in Proc. 3rd Int. Conf. on Logic Programming. London. 1986.

(Sha 83) Shapiro, E.Y.: "A Subset of Concurrent Prolog and its Interpreter." Technical Report TR-003. Institute for New Generation Computer Technology. 1983. Tokyo.

(SC86) Sterling, L. and Codish, M.: "Pressing for Parallelism: A Prolog Program Made Concurrent." J. Logic Programming. No. 1. 1986. p. 75-92.

(Ued 86a) Ueda, K.: "Guarded Horn Clauses." Doctor's Thesis. Information Engineering Course. The University of Tokyo. 1986. (This very read-worthy thesis is combines some of Ueda's earlier papers with new material.)

(Ued 86b) Ueda, K.: "On the Operational Semantics of Guarded Horn Clauses." To appear as Technical Memorandum. Institute for New Generation Computer Technology. 1986. Tokyo.